Volume 26, Number 3

differences

Dossier: Étienne Balibar on Althusser's Dramaturgy and the Critique of Ideology

Althusser's Dramaturgy and the Critique of Ideology

Editors' note: The following text was originally given as the Roger B. Henkle Memorial Lecture at Brown University on October 7, 2013. It has been revised for publication in *differences*.

*H*ow should we explain that, in certain languages at least (notably English, Italian, and Spanish), a renewed interest is taking place in the works and ideas of Louis Althusser, a philosopher widely known as the "inventor" of the "structuralist" brand of Marxism in the 1960s and 1970s who died in 1990 but had already retreated from the public and intellectual scene by 1980, when, in a scandalous episode of criminal madness, he murdered his wife and was confined, at least for some time, in a mental hospital? A very simple reason, and I want to begin with this because it is also a way to acknowledge my debts, lies in the fact that in recent years, several scholars of various generations—some who knew Althusser personally or had met him, like Emilio de Ípola, others who knew him indirectly through common friends and professors, like Warren Montag and Vittorio Morfino, or still others who "simply" encountered him in the course of their investigations, like Judith Butler, Slavoj Žižek, and Mikko Lahtinen—have published

Volume 26, Number 3 DOI 10.1215/10407391-3340324

an impressive number of commentaries and interpretations. These works deliver a new, and in some respects more exciting, picture of the author of *Reading Capital* than simply a contributor to the historical debates on dialectical materialism that are indeed very far from us today.[1] These new readings were to a large extent made possible by the fact that posthumous publication of Althusser's writings has considerably added to the existing corpus, expanding his work in many different directions, making his relationship to theory and to politics appear a more complex one, and highlighting at the same time the continuities and the discontinuities between different "periods" of his activity. All this takes place at a conjuncture that I believe makes it possible to better understand what formed the convergent interests but also the deep fractures within the "philosophical season" of the 1960s in Europe. The time for learned academic commentary has come, no doubt, but unexpected turns of intellectual history, and political history in the broad sense, have also taken place, which have largely neutralized the effects of a philosophical reaction that—perhaps prematurely—proclaimed that we had better forget the old issues of structure and *praxis*, discourse and power, dialectics and genealogy, if we wanted to think in the present.

It is in this spirit that I want to offer a partially new description of Althusser's quest for a critical concept of *ideology*, clearly one of the central aspects of his contribution to "theory" and the linchpin of his project of destabilizing Marxism from the inside. While a critique of ideology no doubt formed the core of the idea of "historical materialism," Althusser always insisted that the concept Marxist theorists (and others) needed to achieve such a goal should be *anything but* the concept of "ideology" that Marx had used; it should be a different one if not an antithetic one. This is, of course, the old *topos*: for Marx, against Marx. It would account for only half of my title, and it is not in this general epistemological manner that I want to return to the issue in the current context.

What strikes me in particular in recent commentaries on Althusser is the place, apparently disproportionate with the dimensions of the texts, that is now granted to some of Althusser's writings about *art*, particularly theater and painting. These commentaries propose not that we read Althusser's texts as *applications* of theory within a particular field (say aesthetics or culture), but rather that we view them as "analyzers," theoretical *dispositifs* or *machines* constructed by Althusser to resolve theoretical problems and identify the objects of theory. This is probably not unique to him—remember in particular Lyotard's use of Duchamp, or Deleuze's use of Proust and Kafka, or Derrida's of Artaud. But in his case, the reversal of the "normal" philosophical attitude is particularly striking because although his essays do not avoid a few considerations on art in general, its social and cognitive functions or its specific mode of being, they are in fact essentially descriptions of singular *experiences* resulting from an "encounter" with a work or a group of works, an "event" in other words, but from which general consequences are drawn for a much larger field. This proves particularly adapted (but also uneasy, from an epistemological standpoint) in the case of a reflection on the issue of ideology, ideological domination, and the "dominant ideology" because, in a symptomatic circularity, such a reflection requires both a description of the processes or procedures of *subjection* and *subjectivation* that form the essence of ideology *and* a "performative" gesture allowing for a "subject" to become located, as interpellating interpellator, within the ideological mechanism itself in order to reveal its coherence and insecurity. This is, Althusser seems to suggest, something made possible not by art *in general*, as an institution or a cultural phenomenon, but only by specific works of art in specific circumstances.

I can readily mention two major examples, both drawn from essays written in the same crucial years between 1961 and 1965, where what would become known as "Althusserianism" was taking shape. The first is an essay from 1965–66 on the canvases of Althusser's friend, the Italian painter Leonardo Cremonini, called "Cremonini, Painter of the Abstract," to which I will, regretfully, make only a quick reference here.[2] The second (chronologically first) is an essay (first published in 1962 and included as a chapter in *For Marx* in 1965) on a performance by the Piccolo Teatro di Milano in Paris in July 1962 with the title "The 'Piccolo Teatro': Bertolazzi and Brecht. Notes on a Materialist Theater." I had once somewhat blindly remarked, when asked to write a preface for the new edition of Althusser's *Pour Marx* in 1996, that this essay formed the "geometrical and theoretical center" of the book, although it was never acknowledged and treated as such ("Avant-propos" viii). But this is no longer the case, since fascinating commentaries have been produced by, in particular, Banu Bargu, Marc-Vincent Howlett, Warren Montag, and Guillaume Sibertin-Blanc.[3] It is from the Piccolo Teatro essay that I want to start again in order to sketch a more general problematic, or rather an aporetic trajectory following an example provided by Althusser himself in his essay on Rousseau's *Social Contract*, a trajectory in which, through successive *décalages*, he moves away from a particular articulation of theater, politics, and ideology toward a different one. From the Piccolo essay, I will draw the idea that theater—not theater in general, but, as he was keen to insist in a subsequent commentary called

"On Brecht and Marx," a specific *practice* of theater illustrated by Giorgio Strehler and his productions at the Piccolo Teatro—represented for Althusser not only an effective critique of ideology, particularly the dominant "human- ist" ideology of bourgeois society, but also an *alternative way* of under- standing the structure of ideological relations, compared to the *scientific* one otherwise advocated in his works as an "epistemological break" with *theoretical humanism*. From there, I will begin exploring the hypothesis that, in fact, the intrinsic relationship between the structure of ideological processes and the *dispositifs* of theatrical representation was displaced to a new field when, immediately after 1968, Althusser embarked on the project of sketching a "general theory" of ideologies, the best-known result of which is the essay from 1970, "Ideology and Ideological State Apparatuses," where the central notion (which is also a metaphor) is "interpellation."[4] I will also suggest, through recourse to the posthumous book *Machiavelli and Us*, the manuscript of which was essentially completed in the years immediately following, that Althusser was not unaware of the aporias of his model of ideological interpellation, particularly when considered from the point of view of a revolutionary politics. Surprisingly, the way he sought to overcome the aporias was through a new philosophical detour: this time not through Spinoza but through Machiavelli in the form of a definition of the "political practice of the *Prince*" as "ideological policy" whose principal instrument is a staging or mise-en-scène of his own passions. Taken together, I sug- gest that these two constructions form a *dramaturgic model* of the political function and political transformation of ideology.

"Je me retourne . . .": The Interpellation from Milan

I cannot summarize in full detail Althusser's essay on the Pic- colo Teatro. That could be useful, but it would also be complicated because it would add a third layer of narration to what is already, at least in part, a description of the experience of a production that was touring Europe after being inaugurated in the city of Milan. It should be recalled that, in the postwar period in Italy, France, Britain, and Germany, theater was a popular art mixing high cultural and, most of the time, political ambitions with a genuine appeal not only to the bourgeois elites but to the educated middle classes and the politically motivated aristocracy of the working class. This was also a moment of heightened ideological passions, marked not only by the vicissitudes of the Cold War and the interrupted "de-Stalinization" of the Communist bloc but also by the dramatic developments of the colonial wars of liberation. Giorgio Strehler, an Italian director of Italian-Austrian origin who had founded Il Piccolo Teatro di Milano just after the war, was already considered one of the greatest figures of European theater. Although not officially a "Brechtian," he had offered remarkable performances of some of Brecht's plays, in particular a famous *Life of Galileo*. In Paris in 1962, he presented an adaptation of a relatively obscure "realist" Italian playwright from the late nineteenth century, Carlo Bertolazzi's *El nost Milan*, which described rather than properly narrated the story of a poor young girl from the slums who, after being raped by some scoundrel subsequently murdered by her loving father, abandons the father when he is about to be jailed, apparently to look for money in the "real" world, that is, to become a prostitute. The spectacle had been scorned as bad melodrama by the critics, but Althusser's lengthy and elaborate interpretation rehabilitated it and, by the same token, played an important role in aesthetic discussions of the time about realism, critique, and irony in art (this being also the period when the avant-garde theater of the "absurd" with Beckett and Ionesco was blossoming in France). Althusser and Strehler became friends and encountered one another in Italy in the following years, together with Strehler's close associate, Paolo Grassi.

Althusser's article consists of two parts of roughly equal length. The first is devoted to a description of the play, highlighting the paradoxes of a succession of three acts, each of which reproduces essentially the same dramaturgy, by juxtaposing rather than articulating two kinds of pictures with different visual content and rhythm: on the one side, a static and neutral presentation of the immobile, desperate, and silent world of the subproletarians, who expect nothing because nothing can happen in their lives, neither work nor struggles nor history; on the other side, taking place in the margins of this world of misery and resignation, or as Althusser writes (retrieving an old category of classical theater), "in the wings" (*à la cantonade*) ("'Piccolo'" 138), the dramatic moments of conflict between the idealist generosity of the father and the cynicism of the rapist, with whom the daughter will side (albeit after his death), in the form of a spectacular transgression of human feelings, which is also shown onstage as an escape from the night of impotent dreams into the risky violence of the day: "Erect, Nina goes out into the daylight" (qtd. in Althusser, "'Piccolo'" 133). With this description goes a double argument: First, that the critics have been unable to perceive the real effect of the production, which is not to endorse a melodramatic perception of the life of the poor, but to radically criticize the melodramatic form of consciousness by juxtaposing it optically, but without explicit interaction, with the description of the *existence* (or conditions of existence) of which, in Marx's words, it is but the ideological aroma. Second, that the critical effect of the play as restructured and interpreted by Strehler and its emotional capacity to affect the spectators both arise from what Althusser calls an immanent or *latent structure* of the dissociation of times, experiences, and imaginaries, which is not pedagogically *explained* to the spectators but is *inherent* in the antithetic visions of the silent crowds and the agitated protagonists and is communicated to the audience almost physically by virtue of the discrepancy of their respective rhythms and the heterogeneity of their actions.

In the second part of his article, Althusser uses the same idea of the latent heterogeneous structure—where the conflict endowed with a critical and political meaning is represented by the paradoxical display of a "non-relationship that is the relationship"—to propose a rectified interpretation of the critical function of Brecht's "epic theater."[5] He argues that in Brecht's major plays, particularly *Mother Courage* and *The Life of Galileo*, the critical effect does not proceed from a psychological phenomenon, which would be the "distanciation" of the spectator from the spectacle ("distanciation" being the word into which Brecht's *Verfremdungseffekt*, literally, "effect of estrangement," was rendered in French), allowing us to break our "identification" with the characters in the play in order to be able to criticize politically the society of which they are the products and the victims. Rather, the critical effect would come from the fact that the same kind of latent structure, a structure of disjunction or even disruption of consciousness, is incorporated in the scenario, the distribution of characters, situations, and actions, and therefore in the performance itself. It is this shift from psychology to structure, from intentionality to a latent dissociation of consciousness, that should be not only described but actively performed by the theater, giving rise to a critique of ideology that consists not in arguing discursively against its subjection to power or domination, but in making paradoxically "visible" or "perceptible" what is in principle invisible, namely, ideology's grip on the consciousnesses of its subjects (as well as the limits of this grip in certain situations of exception). This is what Althusser called the emergence of a materialist theater, where "materialist" has the sense of destitute of ideology. Note that the idea is very similar to what, in "Cremonini, Painter of the Abstract," Althusser also attributes to certain encounters with painting, except that—in the case of Cremonini—painting makes it (relatively) easier to understand what it means to display the invisible (or the relationship of subjects to their imaginary conditions of existence) because the alienated character of this invisible relationship is allegorically displayed in the uncanny redoubling of mirrors, or the mirror-effect of inhuman pictures of the human. In the case of Strehler's theater, however, it is the *active* dimension of the critique that is (relatively) easier to understand, or the *transition from passivity to activity*, from powerlessness to empowerment, because a certain practice of the theater appears as a "machinery" or "dispositive" that has the power to *attract* the spectator's consciousness into its fictitious "world" only to *eject* her *into the real world* after it has been dislocated by the machine itself. The power of *fiction* is to dismantle or invert the *imaginary* in order to allow for the acknowledgment of the *real* and to produce a "real effect."

At this point, it would, of course, be interesting to discuss several questions of interpretation and criticism that are linked to the "dialectical" models between which Althusser is moving. An important point regards the exact nature of his relationship to the Brechtian doctrine of epic theater. This point is all the more intriguing because in a later text, "On Brecht and Marx," which remained unfinished but was published posthumously, Althusser drew an explicit parallel between Brecht's practice of theater and Marx's practice of philosophy, arguing that they both wanted not to overcome theater or philosophy but to introduce a dislocation or a "play," a disjointedness or out-of-jointedness, in the relationship between their constitutive elements that was the condition for their being turned around against the effects of the dominant ideology to which, in a sense, they still belonged.[6] Put briefly, it seems to me that Althusser's intention was to use the lessons he would draw from Strehler's spectacle not only as a critical instrument against the dominant interpretation of Brecht's theater as "critical theater" but against Brecht's own consciousness of the critical mainspring of his theater, insisting in particular on techniques of distanciation in the play of the actors. Much more important, of course, are the references to a system of Freudian concepts, even if freely used, which take their departure from the allusion to a "scenic" structure of the unconscious, where, according to Freud in *The Interpretation of Dreams*, "contradiction is ignored," which Althusser translates as "the opposites are simultaneously given" or "displayed" as if theater, or something of the theatrical machine, would bring into the open the—normally imperceptible—logic of the psychic conflict. This holds as well for the rather insistent—but never fully admitted—analogy between the process of the dissociation of ideological consciousness produced by the theater and a psychoanalytic cure, either a Freudian re-enactment of the libidinal fixations that allows their disentanglement or, even better, a Lacanian "crossing of the fantasy" (*traversée du fantasme*) that, during the same period, as indicated by Safouan, Lacan was giving as the formula explaining what it means to achieve the goals of a cure. But probably the most interesting reference is to Hegel, whose dialectics of consciousness and self-consciousness in the *Phenomenology* is omnipresent in Althusser's text, where it nevertheless appears at the same time as both instrument and object of the critique. It is as if Althusser had wanted to explain that theater, by virtue of its spatial conversion of the structures of time and the shifting positions it assigns to its heterogeneous subjects, the actors and the specta- tors, paradoxically makes it possible to materialize the impossible, namely, the presentation of what Hegel called "the back of consciousness," or the scene on which its limitations and distortions are defined but also subject to refutation. From this point of view, Althusser's essay is an astonishing counter-Hegelian reformulation of Hegel himself.

Finally, although this account of Althusser's argument is trun- cated, it allows us, I believe, to understand a central point of Althusser's critique of ideology, which remains true throughout his successive attempts with different models and from which important consequences derive. This is the fact that what a "materialist" experience of theater (which is the experience of a "materialist" theatrical practice) provides is not so much a "representation" of the ideological phenomenon of *misrecognition* of the social reality (particularly class antagonisms), to which a materialist or scientific or communist "critical" consciousness, awakened among the audi- ence in Brechtian fashion, could be opposed. But it is, rather, a *presentation* on the stage (in short, a *staging*) of the singular event or moment in which a "distanciation" (or "estrangement") with respect to *recognition*—therefore with the basic mechanism of ideological conviction or belief or subjection—is *taking place* as an action or a performance. In turn, the presentation of this action calls for a very special sort of participation, provided it is internally supported by the latent structure that attracts all the subjects and divides each of them.

Here we may remember that linguistic factors play a role: in French, *représentation* names both what the English call a "representation" and what they call a "performance" or a production (for a spectacle). But Althusser, following the Hegelian-Marxian terminology, is also thinking of the difference between a *Vorstellung*, which is cognitive and psychologi- cal, and a *Darstellung*, which is dialectical and theatrical. He suggests that the machine that makes the ideological fabric visible is also the one that forces a subject called a spectator to break with its conformism, if only momentarily or instantaneously. What derives from this is a strategic shift in the understanding of critique. It is not, in fact, *recognition*, whether as acceptation of a belief or authority or as mimetic association with others, that is built on the basis of some "misrecognition" of reality, but just the reverse: misrecognition is made possible by the deep structure of recognition, the "specular" process taking place in the back of consciousness that is consciousness itself. Therefore, to break with the contents of the dominant ideology, or to liberate oneself from its power, from the "stories" that it tells us and has us tell ourselves permanently, always presupposes a capacity to disrupt recognition, in other words, one's identity. To put it more clearly, it presupposes *situations* in which such a capacity is prompted, if not forced. But, according to Althusser's description of his experience in the audience of Strehler's production, "theater" is a social and aesthetic machine that not only shows how such a disruption or dislocation can happen but may make it happen. And this is because it duplicates (or iterates) the representation of the imaginary in a manner that may make it impossible to recompose. Such a theater, of course, is not the classical theater where, according to Althusser (who is, nevertheless, forced immediately to allow for "exceptions," mentioning Shakespeare and Molière), the relationship between stage and audience is precisely a specular one, or one of ideological recognition, with the stage displaying for the audience its own idealized identity; and it is also not exactly the Brechtian "epic theater," where it is supposed that the spectacle and the critical consciousness are divorced, repelling instead of attracting each other. Rather, it seems to be a disposition of several "scenes" on the stage (in French, it would be a single word: *des scènes sur la scène*) or, we might say, a "double installation," whereby the spectator is brought on the scene in order for the scene to intrude into the consciousness of the spectator and produce aftereffects in her life. This is again the idea, or the metaphor, of a "distanciation" that is also a "dislocation," which becomes a "displacement," displacing "agency" as such or displacing the agents in order to displace their actions. We may call this the "play" in the mechanism or the farewell to identity and stability.

No doubt, there is something in Althusser's text at the same time fascinating and enigmatic that various readers have tried to express (as I did myself). It is as if he were not just describing a mechanism or a process but recalling an experience, an interpellation: not the interpellation *of* (by) ideology, as he would later theorize, but the interpellation *out of ideology*, by "the real," as it were, which is presented or embodied on the stage by the *character* called Nina and her opposition to the crowd. This is expressed in a quick but lyrical phrase at the end: "Je me retourne" (152). I turn back or I look back. There is no rupture with ideology that is not accomplished in the first person, that is, as a subject, denoting a *conversion* in both the physical and the spiritual sense. But this takes place because theater forces a subject to identify in a contradictory manner, simultaneously, with antithetic "others" who nevertheless appear the same as oneself: in this case, "we," who eat "the same bread" and share "the same history" as the poor on the stage, and "she," the rebel whose instant rage against the myths of reconciliation we come to adopt. This is why Althusser is so insistent on the "unresolved alterity" that lies at the heart of such a dramaturgy, but also why he remains attached, more than ever, to the dramatic image provided by Hegel—that of a consciousness fatefully turned against itself: "Hegel was right: [the hero's] destiny was consciousness of himself as of an enemy" (147).

Moses or Caesar: Politics of Ideology

What I want to offer now is not exactly another general presentation of the topic of subject-formation in Althusser's well-known essay "Ideology and Ideological State Apparatuses," which remains, perhaps, of all his contributions to critical theory, the most frequently discussed and referred to in our academic programs. This essay has an interesting characteristic: although its internal aporias, or perhaps its weaknesses, are repeatedly indicated, the general theme of the essay, and particularly the specific "performative" effect to which Althusser attributed the name "interpellation," keeps returning in reflections that combine the two issues covered, in French as well as English and other "Latin" languages (English being, in this case, also a Latin language) by such terms as "subjection" and "subjectivation." This is what I have called elsewhere the great historical wordplay, or portmanteau word of European transcendental philosophy, namely, the conjunction of self-reference, or identification of the subject, and subjection to power or authority, therefore a phenomenon of constitutive domination (Balibar, "Citizen"). Among the many commentaries, of course, I single out Judith Butler's detailed discussion in *The Psychic Life of Power*, where Althusser's notion of interpellation occupies the whole of chapter 4 and returns in other chapters, counterposing Freud and Foucault.[7] I do this for two reasons: the first is that Butler particularly emphasizes the *circular* character of the mechanism, or the ideal model of subject-formation, which is subsumed by Althusser under the formula "Ideology interpellates individuals as (or perhaps better: into) subjects." The circle comes from the fact that within the field that Althusser is describing there is no way to identify what "individuals" are, if not as already existing subjects, so that the effect presupposes its own result. This is immediately illustrated in the allegorical scene through which Althusser introduces his notion, that of an individual hailed in a street, from behind, by a police officer who simply calls "Hey, you there!," immediately prompting a reaction from the individual who turns back or looks back (*il se retourne*) as if he were already certain that he is exactly the person interpellated; this would show that the elementary mechanism of recognition, associated with an originary guilt, is presupposed by the constitution of ideology. But interestingly, Butler does not see this as a weakness of the model per se; on the contrary, she interprets it—rightly in my opinion—as an indication of the fact that Althusser is assuming the circularity, describing a retroactive effect and more generally analyzing what she calls a *tropological space*, playing on two meanings of the word *trope*: First, as a rhetorical figure or an effect of discourse but also etymologically a conversion or an action of turning oneself—in this case toward the figure that one was already but that was located, so to speak, behind one's back. The second is that, having assumed a circularity beyond what Althusser himself recognizes, Butler feels able to suggest a way out of what most readers have perceived as the utterly deterministic and for that reason also fatalistic character of Althusser's account of subject formation, or recognition of the subject that one was already, which seems to allow for no margin of interpretation, no line of escape—except for a tragic notation in passing, where Althusser refers to the fact that there are "bad subjects" who refuse to turn around, to answer the call of the subjecting authority, at the risk, in fact, of their lives or their mental integrity. Butler's solution, as we know, is based on the idea that if a trope or a discursive gesture needs to be actually enacted and reiterated again and again to assert its power (as Althusser indicates a little later by provocatively borrowing from Pascal a "materialist" model of the creation of belief through the infinite reiteration of ritual gestures of subjection in the practice of prayer, whether physical or mental), this reiteration by its very nature also involves a possibility of disturbance or trouble (*subject trouble*, as it were), even the possibility of a *reversal* that she calls "counter-interpellation."[8]

This poses important problems, both from the point of view of an internal interpretation of Althusser's argument and from the point of view of the political meaning of the whole idea of "interpellation"—I am tempted to say simply the *politics* that is engaged by the fact that one refers the power of ideology to this kind of performative effect. It seems to me that Butler's rewriting of Althusser's model, arising from a deep understanding of the structure of the "scene," is made possible by the fact that, like most commentators outside of Marxist theory, she focuses on the *second half* of Althusser's essay, which describes the "ideological mechanism," leaving aside the first half, where Althusser defines the function of ideology as a "reproduction of the relations of production" ("Ideology" 148), that is, a reproduction of the type of subjectivity and identity that is necessary for individuals to work as "voluntary" bearers of an exploited or subjected labor force. More precisely, it is as if Butler had kept a formal notion of "reproduction," understood as repetition or reiteration, to import it into the field of discourses and affects, leaving aside its relationship to *production* in the Marxist sense. It is important to recall here that Althusser's essay—in fact, a *collage* or product of cutting and pasting portions of an unfinished manuscript—really consists of two separate parts, widely different in style and object, whose enigmatic unity was indicated in the original text through a series of dotted lines and which precisely generated the fruitful character of the essay because they made it impossible for interpreters to use or discuss it without transforming it. Once again, important translation effects are at play here, since in French *répétition* also means "rehearsal" of a performance and thus, in a sense, always already takes place on a stage, whereas the standard equivalent in German, *Wiederholung*, is also for us indissolubly associated with the Freudian problematic of the death drive and its symbolic effects. No wonder, of course, that in a highly overdetermined gesture, Butler titled her chapter on Althusser with a parody of a famous phrase from Shakespeare's *Hamlet*: "Conscience doth make subjects of us all" (3.1). She would thus indicate that Althusser's seemingly marginal remark in the essay, *à la cantonade*, referring to his description of the policeman's interpellation as "my little theoretical theater," should be taken entirely seriously and pursued as an investigation of its structure and prerequisites.

This is what I want to do myself, in a manner that is partly complementary, partly divergent from hers, by returning to Althusser's text and trying to extricate more of its intrinsic dramaturgy to suggest a possible *displacement* of the reading that is made possible by the insertion of the essay in its context. Let me first recall that the circularity of the procedure of interpellation "as subjects" and the theatrical "element" in which the model is located, namely, the fact that such "actions" as interpellation (and *nomination*, "calling" in the double sense, to begin with) and answer, response, responding, and assuming responsibility are clearly always taking place *on a stage*. This is the whole problem with the issue of the institutional "conditions" of possibility of performative statements, namely, the fact that the speakers must *play their roles*. But here, with the question of the effectivity of interpellations, we are immediately forced to take into account a much wider spectrum of experiences, social forms, and institutions, where the theatrical stage at the same time occurs as a *general model* for the staging of discourse and as *one case* among many others, where the "scenes" are not only located in theaters but also in civic spaces, agoras, tribunals, temples, private meetings, and ceremonies, or also metaphorically on the "world's stage," which is the encompassing space for the staging of life and the assumption of roles, *personae* in Latin, which also means "masks." So we can see that Althusser (and Butler) are in fact taking part in a very long tradition, offering *variations*, as it were, of a theme, the *theatrum mundi*, that has a long existence in philosophy and art from the Stoics to Shakespeare and Descartes, and indeed in Hegel, Marx, Freud. On the other hand, returning to the aporia that is widely identified by readers in Althusser's "scene of ideology," or model of the ideological mechanism as a scene of interpellation, what I want to emphasize is the fact that this aporia is not separable from the assumption that Althusser's explanations have a *political* intention, that they are supposed to indicate why processes of *reproduction* of the social order and the social structure, based on certain forms of domination, are cemented by ideology, whose intrinsic coherence would act as a *guarantee* for the class relationship. At the same time, this "ideological reproduction" would form a place of revolutionary intervention, marking not a deterministic necessity but rather an intrinsic fragility or contingency. Now the fact is that as it is presented in the text, the mechanism of the ideological constitution of subjects, or the transformation of individuals into subjects, which has always already taken place since there is no *originary place outside of ideology*, is a mechanism that offers no way out ("Ideology" 175). Even the "bad subjects" are trapped—perhaps more than the others.

It is quite clear to me that Althusser's description is deeply influenced by Freud's analysis of the "identification processes" that shape, at the same time, the ideal construction of the ego-ideal and the formation of social groups or "masses" (*Massenbildungen*).[9] But Freud's analysis leaves no room, except madness, for a subjectivity that would become liberated from every identification, and this is also formally the case in Althusser. There is "freedom," of course, but only in the sense of *shifting from one identification, one interpellation,* to another, for instance letting oneself become interpellated and subjectively constituted by the "Revolution" instead of the "State" or the "Nation" or the "Market" or the "Republic" or, indeed, "God." There is no "anarchic" freedom in the sense of living, thinking, and acting in the void, the absence of every interpellation, every ideal, that Freud calls an ideal object of love, and Althusser a "Subject" with a capital *S*. It could be argued that this other circularity, the infinite circularity of the imaginary "Others" from which, qua subjects, we expect interpellation, forming like a prison with many cells and no release, reflects the deep pessimism that invaded Althusser (and others) after '68. But it should be noticed as well that he doesn't say (and in fact nothing in his text says) that different interpellations, which *have the same ideological structure, the structure of "ideology in general,"* produce the same historical and political effects. The theory doesn't say that the political effects are the same if your model of interpellation is patriotism or internationalism or the Subject is God as inflexible Legislator or God as suffering Servant. Perhaps it says just the opposite: that the effect remains essentially *indeterminate* until it becomes determined in a given conjuncture, both by the internal "logic" of the specific discourse of interpellation and by the external conditions of its insertion into the processes of reproduction of the existing order—a combination in which there must probably always remain something *aleatory* or contingent. It remains now to be seen if this could be investigated by means of a fuller use of the "dramaturgic" model that, in agreement with Butler, I have identified in the text.

The first element that I find striking in Althusser's examples of interpellation concerns his insistence on the *staging of the voice* that "interpellates" the subject as a voice whose origin—or, if you like, whose speaking "mouth"—is concealed or *hiding*, not only behind a *mask* as in the ancient model of the *persona*, which keeps governing so much classical reflection on the theater (including Diderot's and Brecht's theories on the *paradoxe du comédien* and the "distanciating techniques" borrowed from non-Western theater),[10] but behind a *veil* or a *curtain* (or a *cloud*), which is the veil of transcendence. To put it better so as to keep within the limits of a "materialist" description of the theatrical machinery: it is the veiling effect that produces an effect of transcendence, the effect of *withdrawing the origin* of the interpellation, removing the possibility of identifying an author, except through the tautologies asserting his authority. *I am who I am*, says the voice that interpellates Moses from behind the Burning Bush. Here, of course, we need to move from one "theater" to another, from the everyday scenes of authority, identification, and interpellation to the grand historical and cosmic scene where the source of the dominant ideologies—perhaps only the dominant ideologies *of the West*, which are based on a certain representation of the Law—are traditionally staged. And this produces two consequences. The first consequence is that the concealment of the origin of the voice becomes part of a generic machine, the *Machine*, as it were, that will have to be indefinitely reproduced *within* the ideological world, at the same time setting the pattern that everyday interpellations reiterate. (All judges and police officers stage their interpellation in order to reenact the arch-interpellation of the Law; each priest or pastor stages his admonitions as repetitions of the Revelation; *each of us* stages the "voice of conscience" in the internal theater as one that speaks unconditionally but from nowhere.) And second, it means that the little subjects cannot receive the voice, respond to it, or transmit it to others without *filling the void* with some sort of imaginary, if only the projection of their own desire for subjection. This is why Althusser explains that a new *circle* must take place: that of the imagination of the Other Subject by whose mediation or intermediary a given ideology would interpellate individuals as *its* subjected subjects. This circle—which is a circularity between the stage and the backstage or a re-creation of a backstage each time a subject imagines herself called by (and toward) a transcendent Subject (that is, a power whose authority is beyond contestation or even comprehension)—is theatrical in its very nature, but it is also *fragile* in the sense that, circumstances permitting, it arouses skepticism and rebellion or heresy as easily as obedience and devotion.

Here we think of Lacan (whom Althusser had partly read), of course, and his thesis (since the Seminar on psychoses from 1955–56) that "there is no Other of the Other" which would warrant it—except that, as we know, Althusser's thesis, right or wrong, was always that the symbolic orders of authority and law are no more than formations crystallizing the social imaginary. The stronger inspiration of this model, in fact, which the reference to Moses clearly indicates, is the description and interpretation of the revelation on Mount Sinai proposed by Spinoza in the *Theological-Political Treatise*. It is from there that Althusser may have borrowed not only the idea that the Prophet or Legislator can enunciate the Law as an Absolute only on the condition of adapting his own imaginary to the dominant imaginary of the people or the mass (an idea that we will retrieve in Althusser's interpretation of Machiavelli's *Prince*) but also the idea that the *interpellated* Legislator or Mediator can transmit the interpellation that he has received to those for whom it is ultimately destined (that is, ordinary men, the people or the "herd") only at the risk that this challenge may *backfire* onto the imagination of the originary voice, or the Hidden Mouth itself—as in the episode of the Golden Calf (another staging, or form of "performative reversal"). Perhaps Althusser does not entirely say this, but his example, with the religious and philosophical connotations that it carries, says it for him. And this, of course, is where we could locate his own virtual introduction of a counterinterpellation, or the idea of a "play" that *diverges* in an unpredictable manner from the written script.

But to this we must now add another element. If we reassemble the separated developments of the two "parts" in the ideological state apparatuses (ISAS) essay—the one on "social reproduction" of the structures of domination and the one on "interpellation of individuals as subjects" through the mediation of an imaginary Subject (or Other)—we reach the supposition that there is indeed *someone or something*, some "force," acting behind the scene or, rather, behind the theater itself (perhaps in some hidden box, as in Walter Benjamin's allegory of the automaton chess player of Maelzel). This instance or agency, in Althusser's conception, is *the state* in its broad or generic sense—that of a concentrated political power securing the reproduction of the dominant class structure and also, we are led to understand, *selecting the individuals* within society to return them as "subjects" adapted to their productive functions. This would be a banal Marxist (or, more generally, anti-authoritarian) indictment of the political function of the state as instrument of class domination if it were not for a strange internal dislocation: the State, like God himself, is efficient in "identifying" its own subjects and imposing on them the circularity of recognition *only* on the condition of *withdrawing* from any visible place in the process or the circuit of reproduction. This is particularly developed in a later text: a public lecture delivered in Grenada, Spain, in 1976, with the title "The Transformation of Philosophy," where Althusser explains that the ideological power of the state lies in imposing on the subject's consciousness a "unity" or "identity" that it does not necessarily possess at all but is always *supposed to possess*. In order to be active within reproduction as an "ideological power,"[11] the State must in fact be *absent* from the processes of reproduction—or it must, like the Freudian unconscious, according to Lacan, be acting (that is, it must think, or make think) "where it is not . . ."

You will say: this transposition of the structuralist idea of the "absent cause" into an allegory of the power that dislocates or "decenters" itself in order to remain an empty place of attraction for the imagination of the subjects does not really solve the *political* problem of liberation *from ideology* as such. At the very best, it indicates in political-theological terms where a counterinterpellation or a heretical gesture could "interrupt" the play, deviate it, or "cut" into it. But on the other side—the "Marxist" side, we might say—it seems to introduce a redoubtable *dilemma*: since the mechanism of "interpellation" from which derives the imaginary circle of specularity, binding together the Big Subject and the little subjects, therefore the hypothesis of the "absent State" installing the machine for its own retreat, is presented as a description of "ideology in general," independent of historical transformations (or "eternal," as Althusser writes provocatively in the same essay), would this mean that we should look elsewhere for an *interpellation without a State*? Or should we admit that the "State" is just as eternal as ideology itself, albeit perhaps with other names and other forms of organization, such as—why not?—"Revolution" or "Communist Party"? Would "Revolution" perhaps be the new name of the State, thus calling indefinitely for its own "counterinterpellations" or "revolutions within the revolution," not to say "counterrevolutions"?

It is here that, to provide an ultimate *décalage*, I want to refer to the posthumous book *Machiavelli and Us*. With the exception of some marginal corrections and additions, it was written mainly between 1972 and 1976 and then kept private by Althusser (who would show it only to a few friends and interlocutors).[12] I have written previously that this was in a sense Althusser's *point d'honneur* during a period of bitter struggles, of personal and political misfortunes, and of failed attempts to adapt orthodox Marxist categories to an increasingly escaping reality. It is a book that has the same stylistic qualities, sharp and passionate, as only one or two others in Althusser's career (the book on Montesquieu and the *For Marx* collection, in particular). But what interests me more in this circumstance is the fact that it provides a transformation of the problematic of the ISAs, which is also a way of once again rewriting the dramaturgy of ideology and its internal tensions. Considering Machiavelli's *Prince* from the beginning as a *work of art* but also an *artifice* or a textual "machine" that "grips us" readers ("Il nous saisit")—that is, it interpellates us today (as it did in the past for Spinoza, Rousseau, Hegel, and others) and leaves us uncertain and troubled with respect to its exact intentions—Althusser would also suggest that not only had Machiavelli written his book *in the conjuncture*, under its specific constraints and urgencies (which, according to him, is very different from writing *on the conjuncture*), but he can also only be read *in a conjuncture*, where, depending on the specific problems of the time, it will produce incommensurable effects. The "theaters" involved here are theaters of politics, which also very much resemble *theaters of war* in a generalized sense.

Let us now jump directly to the final section of *Machiavelli and Us*, called "The Political Practice of the New Prince." What we find there is not only a speculation on the uncertain combinations of *fortuna* and *virtù* in the aleatory situations of history, but the idea that this "war" (whether a "war of movement" or a "war of position") essentially presupposes the invention of a politics of ideology. This is linked with a presentation of the prince (or rather the *new Prince*, who *inaugurates* a regime of power and seeks to stabilize it) that makes him neither the embodiment of the State, the bearer of the monarchic or presidential function exercising *leadership*, nor a "Legislator" in the ancient sense, repeatedly discussed in political theory after the privileged example of Moses. Rather, the new Prince is presented as an *agent* who is also an *actor* on the historical stage. And in fact this is possible only because he is at the same time the *director* who sets the stage for his own *acting* or *performing*. This is necessary because, according to Machiavelli as Althusser reads him, the determining element in securing "national" support for his own power and project is the capacity to change, channel, and control the *opinion of the people*. More precisely, what matters is the opinion of the *majority of the people*, which is always made of ordinary, relatively poor people (the *popolo minuto* of the Italian cities, as opposed to the rich and the noble class, the *popolo grasso*). It is the opinion or representation that the people have acquired of the person and the actions of the Prince, therefore the "figure" of the Prince as a ruler in the imagination of the people, that is decisive for the success of his own action—as long as it can last (which, as we know, is never *ad infinitum*). This leads Althusser to insist on the fact that, in the Prince's *art*, which aims not so much at attracting the *love* of his subjects (a highly ambivalent affect, easily turned into its opposite) but rather at inspiring *fear without hatred*, the Prince must be able to "play" in public with his own passions, to offer them for elaboration in the imaginary of the people (we are tempted to say identification and counteridentification). A very difficult task indeed, which seems to require quite antithetic capacities and dispositions: a political passion subjecting the other passions (including the passion for power, riches, and admiration), on the one hand, and a "ruse of the ruse," on the other, indicating *when to feign and when not to feign*, or, in other words, when to speak the truth and when not to speak the truth to the people—following a "rule of veridiction and dissimulation," *norma veri et falsi*, we are tempted to say with Spinoza (another careful reader of Machiavelli). But the ultimate condition, according to Althusser's reading, remains an *objective* one, albeit one entirely located in the *material field of ideology*: this is the negative condition of never offending the "general ideology" of the poor, the ordinary people, which is defined here as religion and morality, or the idea of the holy and the idea of justice.

Let me conclude briefly by saying that this new description sketches a "politics of ideology" in the double sense of the genitive (using ideology itself as an instrument in the field of ideological formations) based on the perception of its subjective constitution. It could be defined, therefore, as a play with interpellation and the limits of interpellation. Clearly, it is "aleatory" both in its conditions and its results: this is a politics without guarantee, hence without certainty. The most interesting question to ask, however, concerns its political orientation in terms of where this kind of "autonomy of the political" would lead: whether toward the *conservation* of or a *revolution* in the existing social order. In fact, it is certainly not "conservative." Althusser was continually returning with more or less sympathetic feelings to Gramsci's attempts to "translate" Machiavelli into the language of a revolutionary strategy for the contemporary Communist Party endowed with a "hegemonic" capacity. He was also an avid reader of Montaigne's and Pascal's considerations on the costuming of magistrates and a commentator of seventeenth-century theorists of the *apparatus of the state* in the sense of pomp and ceremony (whence he may have borrowed his terminology as much as from Marx's and Lenin's "State apparatus"), combining thus a machinery and a show. It seems to me that his reading of Machiavelli has certain affinities, on a different terrain, with Benjamin's distinction between "mythical" and "divine" violence (an author he certainly had not read), except that here what is at stake is conservative versus disruptive uses of the imaginary, or the collective figurations of ideology. But none of this, it seems to me, entirely resolves the "aporia" of an action of the masses (or the people) *upon their own imaginary* that would use the artifices of visualization and representation in order to orient it toward actions that are in their own interest, following ideals in which they believe—without believing "blindly," as it were, or in which they believe *with a distance.* The difficulty seems to be the same as the one already encountered by Spinoza at the end of the *Theological-Political Treatise* when asking how it could be possible that a "power of the multitude" not be terrorized by the multitude, or by the enormity of its own power.

This allows me a final, very formal remark. In a sense, what I have read in two series of texts was, first, a description of *theater as politics* and, then, an attempt at conceptualizing *politics as theater.* In both cases, what appears is that the key—or *one key,* but an important one—to understanding Althusser's ruminations about ideology lies in the fact that, for him, *ideology is always already a dramaturgy.* History appears not only as a succession of "modes of production" but as a series of "productions" in the sense of performances, where one *staging* (or mise-en-scène) can become corrected and its effects transformed only through another mise-en-scène, and so on indefinitely. He had written toward the end of the preface to *Reading Capital* that, from a materialist point of view, "history" should be conceived as "a theater without an author." I am not sure whether this was Marx's view—not so much because of the repudiation of the "author," but because of the "theater," although it is striking to see how often Marx speaks in terms of stages, scenes, intrigues, and genres, notably in the famous assertion that historical events always occur twice, "first as tragedy, then as farce."[13] But it was certainly one of Althusser's obsessions. And he may have fancied himself at times not as an author (I believe that he hated authorship as much as Foucault did, if not more), but as a *metteur en scène*, a stage director in the field of theory or in the field of that specific politics of ideology with which he identified philosophy under the name of "class struggle in theory," a director whose action is incorporated and occulted in his own production ("Philosophy" 19–21).

ÉTIENNE BALIBAR is Anniversary Chair of Contemporary European Philosophy at Kingston University London and visiting professor at Columbia University. His books include *Reading Capital*, with Louis Althusser, Roger Establet, Pierre Macherey, and Jacques Rancière (Verso, 1965/2015), *Identity and Difference: John Locke and the Invention of Consciousness* (Verso, 2013), *Equaliberty: Political Essays* (Duke University Press, 2014), and *Violence and Civility: On the Limits of Political Philosophy* (Columbia University Press, 2015).

Notes

1   See Butler, *Psychic* and *Excitable*; de Ípola; Lahtinen; Montag, *Althusser*; Morfino; Žižek.

2   A complete history of the Cremonini essay's elaboration, along with an analysis of its relationship to other "encounters" between French philosophers and painting mediated by politics, can be found in Sarah Wilson's beautiful book *The Visual World of French Theory*.

3   See Bargu; Howlett; Montag, *Louis*; Sibertin-Blanc.

4   "Ideology and Ideological State Apparatuses" first appeared as a separate essay in the journal *La Pensée* in 1970. This is the text that has been used and discussed for years (as translated into English by Ben Brewster and published in *Lenin and Philosophy and Other Essays* in 1971). The longer manuscript from which it was extracted has been published posthumously in French as *Sur la reproduction* and translated into English by G. M. Goshgarian as *On the Reproduction of Capitalism: Ideology and Ideological State Apparatuses*. I use the original French version here and have retranslated quotations from it.

5   It can be recalled here that Brecht, who had created his own theater in East Berlin, Das Berliner Ensemble, after leaving the United States under the pressure of the McCarthy prosecutions, had come to Paris in 1955 on a tour with

Mother Courage and other plays, where he had been hailed by the left intelligentsia, particularly Roland Barthes in an enthusiastic series of articles, as the bearer of a genuine aesthetic "revolution." For a complete set of references to the articles written by Barthes on Brecht and an illuminating commentary, see Carmody.

6   I am relying here on the commentary offered by Warren Montag in his first book on Althusser, *Louis Althusser.*

7   See also Butler, *Excitable.* On Butler's reading of Althusser, see Macherey.

8   See Butler, *Psychic* 109, 129–31. See also Butler's introduction to *Excitable.*

9   Althusser's personal notes on Freud's *Massen* are dated the same year as the writing of *On the Reproduction of Capitalism.* See note 4.

10   See Barthes; von Held.

11   "The State is the first ideological power," Engels wrote in *Ludwig Feuerbach and the End of Classical German Philosophy.*

12   I was not one of them, hence my surprise when it was published after his death in 1994.

13   From Marx's *Eighteenth Brumaire of Louis Bonaparte.*

Works Cited   Althusser, Louis. "Cremonini, Painter of the Abstract." *Lenin* 229–42.

——————. "Ideology and Ideological State Apparatuses." *Lenin* 127–86.

——————. *Lenin and Philosophy and Other Essays.* Trans. Ben Brewster. New York: Monthly Review Press, 1971.

——————. "On Brecht and Marx." Trans. Warren Montag. Montag, *Louis* 136–49.

——————. *On the Reproduction of Capitalism: Ideology and Ideological State Apparatuses.* Trans. G. M. Goshgarian. New York: Verso, 2014.

——————. "Philosophy as a Revolutionary Weapon." *Lenin* 11–70.

——————. "The 'Piccolo Teatro': Bertolazzi and Brecht. Notes on a Materialist Theater." *For Marx.* New York: Verso, 2005. 129–52.

——————. "The Transformation of Philosophy." Trans. Thomas E. Lewis. *Philosophy and the Spontaneous Philosophy of the Scientists.* London: Verso, 1990. 241–66.

Althusser, Louis, and Étienne Balibar. *Reading Capital.* Trans. Ben Brewster. London: Verso, 1970.

Balibar, Étienne. "Avant-propos pour la réédition de 1996." *Pour Marx.* By Louis Althusser. Paris: La Découverte, 1996. i–xiii.

——————. "Citizen Subject." Trans. James Swenson. *Who Comes after the Subject?* Ed. Eduardo Cavada, Peter Connor, and Jean-Luc Nancy. New York: Routledge, 1991. 33–57.

Bargu, Banu. "In the Theater of Politics: Althusser's Aleatory Materialism and Aesthetics." *diacritics* 40.3 (2012): 86–111.

Barthes, Roland. "Diderot, Brecht, Eisenstein." *Image, Music, Text*. Ed. and trans. Stephen Heath. New York: Noonday, 1977. 69–78.

Butler, Judith. *Excitable Speech: A Politics of the Performative*. New York: Routledge, 1997.

——————. *The Psychic Life of Power*. Stanford: Stanford UP, 1997.

Carmody, Jim. "Reading Scenic Writing: Barthes, Brecht, and Theatre Photography." *Journal of Dramatic Theory and Criticism* 5.1 (1990): 25–38.

de Ípola, Emilio. *Althusser, El infinito adiós*. Buenos Aires: Siglo Veintiuno, 2007.

Engels, Friedrich. *Ludwig Feuerbach and the End of Classical German Philosophy*. *Marx/Engels Internet Archive* 1994. https://www.marxists.org/archive/marx/works/1886/ludwig-feuerbach/ (accessed 15 July 2015).

Howlett, Marc-Vincent. "Le théâtre n'est-il pour Althusser qu'un 'risque fictif'?" *Lire Althusser aujourd'hui*. Spec. issue of *Futur Antérieur* (Apr. 1997). *Multitudes: Revue politique, artistique, philosophique*. http://www.multitudes.net/Le-theatre-n-est-il-pour-Althusser/.

Lacan, Jacques. *The Seminar of Jacques Lacan: The Psychoses*. Book 3. Ed. Jacques-Alain Miller. New York: Norton, 1997.

Lahtinen, Mikko. *Politics and Philosophy: Niccolò Machiavelli and Louis Althusser's Aleatory Materialism*. Trans. Gareth Griffiths and Kristina Köhli. Chicago: Haymarket, 2011.

Macherey, Pierre. "Judith Butler and the Althusserian Theory of Subjection." Trans. Stephanie Bundy. *Décalages* 1.2 (2012). http://scholar.oxy.edu/cgi/viewcontent.cgi?article=1031&context=decalages.

Marx, Karl. *The Eighteenth Brumaire of Louis Bonaparte*. *Marx/Engels Internet Archive* 1995, 1999. https://www.marxists.org/archive/marx/works/1852/18th-brumaire/ (accessed 15 July 2015).

Montag, Warren. *Althusser and His Contemporaries: Philosophy's Perpetual War*. Durham: Duke UP, 2013.

——————. *Louis Althusser*. New York: Palgrave Macmillan, 2003.

Morfino, Vittorio. *Plural Temporality: Transindividuality and the Aleatory between Spinoza and Althusser*. Leiden: Brill, 2014.

Safouan, Moustafa. *La Psychanalyse: Science, thérapie—et cause*. Paris: Éditions Thierry Marchaisse, 2013.

Sibertin-Blanc, Guillaume. "De la théorie du théâtre à la scène de la théorie: Réflexions sur '"Le Piccolo": Bertolazzi et Brecht' d'Althusser." *Le moment philosophique des années 1960 en France*. Ed. Patrice Maniglier. Paris: PUF, 2011. 255–72.

von Held, Phoebe. *Alienation and Theatricality: Diderot after Brecht*. Oxford: Legenda, 2011.

Wilson, Sarah. *The Visual World of French Theory*. New Haven: Yale UP, 2010.

Žižek, Slavoj. *The Sublime Object of Ideology*. New York: Verso, 1989.

Theatrical Machines

*B*alibar's impressive effort to revisit and reanimate Althusser's engagement with theater opens up several new theoretical queries. Among them is whether, and how, the examination of political theater helps us to rethink a critical concept of ideology. And further: how do procedures of subjectivation, which centrally informed Althusser's account of ideology, rely on notions of identification and performativity that are highlighted in very specific ways by political theater, especially the Brechtian version? Balibar reminds us that for Althusser, the mechanism of subjectivation (*assujettissement*: a term that includes both subjection and subject-formation) reproduces social relations but not precisely in a mechanical or deterministic way. The meaning of "mechanical" is immediately important, since for the most part *mechanical* tends to be associated in popular language with *automatic*, yet every mechanism has within itself the possibility of not quite working as smoothly as it should. So though the mechanism is governed by the reproduction of social relations through the reproduction of the subject, there is sometimes "play" in the mechanism, which means that it can veer

Volume 26, Number 3   DOI 10.1215/10407391-3340336

in a different relation, or it can, indeed, fall apart and fail to reproduce in the way for which it is designed.

Most of Kafka's efforts to treat the mechanical foreground this constitutive possibility of breakdown, or malfunction. The wayward machine in "In the Penal Colony" is a particularly graphic example. It is supposed to be a writing instrument that inscribes the final judgment on the prisoner but, in the writing, jerks out of control, periodically stabbing and killing the body that lies within its maw. In that case, the machine, the directions for which have become unreadable over time, loses control but still acts mechanically. We find a similar configuration of the machinic in Freud's notion of the "psychic mechanism," one that starts to move in compulsive tangents precisely when it is overwhelmed by either internal or external "influx." Indeed, the psychic mechanism transcribes and rewrites not only the overwhelming drives that emerge from a psychic interior but also the "stimuli" of historical events, including wars, that traumatize the psychic mechanism and cause it to stutter and repeat compulsively and in a direction that seeks to move toward, or back to, conditions of nonlife. Those forms of compulsive repetition, as we know from *Beyond the Pleasure Principle*, do not yield pleasure and seem rather to be in the service of a rival principle, one that he names the "death drive." That drive is characteristically "machinic" in its repetitions, and it is instigated, or aroused, especially in the wake of war. It matters, in other words, that Freud is trying to understand war psychosis in light of the pleasure principle when he comes up against the limits of his own theory. It is at the point that he discovers forms of compulsive repetition that do not drive toward the satisfaction of the wish that he himself is compelled to leave aside the comprehensive claims he has made for the libido for the previous twenty-five years. How is he to describe, or understand, this new form of repetition, one that seems mechanical and compulsive and that does not seem to be in the service of pleasure? Freud identifies the increasing power of new technologies to deliver mass death as part of what is so very overwhelming to register between the two world wars. Referring to World War I in "Reflections on War and Death," he writes, "[T]he war in which we did not want to believe broke out [. . .] bloodier and more destructive than any foregoing war, as a result of the tremendous development of weapons of attack and defense" (278). And then again, in *Civilization and Its Discontents*, alert to the rise of European Fascism: "[M]en have gained control over the forces of nature to such an extent that with their help they would have no trouble exterminating one another to the last man" (145). The mechanical, understood not only as a more rudimentary form of war technology but as a form of repetition not fully governed, or governable, by conscious plan or wish, unleashed destructive potential that has to be, according to Freud, quite deliberately checked when and where it can. Significantly, the "mechanism" is a figure for the very problem of how the external world impressed itself upon the psyche and how primary drives do, or do not, find expression in the outer world. Indeed, it seems that the "mechanical" belongs neither to psychic nor to historical life, but to the very event of their disturbing convergence.

For all the gravity of this treatment of the mechanical and its special function and character as part of the death drive and/or the destructiveness of war, the "mechanical" can take on other meanings. Walter Benjamin surely seems to concur with Freud when he writes toward the end of "The Work of Art in the Age of Mechanical Reproduction," "[T]he destructiveness of war furnishes proof that society has not been mature enough to incorporate technology as its organ," and then, inverting agency altogether: "[I]mperialist war is a rebellion of technology which collects, in the form of 'human material,' the claims to which society has denied its natural material" (242). And yet, earlier in that same essay, Benjamin points out that photography "is the first truly revolutionary means of reproduction," one that he associates with the "rise of socialism" (224). Indeed, in the midst of a pessimistic account of how mechanical reproduction has contributed to the development of an aestheticized pleasure in the representation of the prospective destruction of humanity, Benjamin remarks that "mechanical reproduction emancipates the work of art from its parasitic dependency on ritual," establishing new possibilities for "exhibition value" (224). Although "democratization" of art is not exactly the term that Benjamin would use, it is clear that art, especially photography and film, is released from traditional strongholds of nation, class, and museum culture precisely in and through its mechanical reproducibility and dissemination throughout the visual field. No subject established this aim for photography and film, though it would appear that these effects follow from mechanical reproducibility as it breaks away from the traditional and ritual functions of art. There is a "breaking away" or "breaking off" in mechanical reproduction, and so a destructive dimension; and yet, this repetition leads in ambivalent directions at the same time: the aestheticization of destructiveness and the accessibility of art to the masses.

The mechanical can work in at least two ways at once, and this suggestion seems to be confirmed in Balibar's reading of Althusser. Although Althusser is not primarily concerned with destructiveness in his formulation of ideology, he is concerned with the conditions under which a subject breaks with a set of primary identifications and comes to critically question a set of ideological convictions or beliefs that have maintained and naturalized the system of domination under capitalism. Althusser foregrounds the way in which there is a certain "play" between what we might call, drawing on Benjamin, the mechanical reproduction of ideology and the psychic mechanism. If the psychic mechanism is not simply formed or determined by social forces, neither is it fully independent of the "play" of forces. As we have seen, in Freud the "mechanism" is a figure for the negotiation of psychic and socio-historical forces that impinge upon the subject. That double-impingement is taken up by a mechanism that produces a series of displacements that do not mimetically reflect the overwhelming conditions of its production.

Although this part of Freud's reflection is not at the center of Althusser's analysis, the idea of the mechanism surely is.[1] Balibar makes an important distinction between a theoretical practice that describes the processes and procedures of subjectivation and a "performative" gesture that helps to locate the subject "within" the ideological mechanism. This second dimension, which will become so crucial to Althusser's consideration of theater, is where the fragility of the mechanism can be found, evidenced most clearly in the wayward production of ideological incoherence or disturbance. If the machine has gone awry, it is not only, or always, in the service of destruction; the contingent or inadvertent effects of the mechanical reproduction of ideology seem to take place precisely by virtue of the psychic dimension on which they rely. *Identification* names that process by which ideology reproduces more or less consistently and where it deviates from its apparent goals. So the question that we bring to the consideration of the critical function of political theater, as it amplifies or revises the account of ideology, is the following: how do identification and misidentification function in the process of subjectivation, and where might we find the performative dimension of identification that exhibits the fallibility of ideological reproduction? This performative dimension is associated for Balibar with what he calls the "dramaturgical model of the political function and political transformation of ideology" (5).

In the first instance, it would seem that the staging of melodrama, as evidenced in the work of Giorgio Strehler, provides the condition not to endorse melodramatic consciousness, but to criticize it. That criticism becomes possible only because the melodramatic loses something of its credibility onstage. But perhaps more importantly, the melodramatic forms of enthrallment that persist throughout ordinary life are explicitly staged so that they can become an object of critical reflection. Such a reflection involves self-reflection, namely, the recognition of how one is in a daily way implicated in that form of consciousness without recognizing it as such. But for this first modality of critical consciousness to emerge, there has to be a form of self-reflection that centrally focuses on identification: I am that character or the other one, or perhaps I am both at once, and my identification is relatively seamless. The scene allows me to track my multiple identifications as an enacted and visual experience that takes place at some distance from who I am, even though I manage to bridge that gap time and again. If I bridge that gap, I am forming myself as a subject in conformity with the norms by which ideological subjectivation takes place.

A more specifically critical concern with identification becomes possible with Brecht's epic theater. That distance that I take from the scene of my identifications follows from a *Verfremdungseffekt*, understood as a practice of "disidentification." I not only say I am that character or that other one, but also, I become self-aware of the lure of identification as well as its impossibility: I am, yet I am not that character, which means that even as I give in to the lure of identification, I know it to be false. This is the operation of *dénégation*, a form of dissociation that allows me to believe and not to believe at the same time (crucial to the "I know, but still" that concedes that the fetish is a displacement and substitution at the same time it gives in to its pull, as if it were the primary object of one's desire). In other words, I become double to myself as a process of simultaneous identification and disidentification. I can ask: what propels me to identify in this way, and what grounds do I have for resisting that identification? In asking this question, I am asking how ideology works through the process of subjectivation and how subjectivation works centrally through identification.

As Balibar points out, it is only from this position of disidentification that the audience can begin to criticize the political character of their society and see themselves as its product. The task is to "make visible" the ideological lure of identification. But then a few questions arise: How does this "making visible" occur? Is the visual field the only one in which it can occur? And how does identification hold within it the possibility for disidentification? And perhaps, lastly, how does disidentification operate in relation to misrecognition (*méconnaissance*), a category so central to Althusser's reading of Lacan for his theory of ideology? It would seem that theater has a specific capacity to make visible those imaginary relations to the conditions of existence that define ideology for Althusser. If we ask through what imaginary relations the real conditions of existence are known, we are already asking about ideology but are also focused on the identificatory practices. In his essay "Freud and Lacan," Althusser makes clear that the imaginary is the domain of the pre-Oedipal, and so the site where identifications can be at play before being "ordered" more formally by the Oedipal complex, which installs, for Lacan, the symbolic domain. Interestingly, Althusser brings the dramaturgical motif together with the mechanical one in that essay: "So the Oedipal phase is not a hidden 'meaning' which merely lacks consciousness or speech—it is not a structure buried in the past that can always be restructured or surpassed by 'reactivating its meaning'; the Oedipal complex is a dramatic structure, the 'theatrical machine' imposed by the Law of Culture on every involuntary, conscripted candidate to humanity" (201). And should we assume that the machine cranks out its results in predictable ways, we read in Althusser that this "structure" has its "concrete variants." And the effects it produces in and as the human subject are the result of having "lived through" and "survived" that conscription process; the subsequent form that the subject takes, including, if not primarily, its gender, bears the visible and nonvisible traces of that survival. How the human animal survives is not precisely predictable. Indeed, the notion of "effect" Althusser explicitly affirms in an endnote appended to this discussion makes clear that it does not belong to "a classical theory of causality," but rather to Spinoza: an effect must be understood as one (variant) modality in which the continuing presence of the cause appears. Indeed, the human subject is always, in his view, "de-centered, constituted by a structure which has no 'center' either, except in the imaginary misrecognition of the 'ego,' i.e., in the ideological formations in which it 'recognizes' itself" (201).

So a seamless identification is the means through which misrecognition is accomplished. I see myself onstage, feel quite pleased with that specular reflection, and affirm that I am that one, or the other one, and leave the theater ratified in my sense of who I am. That "achievement" rests on a misrecognition, since I am not that character, and the recognition of that negation precipitates a decentering of my sense of self, or my "ego" in the Freudian vocabulary. What was it that just staged that happy but mistaken sense of identification, the basis for that mistaken sense of recognition? We cannot precisely find a Subject who inaugurated that process. The scene is constituted by a "structure" that "has no center either." Of course, the ego is constituted within the imaginary and always in a fictional direction, or so Lacan tells us in "The Mirror Stage." In Althusser's terms, the ego, that bounded and knowable sense of self, is founded invariably through misrecognition, which means that every time there is a specular satisfaction, ideology has done its work and our own doubts about who we "are" are temporarily set aside. The self-satisfactions of seeing oneself "as one really is" constitute the triumph of ideology.

So how does that work in theater, and how does the theatrical machine make ideology work, or expose its dysfunction and mobilize its audience? Political theater enacts those relations, depending on the spectatorial distance of the audience that allows both for identification within the scenes acted out and for forms of critique based on disidentification with those very scenes. The capacity to describe the reflexive process of disenchantment and disidentification realized within Brechtian theater (epic theater, in particular) is not by itself sufficient to account for the performative dimension of the theatrical encounter. The audience has to be ejected from the theater into the broader world, dislocated from the lure of those forms of identification (which take place within, and compose, the imaginary relation to the conditions of existence), and also empowered to transform the world in new ways. In other words, the audience has to be mobilized in some way. In a way, historical reality is opened up through the process of disidentification. Balibar claims that it is "[t]he power of *fiction* [. . .] to dismantle or invert the *imaginary* in order to allow for the acknowledgment of the *real* and to produce a 'real effect'" (7). The "real" is outside the ideological conviction; it is what contests ideological belief. Fiction has the capacity to expose the fictive status of the ego within the imaginary and within ideology, but it does this, interestingly, through reference to a "real" that cannot be assimilated into the terms of ideology. Under certain conditions, the wager goes, the disturbance of the field cannot be quelled; the dislocation of the self-satisfied and self-identical ego cannot be reversed, except through a "relocation" within the real that is bound up with potential revolutionary action.

What Balibar claims is true for some forms of fiction is emphatically true for certain kinds of theater, or so Althusser argues. In "On Brecht and Marx," Althusser seeks to draw a parallel between epic theater and Marx's practice of philosophy. Both of them are said to introduce a "dislocation" in theater and in philosophy, or rather in the practices of each. It is in the midst of the reproduction of the practice that the "play" in the machine starts to generate effects that call that form of reproduction into question. In other words, the contingent and generative effects of the mechanical reproduction of ideology enact the power to break apart its own predictable patterns.

As Balibar points out, Althusser draws on the Freudian "scene" in which oppositions coexist without a problem. Althusser refers to a "display" in which opposites are simultaneously given. And yet, what constitutes the scene that we see is not there to be seen. It is only indirectly referenced through the visible display and our identificatory enactments in relation to what we see. There are conditions under which those forms of conflict (or contradiction) can appear, though even then we have to distinguish between forms of theatrical display that let us simply appreciate multiple identifications relieved of the burden of internal consistency or standards of noncontradiction and those that permit the contradiction to take place. Further, there are forms of display that sustain *dénégation* indefinitely ("I know that I am not that character, but I am still that character; who cares whether or not it is true") that effectively manage the potential crisis of the contradiction. For a theatrical piece to operate as a "theatrical machine," it must not only lay bare the psychic conflict to see but also prepare for the lived enactment of contradiction and the crisis that follows. For a dislocation from the self-satisfactions of identity to lead to empowerment or, indeed, to a joyful transformation of the social world, there has to be this ejection of a "critical" audience into the wider public. In other words, misrecognition has to be undergone in much the same way that a psychoanalytic process involves being cured of one's illusions about oneself, a form of mindfulness about the limits of my self-knowing that does not convert to mastery. Having lost one's location in the imaginary, one is now dislocated, and what has broken into the imaginary, what has broken it apart, is precisely the real that is outside the theater, yet constituting the relations in the scene.

In Balibar's view, what we are given is a presentation onstage, or a staging, of the moment in which dislocation takes place within the process of recognition. It is myself or my world that I no longer recognize as I once did, and I am suddenly at a distance, not quite reproducing with the same ease my "conviction" and "belief" and, hence, my "subjection" (8). My belief in how the world is structured proves to be intimately linked with my own location within that world. As I start to regard that structuring process differently (I become "critical" about the mechanical reproduction of ideology), I begin to lose my place within ideology. This means that in ceasing to believe in the ideology I have reproduced and that has reproduced this "I," I lose my coordinates in relation to my world and my sense of self-identity. If I leave the theater in such a condition, I have to locate myself in another way, one that we might call "critical" from within an intellectual field or "revolutionary" in relation to the sociopolitical field.

In this way, political theater drives its enthralled audience toward and over the edge of the proscenium, dumping them off the stage.

If I no longer know myself, or I look over there only to see the promised moment of identification as well as my estrangement from myself, I am hence constituted at a distance from myself. I am not just over there in a character, distanciated from my bodily location and existing now on the proscenium stage, but more fully "estranged" from my usual understanding of myself, itself now clearly constituted through repeated acts of "satisfying" identification. It is at such a moment that externalization and estrangement work together, even though, as we know, they are for the most part distinguished within Marx's early manuscripts. There, the worker externalizes himself in the object and discovers the value of his labor (prior to exchange); he finds himself "estranged" precisely when that object is sold on the market for an exchange value that conceals labor value. In the political theater, however, the sense of externalization that is required for self-understanding is provided by an infrastructural condition that directs attention, and identification, onstage, temporarily dislocating the audience onto the stage only to disabuse them of their identificatory fantasy (their immersion in the imaginary). Usually, theater allows for the specular constitution of the ego within the imaginary (and within ideology) to take place at once, which produces an audience that leaves the theater with a rich feeling of self-satisfaction about who they are and how the world is structured.

The very possibility for mobilization depends upon a dissolution of ideological belief that is irreversible. When forms of recognition are decomposed, and can never be recomposed, an emancipatory trajectory follows, and breaks from, the time and the scene of ideological conviction. Indeed, according to Balibar, in this situation one is not called by an ideology (the usual sense of interpellation), but *called out of* an ideology, extracted, if not ejected. Significantly, the rupture with ideology happens within, and for, the first-person and so at the level of subjectivation. In my view, the point is not to simply shift from one identification to another, since if any identification is understood as commensurate with identity, then it effectively forecloses what Althusser understood as the "alterity" at the heart of all subject-constitution. So the question is, rather, what kind of mobilization can work with disidentification, that is, with a "critical" consciousness that may well be moved by characters and ideals without precisely being captured or lured by the promises of new revolutionary identities.

Imagine Pascal deciding not to mime in advance the act of prayer as a way of producing belief through ritualistic repetition, but standing up quite suddenly in the middle of the act, or miming a cook preparing dinner on the altar, or taking up an electric guitar and unleashing punk music with a small band of skeptics, or, indeed, leaving the church, unceremoniously, to join a gathering crowd on the outside, risking apprehension by the police and being sent to prison.

Balibar draws our attention to the active way a subject is constituted and deconstituted through theatrical machinery, so let us then turn to the problem of performativity as it relates to interpellation and subjectivation. The way that a character is cast onstage and the overall "display" of the theater piece "calls to" the audience, either interpellating them into ideological belief and self-satisfaction or, in the case of political theater (or epic theater, more specifically), calling them out of their ideological moment of self-constitution. Of course, theatrical pieces can do a bit of both, or not very much of either, but we are working here with idealized forms, ones that Althusser understands as potentially or effectively revolutionary. His descriptions of political theater are, in this sense, aspirational if not idealized. Of course, many of us would like to think that really good theater, really political theater, can do precisely this. Althusser himself understands that it is not a question of "applying" a technique or finding a recipe, or even finding the right play. Even the techniques of epic theater have to be situated, he claims, within a broader *practice*, one that he calls "revolutionary." Still, under the best conditions, can we say that theater, conceived as revolutionary practice, not only has the power to reconstitute and deconstitute us as subjects but also to mobilize us to move into the world with transformational aims? Or is its function both transient and allegorical? Or is it critical in some other sense? In Balibar's view, the theatrical stage becomes a general model for the staging of discourse, which suggests that it functions in a more allegorical mode. If it is a model, it can be replicated, perhaps even applied. If it is an allegory, as I would suggest, then there is no precise analogy: something is enacted within the terms of theater that cannot be mimetically replicated within the field of discourse, yet some element in the one resurfaces in the other. The allegorical function compels us to think about a transposability without a strict mimesis. In either case, the "model" cannot translate into a clear prescription regarding how one is supposed to act.

At stake is whether we are really "called out" of ideology and ushered into another, less ideological, relation to the historical conditions of our existence. If there is no "outside" to ideology, according to Althusser, then to what domain are we ejected when we are called out of our imaginary relations? If we were able to transcend all identifications and the misrecognitions that follow, then we would perhaps have a direct line to reality, but that does not seem supported by any of the theoretical postulates we have been considering so far. Is there a way to maintain a critical relation to the historical conditions of our existence without passing through an imaginary of some kind?

Here the relationship between performativity and interpellation becomes important, since even if one is "called out" of an ideological conviction or form of misrecognition, one is still *called*, and there is a voice of some kind, originating from some unknown place that is clearly external to who I am and that I am receiving. Perhaps it is a "revolutionary call," but what is to keep that call from being any less illusory than the call of bourgeois self-satisfaction from which I am now dislocated? There would always still be the task of discriminating among forms of revolutionary calls, deciding which ones reconstitute illusory forms of subjectivation and which make room for the constitution of the subject through forms of unmasterable alterity. Those last would perhaps qualify for a critical and revolutionary form of the subject.

When Althusser argues that a critical dislocation of ideology within the theater produces a new relation between spectacle and audience that spells the "end of identification" for the audience, he doubtless overstates the case, as Balibar rightly remarks. For Althusser, criticality means the end to all identification, a Brechtian view that counters the psychoanalytic basis for his account of the imaginary. If the audience "should cease to identify" and become "critical," then it is unclear whether they would be psychotically dislocated, and so quite unprepared for revolutionary practice. Instead of understanding critical dislocation as a farewell to all identity or to identification, it may well be possible to consider a critical practice of living the condition of the subject, that is, resisting the collapse of identification into identity.[2] Every form of identification that does not resolve into identity is also a form of disidentification: "Yes, you can call me by that name, but I am not really captured by that name; whoever I am does not correspond to the norms conveyed by the name you call me; even if I answer to the call, something in me resists or exceeds the way you call me, and yet I am here, responding."

Every interpellation has to travel through an identificatory process of some kind that leads the one hailed to come forth, turn around, and affirm that "Yes, the one you call is me. I am that name!" or even "No: do not call me that name. That is not how I am to be addressed. I refuse to respond when you hail me in that way." And yet, between the yes and the no, both conditioned by a firm sense of identification, is there not a critical alternative that focuses less on what you call me than on what calls when you call?

In other words, what is the operation of power that is calling when you call and I either affirm or evade the address? If you and I become bogged down in struggles over how to be addressed, which name to be used, and what will make me feel recognized, then perhaps we have engaged in an ideological deflection of the structure of interpellating power. If we fail to ask the question of what calls when you call, we miss the ideological reach and power of the call. Similarly, if we imagine that we are the name we are called, we make the error of overriding that alterity in us that can only be covered over by an ideological capture, such as those performed by strict identity claims.

Of course, the address can act upon any of us, becoming a means of solicitation or injury, and in that sense, every such interpellation is performative. It is speech that either helps to bring into being that which it names (subject-constitution) or speech that sets off a set of effects, understood as consequences, by virtue of acting as it does. The speech act that works in either case depends upon the scene in which it takes place, which means that the performative requires the dramaturgical but is not identical with it. When the police officer calls, "Hey, you there," it matters whether he is speaking in his sleep, citing the utterance in the midst of telling a story, or walking down the street in uniform in proximity to pedestrians. We need the scene to be clarified in order to account for the relative efficacy of the performative. Speech only acts on a person who is in the vicinity of the call. In my earlier consideration of Althusser, I argued that guilt may well be what prompts the subject to turn around, ready to respond to that disciplinary hailing. But I doubt very much that the guilt is "originary," as Balibar suggests. Rather, we might at this moment suggest a link between the readiness of the pedestrian to respond to the interpellation of the police— "Yes, you calling me?"—and the kind of guilt that secures subjectification under conditions of legal violence. In Benjamin's "Critique of Violence," he makes clear that the release from legal violence entails expiation. His view, as I understand it, is that legal violence, namely, the coercive power of the law that pervades ordinary life, establishes guilt as a way of producing a subject who is internally bound to the law. Coercion is not only the explicit use of police force to compel obedience but the matrix of subject-formation that produces a "good" citizen bound by the law from the start. Guilt is what embeds the subject in the law; expiation is part of what "divine violence" enacts when it releases a subject from guilt.

So when on the street, abiding by the law, the subject is tied to the law through an anticipatory guilt. The subject is bound to the law through guilt. The ready turn toward the police who calls is the action of a subject who turns in order precisely to establish his compliance with the law. The greater the compliance, the more intensified the guilt. Although the police calls, it is the entire order of legal violence that calls, the order in which that subject finds his location and his identity. The expiation of guilt constitutes a dislocation, since to what, if any law, is the subject now bound? And if the subject is bound to no law, is the subject no longer a subject?

Of course, for Althusser, the system of domination and exploitation that belongs to capitalism is not concentrated in the legal violence of the state, though strikes, and the general strike in particular, do attack both the contracts that permit exchange to continue and the legal obligation to the state. Althusser's example references the police, so it raises the question of the relationship between legal violence and the broader system of domination whose ideological apparatus produces and reproduces subjects who ratify its necessity and rightness. In the United States, we have witnessed in the last months instances of black men who, when interpellated by the police, ran away, turning their backs. Some of them were killed as they ran (Walter Scott), and others were apprehended for running (Freddie Gray). Indeed, in the case of Freddie Gray, it was reported that he locked eyes with the police officer who called his name and was subsequently apprehended. Was the crime that he failed to look down or that he dared, by looking the policeman straight in the eye, to assert equality (once punishable under conditions of u.s. slavery), or was Gray looking to see if the policeman was looking at him with suspicion, caught up in a circle of suspicion that led ultimately to his death and charges of homicide against the police? Those who run away from the call are not just "bad subjects" but are refusing the legal authority of the police, understanding the call as the threat of punishment, prison, racist violence. Those who are ready to run are no longer convinced, or never were, that the police would offer "protection" and, in that way, do not depend on police power for their secure location in the world. In a sense we might rightly call "postideological," they are less than ready to turn around and yes, "yes, I am the one you are calling." Perhaps they are at such moments freed from guilt because they are struggling to survive under conditions in which the threat of violence permeates the legal structure and its instruments.

What happens, Balibar asks, when we refer the "power ideology" to this kind of performative effect? Balibar offers us this interesting amalgam, *power ideology*, perhaps importing a Foucauldian twist into the understanding of Althusser on ideology. The power does not reside in the speech act or even in the authority of the one who speaks. Nor can it be found simply in the established conventions that authorize the police to speak and act as they do. The "scene" is important to the understanding of ideology, and not only in its empirical dimensions. Some dimension of power is articulated through the scene, in its syntax and its staging. So when we ask what speaks when the police speaks, we are then already within that Foucauldian-Althusserian amalgam, "power ideology," that is neither illustrated nor exemplified in the scene. That operation of power and ideology is *dramatized* or, indeed, acted out, but its full operation is never manifest on the stage. As noted, Balibar understands the scene, structured as it is by powers located outside the scene, as dramatizing the discourse of power. In "On Brecht and Marx," Althusser writes, "[T]he center of the play is not within the play but outside, and one does not see it, ever" (144). And just as with the practice of philosophy, "at the heart of the theatre, it is always politics that speaks" (140). Or again, the function of theater in the service of ideology "consists in smothering the voice of politics" (140). In the scene and on the stage, "one cannot see the face of politics in the theatre with the naked eye" (143).

Balibar situates my own work in a long history of the *theatrum mundi*, which may well be fair, but to evaluate the claim, we have to understand the differences between the performative, the theatrical, and the dramaturgical. If the performative is a speech act, gesture, or embodied action, understood as generative or consequential, then it takes place within a scene, even as it may be a way of "making a scene." For Brecht, the dramaturgical practice is a highly intentional one; directorial intention, or the observational attitude, pervades the stage, the setting, and the acting, all of which set limits on improvisation that does not fulfill the "instructional" mission of the theater. Although Brecht clearly understood that "dislocation" could not always be perfectly planned, there was a limit to the breakdown of "unity" that would lead to the breakdown of the basic model of "epic theatre." And the "theatrical" tends to imply that performance remains restricted to the proscenium stage, which distinguishes it, for instance, from performance, which implies that any number of settings can be animated for staging a performance: the street, the bus, the mall, the museum. The "theatrical" in Althusser depends quite emphatically on the distance between stage and audience, the imaginary or "fourth" wall, maintaining the abyss that separates the two: "[W]e must 'show' that the stage is a stage, artificially erected before the spectators, and not a prolongation of the auditorium" (Brecht, *Brecht* 143). Indeed, Althusser's emphatic insistence on that separation exceeds the Brechtian understanding of the audience who may well become part of the theatrical action at any time, and for whom the loss of the fourth wall is critical.

In Balibar's appropriation of Althusser's remarks on theater, he suggests that the kind of critical dislocation from ideology that happens in the theater can become a model or a sign for a more general disruption of ideology. In this formulation, theater gives us a way of seeing what disruption might be like but in an abbreviated and suspended form. How any of us might move from what we see in the theater to what we do outside the theater remains unclear, at least on this reading. But a second reading, which we have considered above, suggests that theater ejects its audience onto the street as "the people" and generates revolutionary action as a result of the critical dislocation of ideology that happened in the theater. At this point, the distinction between theater and world breaks down, since the illusory conceit of the theater, itself dependent on an imaginary constitution of the ego, loses credibility and no longer works. The crucial distinction between these two formulations can be stated this way: either theater provides the conditions of possibility for the thinkability of revolution, or theater moves us toward revolutionary action. Perhaps there is a third view that is closer to what I have written about performativity. If Balibar is right that theater foregrounds that fragility within the scenes by which ideology interpellates and effects subjectivation, then what possibilities of counterinterpellation emerge from the breakdown of ideological reproduction? I am less interested in how repetition spawns variants as a matter of course than in the possibility of a counterdiscourse that emerges in the midst of breakdown, animating the remnants of a broken ideological machine for critical purposes.

In claiming that ideology is always a dramaturgy, Balibar opens up many important questions about how best to understand dramaturgy in its ideological operation. If it were strictly Brechtian, then the intentional and deliberate plans of the director would be front and center; in other words, dramaturgical staging would presuppose a strong sense of the intentional subject. I am less sure that the mechanical reproduction of ideology proceeds according to directorial control. How would we find such a director? How would we begin the process of making an appointment with him? How much Brecht himself followed a "vanguard" practice of dramaturgy probably has to be probed if we are to understand his notion of dramaturgy as the model for political disruption or revolution.[3] Balibar writes of this dramaturgy that it involves "a director whose action is incorporated and occulted" (20), but on the other hand, as Althusser explains, the theater stages a set of passions lived, such as fear and hatred, but without danger" ("On Brecht" 146–47).

Between the defense of strong directorial intention and the requirement of the imaginary wall for passions to be lived "without danger," the theater remains both autonomous and suspended from the world outside. Hence, what seems foreclosed from this notion of theater is precisely the possibility for less scripted forms of performance in public space, for instance, that may well generate a sense of danger, not so much from the performers, but from social and economic institutions that threaten life or undermine the conditions for livable life. This last possibility comes closer to my own view and resonates with forms of performance art that have taken place in Gezi Park and elsewhere (consider the example of the "Standing Man" in 2013 who, through performance art, complied with the police ban on assembly only to proliferate individuals throughout the square standing in defiance of police power).

The Brechtian inheritance that interests me most is the account of the gestic, or the gestural (Brecht, *Brecht* 104, 136). Benjamin reads Brecht in another direction, understanding the gesture as a human action that has been deprived of its traditional supports. So a frozen or stilted gesture onstage does not reproduce the world in which the gesture comes to make sense and signify in the way it usually does; it is decontextualized, deprived of its usual location within the reproduction of social relations. For Brecht, this isolation and freezing of the gesture is meant to denaturalize the ways that bodily gestures follow from one another, forming perceptual and practical unities. One can see rather clearly how a Brechtian method of this kind might lead to a denaturalization of gender, bringing into relief bodily movements like gait, stride, gesticulations with the hands, expressions, smiles, turns, bends, and stretches, how and whether one leans, holds the mouth or the chin or the lips. Such moments, Benjamin tells us, occur in Kafka's literary work when, for instance, a leg for no medical reason no longer functions as it once did but has to be lifted and placed on a surface as if were dead weight, or two hands clapping are described as an industrial set of hammers. Reification has pervaded motility and coordination, and the body part is not fully separable from the machine or the obduracy of objects in the world. Usually in Kafka there are body parts that have lost their aim, or speech and action work in opposing ways so that a facial expression has nothing to do with what is said. The disjunctive effect is startling. A certain unmasterable arbitrariness now characterizes the relation between what the body does and what the person says. In other words, it would seem that the gesture allegorizes the unraveling of the unified speech act, understood as an embodied act of speech. If we expect a body to perform its words in conformity with the oratorical standard of the speech act, the gesture marks the impossibility of that particular coordination. Indeed, the problem is not that such coordination happens not to be possible now, but that that possibility is now historically lost.

For Benjamin, Brecht provides another way of understanding identification and disidentification: the "one" who follows not as an individual, but as a collective, for whom the reaction is not the same as the individual body gripped in the face of spectacle, bound up with what he or she watches. If anything, the one who watches, as it were, from the perspective of the collective, is "ungripped" by what she sees, considering the action a position of attentive consideration and, especially, of "interest." Those who follow have an interest in what they follow, and what they follow appears in two different but simultaneous ways: when they are seized by what they see, the object is a form of *action with which one identifies*; the second way of seeing, attentive, considered, even critical, is what Benjamin calls *performance.* And so a distinction is introduced between action and performance. The distinction permits Benjamin to describe, on the one hand, that an action can be followed on the basis of one's own experience—and we are not really differentiated from what we see, where we are identified and sympathetic, and where the sympathy fails to differentiate the one who watches from the action watched. Performance, on the other hand, is something mounted by someone else, where one's own way of seeing is interrupted by another's way of seeing; it implies a director whose deliberate forms of orchestration are considered "pellucid." As we consider this deliberate orchestration, we are constituted as a "we" who are implicated together in what we see. As this very plurality, it would appear that we become. And we become capable of attentive and critical thinking. That once rapt body that was, it seems, associated with spectacle and sensation is put out of play. Indeed, to the extent that epic theater takes historical events as its subjects, its point is "intended to purge them of the sensational" (Benjamin, "What" 148). For Benjamin, the "event" will be related to the gesture, that incomplete or fragmented form of action that has been deprived of its traditional supports. Indeed, in his writing on Kafka, Benjamin tells us that the gesture has become the event.

When Benjamin starts to describe interruption (or *décalage*, in Althusser) in Brecht's epic theater, he gives us an example that brings together relations of gender, class, and violence. He describes what he calls a "primitive scene," apparently drawn not from a play, but from a daydream, perhaps, in which "suddenly a stranger enters. The mother is just about to seize a bronze bust and hurl it at her daughter; the father was in the act of opening the window in order to call a policeman [einem Schutzman zu rufen]" ("What" 150). The scene emerges quite suddenly for the stranger and for us, the reader, for we do not have any context for what is happening. It is fair to say that this is an astonishing scene of violence. It matters that this is a domestic scene, since the violence that astonishes us emerges within and from the traditional family and bourgeois life, and the father who, unable to intervene, gets ready to call upon the greater paternal authority of the police to invade the familial territory and stop a potential murder. Indeed, this seems to be violence directed from the mother against the daughter at the heart of the bourgeoisie, one that depends upon police intervention to be thwarted.

　　　　Why is it a statue, a bronze one, that is about to be thrown? This seems like an imitation of some kind, not gold so not the most original and superior form of the head. The German *eine Bronze* is translated as a "bust." What does it mean to take the replica of a head as a murderous instrument to be directed at the daughter? Someone or something has lost its head, perhaps, or the head has become severed from a body and is now a lethal instrument—except that the head is no longer a head but a copy, and has thus already suffered a severing of its own and, as a replica, is clearly deprived of its original body and original scene and is now traveling in worlds where it does not belong. This bronze bust does not act on its own, but if the mother has lost her mind and is now about to throw a head, then some sort of decomposition, displacement, and simulation of the human body has already occurred and set the scene; some alienation of the body or fetishism of the object or relic of ruined work is weaponized. And now it seems that the family—this family, but any family, since there is no context for this family—will also be destroyed or invaded by this inanimate citation of a head that once belonged to a citational body, or should have but never did. Its citational character marks the distance between that "bust" and any possible person it might be replicating. Was it royalty? Was it authority? So something is already lost and seemingly irrecoverable in this scene in which the mother appears to be about to injure or destroy the daughter and the family, precipitating the entry of the police and then, by implication, the courts and the prison. Did the head start this business, or was it, rather, some prior loss of bearing and orientation that established this scene without context, the one that Benjamin suddenly starts to write in the middle of his paragraph, a kind of directorial performative that establishes this nearly murderous moment with a sudden start and stop and does not, cannot, tell us what happens next?

We can see this as a form of alienation, to be sure, an interpretation that would follow the directorial imperative of a Brechtian kind. The human body has come apart and its head has become a commodity that appears on the shelf of the family dining room, as if a beheading has already taken place. Perhaps this is the murderous trace of a certain form of alienated labor, or one of the last remaining relics of the aristocracy that is about to take on new meaning as a lethal weapon. Is there, however, another reading, one in which Benjamin is suggesting that the violent act against the institution of the family and bourgeois life, even the criminal act of murder, is itself a "critical" practice? Benjamin stops the scene quite suddenly, giving us only the gesture, the frozen image, but not the act of violence itself. *The gesture, then, functions as the partial decomposition of the performative that arrests action before it can prove lethal.* Perhaps this kind of stalling, cutting, and stopping establishes an intervention into violence, an unexpected nonviolence through an indefinite stall, one effected by interruption and citation alike. In other words, the multiplication of gestures makes the violent act citable, brings it into relief as the structure of what people sometimes do, but does not quite do it—relinquishing the satisfaction of the complete act for what may prove to be an ethos of restraint, if not a critical act of nonviolence.

The decomposition of the speech act into gesture is not only the sign of critical capacity but of grief for what decomposes as we compose, and for what is no longer possible, and for the loss of those traditional supports—and tradition itself—that cannot be restored. After all, that mother was about to throw a hard piece of some defunct tradition at her daughter, and we do not know which one. We can neither recover that history nor conceptualize the act when gesture becomes the event. In the best of circumstances, such disconcerting moments of citations—these incomplete performances—can bring to a halt what has become both very usual and utterly wrong, allegorizing the intervention into the mechanical reproduction of ideology that seeks to stop its potentially destructive force.

JUDITH BUTLER is Maxine Elliot Professor in Comparative Literature and Critical Theory at the University of California, Berkeley. She is the author of several books, including most recently *Senses of the Subject* (Fordham University Press, 2015) and *Notes toward a Performative Theory of Assembly* (Harvard University Press, 2015).

Notes   1   In "Freud and Lacan," Althusser writes: "It is clear that the object of psychoanalysis may be specific   and that the modality of its material as well as the specificity of its 'mechanisms' (to use one of

Freud's terms) are of quite another kind than the material and 'mechanisms' which are known to the biologist, the neurologist [. . .]. We need only recognize [. . .] the specificity of its object: the unconscious and its effects" (191). And then again, he asks after "the meaning of this primacy of the formal structure of language and its 'mechanisms' as they are encountered in the practice of analytical interpretation, as a function [whose] effects [are] still present in the survivors of the forced 'humanization' of the small human animal into a *man* or a *woman*" (192).

2   See Hall; Rose 91–99.

3   This important question depends in part on how *The Messingkauf Dialogues* are to be read. The *dramaturg* figured there promises to "apply" the lessons of the philosopher, yet is he a model for Brechtian dramaturgy? It is possible to read that figure literally and conclude that, for Brecht, theater should become propaganda. It is, however, more likely that the figure of the dramaturge is hyperbolic, if not self-mocking.

Works Cited

Althusser, Louis. "Freud and Lacan." *Lenin and Philosophy and Other Essays*. Trans. Ben Brewster. New York: Monthly Review Press, 1971. 195–219.

——————. "On Brecht and Marx." Trans. Max Statkiewicz. *Louis Althusser*. By Warren Mantag. New York: Palgrave Macmillan, 2003. 136–49.

Balibar, Étienne. "Althusser's Dramaturgy and the Critique of Ideology." *differences* 26.3 (2015): 1–22.

Benjamin, Walter. "Critique of Violence." *Reflections: Essays, Aphorisms, Autobiographical Writings*. Ed. Peter Demetz. Trans. Edmund Jephcott. New York: Schocken, 1986. 277–300.

——————. *Illuminations: Essays and Reflections*. Trans. Harry Zohn. Ed. Hannah Arendt. New York: Schocken, 1976.

——————. "What Is Epic Theatre?" *Illuminations* 147–54.

——————. "The Work of Art in the Age of Mechanical Reproduction." *Illuminations* 217–52.

Brecht, Bertolt. *Brecht on Theatre: The Development of an Aesthetic*. Trans. John Willett. London: Methuen, 1964.

——————. *The Messingkauf Dialogues*. Trans. John Willett. London: Metheun, 2012.

Freud, Sigmund. *Civilization and Its Discontents*. 1920. *The Standard Edition of the Complete Psychological Works of Sigmund Freud*. Trans. and ed. James Strachey. Vol. 21. London: Hogarth, 1957. 64–148. 24 vols. 1953–74.

——————. "Reflections on War and Death." 1915. *The Standard Edition*. Vol. 14. 1957. 273–300.

Hall, Stuart. "Who Needs 'Identity'?" *Questions of Cultural Identity*. Ed. Stuart Hall and Paul du Gay. London: Sage, 1996. 2–16.

Rose, Jacqueline. *Sexuality in the Field of Vision*. London: Verso, 1986.

Althusser's Authorless Theater

*A*lthusser once made what he called the "simple observation" that in a "conflictual situation [. . .] one cannot see everything from everywhere" (*Writings* 111). Although the situation in question was class society (and therefore class struggle), Althusser's work as a whole allows, or perhaps compels, us to understand even theoretical texts as conflictual situations, that is, as sites of active antagonism visible only from certain positions in the topography of theory and intelligible only to those who occupy these positions. Balibar's essay "Althusser's Dramaturgy and the Critique of Ideology" occupies a position that allows us to see, if not "the essence of that conflictual reality" (Althusser, *Writings* 111), an important part of it, which, moreover, had been systematically overlooked even by Althusser's most perceptive readers—not hidden, but simply unseen, its "fleeting presence" in the "field of the visible" unperceived (Althusser and Balibar, *Reading* 26). The very idea of the field of the visible may be understood as a philosophical dramatization, if not a translation, of the idea expressed in the Greek θέατρον (*theatron*, derived from the verb θεάομαι, "to behold" or "to look upon"), a space where something is exhibited or placed in order to be seen. Indeed,

Volume 26, Number 3   DOI 10.1215/10407391-3340348

reading Balibar's essay, we cannot help but ask ourselves how, with few exceptions, we failed to see the theatricality of Althusser's practice of theory.

The answer to this question lies in what we behold when we enter Althusser's little theater of philosophy (*notre petit théâtre théorique*): a contradiction or, more precisely, a contradiction that opens onto a series of contradictions inseparable from Althusser's dramaturgy, his staging of the fact that philosophy is by its nature compelled to perform (that is, act or act out) its theses in the field of visibility, that is, the theater proper to it. His dramaturgy might be summarized as the work of staging philosophy's staging of itself, like a play about the way plays are "made," a play within a play, a metacommentary or metatheater that nevertheless cannot step outside that which it dramatizes or that on which it comments. And nothing that Althusser has written illustrates more dramatically the aporia that makes his work what it is than the notion of the authorless theater (*un théâtre sans auteur*), which makes a brief appearance near the end of his introduction to *Reading Capital*. Balibar's title, "Althusser's Dramaturgy," declares both the dramaturgy at work in his texts and the theory of dramaturgy exhibited in them to be Althusser's. In doing so, he reminds us that there can be no concept of the authorless theater or perhaps even of authorlessness itself without an author or, more precisely, without the attribution of authorship.

The phrase "attribution of authorship," following the second part of Balibar's title, takes us to what Althusser called the "central thesis" of his theory of ideology ("Ideology" 170); in fact, attribution of authorship might be understood as a form, perhaps the form, of the interpellation of the individual as subject. In an important sense, Althusser's theater of ideological interpellation is a world of individuals in which each, without any original authorship or authority, must be interpellated as the author of speech and acts, which in turn must be attributed to an author. Individuals, each separated from every other, are retroactively "recruited" to serve as the point of origin or creation from which the intention or meaning of a work may be deduced and to which responsibility (both causal and legal) is assigned for the work that henceforth will be called his or her own. In a sense, then, Althusser's theory of the interpellation of individuals as subjects/authors presupposes the authorlessness of works as its necessary condition: because a given work originally "belongs" to no one, it can be assigned to anyone, the reasons (which often seem "obvious," and obviousness is the first sign of the work of ideology for Althusser) for the assignment furnished after the fact. But this attribution or ascription is not an illusion or even a fiction to be dispelled by knowledge; it has a material existence insofar as it is staged and performed by means of the machines and apparatuses necessary to the production of the theatrical effect that allows the audience not simply to "suspend its disbelief" but to do so willingly and accept as credible the "role" of the author played, authoritatively, by an actor.

It would appear, then, that Althusser demonstrates the necessity by which even Foucault's question at the conclusion of "What Is an Author?," a question that is itself a citation placed in quotation marks and therefore marked as a "borrowing" of what rightly belongs to someone else (in this case, Beckett, "what matter who's speaking?"), calls out to be authored or to be recognized as having been authored in a way that we are not free to ignore; it thus calls upon, calls up, or calls out an individual who will assume the burden of authorship. Thus, in a way that bears some similarity to Ernst Kantorowicz's notion of the king's two bodies, the living individual is nothing more than a *Träger*, a bearer or support of the legal/ideological individual, the subject who provides the unity and continuity that the former cannot possess. But it is above all Hobbes who haunts Althusser's dramaturgy, his absent presence never allowing us to forget that "author" and "actor" are simultaneously literary/theatrical and legal terms. In chapter 16 of *Leviathan*, Hobbes defines *author* as "he that owneth his words and actions," a definition that severs authorship from any necessary role in the creation of what the author owns (in opposition to the Latin *Auctor*, which most commonly refers to the doer of a deed or the producer of an object, utterance, or text) and thus dissolves any natural (or prelegal/political) relation between person and thing. Hobbes seeks to undo the forgetting of origins that confers on the notion of person its natural relation to the human individual by recalling that in Roman theater it signified a mask or disguise: "[T]he word Person is latine: instead whereof the Greeks have Prosopon, which signifies the Face, as Persona in latine signifies the Disguise, or Outward Appearance of a man, counterfeited on the Stage; and somtimes more particularly that part of it, which disguiseth the face, as a Mask or Visard: And from the stage hath been translated to any Representer of speech and action, as well in Tribunalls, as Theaters" (*Leviathan*, ch. 16). Thus, author ("he that owneth his words and actions") and actor ("as representing the words and actions of an other") are the two forms personhood takes, meaning that both have a common origin in theatrical performance, namely, in the persona or character one "counterfeits" on the stage or the mask worn by one individual to speak in the guise of, or disguised as, another.

But Hobbes takes his argument even further. The idea of disguise or mask might appear to suggest the primacy of author over actor, as if the latter imitates (in theater) or represents (in law) what the former has said or done, the words or actions attributable to the author as his own. Instead, "a Person, is the same that an Actor is, both on the Stage and in common Conversation; and to Personate, is to Act, or Represent himselfe, or an other; and he that acteth another, is said to beare his Person, or act in his name" (Hobbes, *Leviathan* ch. 16). Hobbes has thus led us to a rather surprising conclusion: every author "personates," represents, or plays himself to another; he must wear the mask that represents him in order to act the part of himself. The author, too, then is an actor, in no way external and prior to the drama that was thought to issue from him, but rather one of its players, the individual given the part of devising the parts and wearing the mask that identifies him as the one without a mask, that is, the author of the authorless theater. From this perspective, Althusser's little theater of ideology may be seen as a kind of parody that performs authorship in order to set it against itself, or perhaps more accurately to dramatize the conflicts without which it would not exist.

To understand how Althusser stages his authorless theater, we must turn to the text itself, to the phrase to which, following Balibar, I have attached so much significance. It is noteworthy that it appears not in Althusser's writing on theater or art but in the penultimate paragraph of Althusser's contribution to *Reading Capital* ("The Object of Capital"). Printed in italics, *un théâtre sans auteur*, the final four words of the paragraph resound like a musical phrase in the blank space, the print version of silence, between paragraphs:

> *It is sometimes directly exposed in Marx's analyses, in passages where it is expressed in a novel but extremely precise language: a language of metaphors which are nevertheless already* almost perfect concepts, *and which are perhaps only incomplete insofar as they have not yet been* grasped, *i.e., retained and elaborated as concepts. This is the case each time Marx presents the capitalist system as a mechanism, a machinery, a machine, a construction [. . .]; or as the complexity of a "social metabolism" [. . .]. In every case, the ordinary distinctions between outside and inside disappear, along with the "intimate" links within the phenomena as opposed to their visible disorder: we find a different image, a new quasi-concept, definitely freed from the empiricist antinomies of phenomenal subjectivity and essential interiority; we find an objective system governed in its most concrete determinations by*

the laws of its erection *(*montage*) and* machinery, *by the specifications of its concept. Now we can recall that highly symptomatic term "*Darstellung," *compare it with this "machinery" and take it literally, as the very existence of this machinery in its effects: the mode of existence of the stage direction (*mise en scène*) of the theatre which is simultaneously its own stage, its own script, its own actors, the theatre whose spectators can, on occasion, be spectators only because they are first of all forced to be its actors, caught by the constraints of a script and parts whose authors they cannot be, since it is in essence* an authorless theatre. *(192–93)*

This passage marks the crescendo in Althusser's text, after which his phrases begin their descent to the last word of the next and final paragraph: *silence* ("Forty lines, then silence" [193]). This silence is Marx's silence, the silence of *Capital*'s incompleteness, but it is also Althusser's silence, a silence in commemoration of Marx's silence that simultaneously marks the silence proper to Althusser's own text, a silence all the more resonant in that it punctuates the torrent of words and concepts that fill the final pages of "The Object of Capital," as if Althusser sought to imitate and not just indicate the abrupt breaking off of Marx's text. But Althusser insists that we must differentiate between silences: the "deafening silence" that follows the last word of volume 3 of *Capital* is merely one kind of silence. There is another silence, another kind of silence: that which is "underneath the words uttered," a "discourse of the silence, which, emerging in the verbal discourse, produces blanks in it, blanks which are lapses in its rigour, or the outer limits of its effort: its absence, once these limits are reached, but in a space which it has *opened*" (30). This extraordinary statement, which if Althusser is to be taken seriously must apply to his work as much as Marx's, concerns both the silence external to the text, the silence that it leaves in its wake, the fissure that it has forced open and that cannot be closed, as well as the silence internal to it, the discourse that silence pronounces but that is audible only in the act of enunciation, which hollows itself out as it is spoken. "We cannot fail to hear behind the word that is uttered the silence it conceals, to see the blank of suspended rigour, scarcely the time of a lightning-flash in the darkness of the text: correlatively, we cannot fail to hear behind this discourse which seems continuous but is really interrupted and governed by the threatened irruption of a repressive discourse, the silent voice of the real discourse" (143). It is this internal silence that Althusser, in reading Marx, seeks to "make speak" and that we must recognize in Althusser's own commentary on the silences of *Capital*, the silence in his text that speaks to us even if we do not hear it.

But Balibar's remarks on Althusser's dramaturgy compel us to recognize another modality of silence. (We should recall that Althusser spoke of the different modalities of material existence, and silence possesses a material existence in that it produces effects.) Beyond the symptomatic silences, the lapses and elisions that interrupt Althusser's account of Marx's silences, is the silence specific to the dramaturgy itself, that is, the silence that is staged by *Reading Capital*. We might well think of those contemporaries of Althusser who experimented with silence. Rather than punctuate speech with silence, they tended to stage a silence punctuated by speech (or sound): Beckett, who sought increasingly to shift the balance in favor of silence over speech in the works contemporaneous with *Reading Capital*, above all *Film* (1965); and John Cage, who composed a silent score (*4'33"*) to explore the silencing of silence in everyday life. Perhaps Althusser's observations on the relation of absence to presence in the paintings of Leonardo Cremonini can be understood according to a kind of parallelism of the visual and the auditory as simultaneously directed at the sound/silence relation. Just as there are words that install silence or that bring with them a silence that oozes through the sounds or letters in which it is enveloped, escaping with a volume and force that pries them apart, so there exist lines and figures that make absence visible, that is to say, present or at least presentable: "[H]e never 'painted' anything but the absences in these presences," the figures of what appear to be human beings, animals, and plants.

> *The structure which controls the* concrete *existence of men, i.e., which* informs the lived ideology *of the relations between men and objects and between objects and men, this structure,* as a structure, *can never be depicted by its presence, in person, positively, in relief, but only by traces and effects, negatively, by indices of absence, in* intaglio (en creux). *[. . .] Cremonini can never paint a* circle *without simultaneously painting* behind the scenes, *i.e., alongside and away from the circle, but at the same time as it, and near it, something which rejects its law and "depicts" the effectivity of a* different *law, absent in person. ("Cremonini" 237)*

Precisely because they concern strategic or aesthetic choices, these examples, however, suggest that there is an author behind Althusser's authorless theater, as if he sought to produce the effect or illusion of authorlessness that would serve as the greatest affirmation of his mastery and "authority." In fact, Althusser's account in the passage from *Reading Capital* cited above leaves no room for such an interpretation: the theater is "the mode of existence of the stage direction (*mise en scène*)" and thus "is simultaneously its own stage (*scène*), its own script (*texte*), its own actors," all of which are set into motion and put to work in the course of the performance (*Darstellung*), which is irreducible to what comes before and annexes these elements and transforms their meaning and function. This is the significance of the repeated formula "its own" (*sa propre*): it is no longer the script that is performed or the actors that perform it but a script written by and in the performance itself, a script written "simultaneously" with its performance and the actors, bearers of a role assigned to them, more acted than acting, brought to life, as it were, by the performance attributed to them. The author is no less a product than they, an origin assigned retroactively by the performance itself, recruited to play the role of creator, but offstage, in the wings, an absence dressed up in the costume of presence, a costume woven of sound and silence, like Beckett's Godot, present only through his emissaries, his words clothed in theirs. The stage itself—and the French word here is *scène*, which denotes not simply the stage as a defined space but also the scenery or scenic elements of theater—is staged as if there exist only singular scenes whose elements in the strict sense do not exist prior to their being staged.

These reflections lead, in turn, to the question of the spatial boundaries of this theater, of what can be determined as its interior and exterior, that is, to the question of the spectator. The theater of which Althusser speaks is a "theatre whose spectators can, on occasion, be spectators only because they are first of all forced to be its actors, caught by the constraints of a script and parts whose authors they cannot be, since it is in essence *an authorless theatre*." To follow his argument here is to arrive at the conclusion that the very division of audience and actors, of stage and "house," as one says in English (the Greek *theatron*, the space from which one beholds a spectacle), is internal to the theater that, as Althusser will soon say of ideology, has no outside. In fact, Balibar shows that it is possible to see the notion of ideology developed in the ideology and state apparatuses (ISAs) essay as profoundly theatrical, not in the sense that it is the site or scene of illusions or deception, but rather because ideology can be understood as composed of ideas only on the condition that ideas are conceived as always already staged and performed. Ideas are things, as Spinoza put it, but not things constituted and defined prior to their performance; on the contrary, they only exist *in actu* (*Ethics* 2:11). Althusser's analysis suggests that author and spectator are constituted as symmetrical figures, the one, the origin, and the other, the destination of the work. Both are positioned or staged off-stage, one as cause and the other as recipient or patient in the Latin sense (derived from *patior*), the one who undergoes, bears, or suffers something, the effects of the theater. The spectators "are forced to be its actors," forced to say the "lines" provided to them; they are constrained to say that they are only spectators and not participants and are free to exit the theater at any time. The author is the scribe who reproduces a text in an act whose primary effect is that peculiar form of forgetting whose most important effect is the sense of authorship.

What exactly do we mean when we say that ideology is performed or, to distance our analysis for the moment from the notion of speech acts that offers a too familiar way out of the difficulties engendered by Althusser's theory as understood by Balibar, *staged*? It is here that the term *machinery*, together with the allied terms *machine*, *mechanism*, and *apparatus*, takes on a dual function that is expressed in a concept that, while metaphorical, is "almost perfect, incomplete only because its perfection has yet to be grasped" (Althusser and Balibar, *Reading* 192). One of the functions, or rather set of functions, of the concept of *machinery* derives from the meaning of the term in theater: stage machinery. These are the apparatuses used to induce in the spectator the suspension of disbelief proper to the theater, its spectacle, the changes of scenery that denote change of location, lighting to suggest time change (day to night), sounds, and so on, even the machine that delivers a god to the stage. Althusser has appropriated "machinery," in this sense, to insist that ideology is not belief, false consciousness, or illusion, all of which terms locate ideology in the mind where its power is diminished through critique, the rational criticism of irrational ideas. Ideology is a machine or machinery with a perfectly objective and material existence. One doesn't change a machine by criticizing it, especially if it is a machine of subjection for which criticism is the lubricant that reduces the friction between its parts.

Althusser's notion of the ISA is in this sense borrowed from both Engels and Lenin, who referred to the state as a machine and its parts, machinery, or apparatuses, above all to counter Hegel's notion that the state is "the reality of the moral idea [die Wirklichkeit der sittlichen Idee]" (*Elements* 3:257) or "the image and the reality of reason [das Bild und die Wirklichkeit der Vernunft]" (3:272), as if the state emerged in order to realize a preexisting idea in whose image it was created. But Marx, according to Althusser's reading, introduces the notion of society as a whole as a machine in order to make (as quoted above) "the ordinary distinctions between outside and inside disappear, along with the 'intimate' links within the phenomena as opposed to their visible disorder: we find a different image, a new quasi-concept, definitely freed from the empiricist antinomies of phenomenal subjectivity and essential interiority; we find an objective system governed in its most concrete determinations by the laws of its *erection* (*montage*) and *machinery*, by the specifications of its concept." The antinomies of inner and outer and phenomenal and noumenal are excluded from any understanding of the "objective system" that constitutes the reality of the machine, which, being constructed, can be deconstructed, taken apart and replaced. But the state and, indeed, the "phenomena" often designated in Marxist writing as "superstructure" will not simply vanish as if they were emanations from what no longer exists. Politics, law, religion, and culture must all be understood as composed of machines or apparatuses that concur in the production of an effect, the effect of subjection, rather than as systems of belief or values. But the problem of the metaphor of the machine or mechanism is that it is too easily assimilated into a functionalist account of what must appear as a social order: all its parts must perform their proper function for the machine to work as it should. It is perhaps for this reason that Althusser preferred the term "apparatus" (*appareil*) to that of "machine" in order to theorize the "existence of this machinery in its effects," as if the apparatus were a certain type or modality of machine, a montage of sorts, assembled only in and through its effects: a designerless machine or perhaps the designerless machinery of an authorless theater.

We may now appreciate the importance of theater for Althusser, the theoretical imperative that led him to discover the existence of a theater without boundaries or limits in which he, moreover, without his knowledge or consent, was an actor playing a part. Let us recall the final paragraph of "The 'Piccolo Teatro': Bertolazzi and Brecht," written three years before *Reading Capital*: "I look back, and I am suddenly and irresistibly assailed by the question: are not these few pages, in their maladroit and groping way, simply that unfamiliar play, *El nost Milan*, performed on a June evening, pursuing in me its incomplete meaning, searching in me, despite myself, now that all the actors and sets have been cleared away, for the advent of its silent discourse? [Je me retourne. Et soudain, irrésistible, m'assaille la question: si ces quelques pages, à leur manière, maladroite et aveugle, n'étaient que cette pièce inconnue d'un soir de juin, *El nost Milan*, poursuivant en moi son sens inachevé, cherchant en moi, malgré moi, tous les acteurs et décors désormais abolis, l'avènement de son discours muet?]" (151). It is only after leaving the scene from which there is no exit, not because the exit is blocked but because its boundary recedes before us as we approach it, and after an interval of time contracted into an instant that Althusser turns around or turns back (*Je me retourne*) as if in response to an interpellation or a call ("If we suppose that the imagined theoretical scene takes place in the street, the interpellated individual turns around [Si nous supposons que la scène théorique imaginée se passe dans la rue, l'individu interpellé se retourne]" [Althusser and Balibar, *Reading* 174]) only to find that in turning around he is playing the role assigned to him, the part of the one who has no part in the play, wearing the mask that marks him as the one who does not wear a mask. The question that "suddenly and irresistibly" assails Althusser as he arrives at the conclusion of his essay is whether he is indeed the author of "these few pages" (*ces quelques pages*) or whether they are nothing more than this little-known play (*n'étaient que cette pièce inconnue*) writing itself through him, unbeknownst to him, in pursuit of its final moment, a moment that it will never find. In a letter dated July 30–31, 1962, Althusser describes the essay on Bertolazzi and Brecht as driven by terminological problems and a sense that he could not find the terms to explain the activity proper to a materialist theater: "To replace one word with another means that one must find this other word, to find it, one must first look for it, to look for it and find it, nothing is better suited to the task than writing (a kind of prospecting, or foraging)" (*Lettres* 200). The search to complete the incomplete meaning opens onto the unfinishable work of substitution: behind the masks are only other masks; behind the machinery, only the machines that produce the machines; behind Althusser's words, other words; so many traces of a meaning that has never been and never will be present. Althusser, foraging for terms in the space of an absence and surrounded by silence, stumbled upon the fissure that history had opened and through it saw himself: an actor on the stage of the authorless theater, transcribing the words of its silent discourse and reading them aloud, a maker and destroyer of machines, the dramaturge of an unknown world.

WARREN MONTAG is a professor of English at Occidental College in Los Angeles. He is the editor of *Décalages: An Althusser Studies Journal*. His most recent book (with Mike Hill) is *The Other Adam Smith* (Stanford University Press, 2014).

Works Cited   Althusser, Louis. "Cremonini, Painter of the Abstract." *Lenin* 229–42.

—————. "Ideology and Ideological State Apparatuses." *Lenin* 127–86.

—————. *Lenin and Philosophy and Other Essays.* Trans. Ben Brewster. New York: Monthly Review Press, 1971.

—————. *Lettres à Franca (1961–1973).* Paris: Stock/IMEC, 1998.

—————. "The 'Piccolo Teatro': Bertolazzi and Brecht. Notes on a Materialist Theatre." *For Marx.* Trans. Ben Brewster. London: Verso, 1969. 131–51.

—————. *Writings on Psychoanalysis: Freud and Lacan.* Trans. Jeffrey Mehlman. New York: Columbia UP, 1996.

Althusser, Louis, and Étienne Balibar. *Reading Capital.* Trans. Ben Brewster. London: Verso, 1970.

Balibar, Étienne. "Althusser's Dramaturgy and the Critique of Ideology." *differences* 26.3 (2015): 1–22.

Foucault, Michel. "What Is an Author?" *Language, Counter-Memory, Practice: Selected Essays and Interviews.* Ithaca: Cornell UP, 1980. 113–38.

Hegel, G. W. F. *Elements of the Philosophy of Right.* Trans. S. W. Dyde. Ontario: Batoche, 2001.

Hobbes, Thomas. *Leviathan.* Project Gutenberg. N.pag. 11 Oct. 2009. www.gutenberg.org/files /3207/3207-h/3207-h.htm.

Kantorowicz, Ernst H. *The King's Two Bodies.* Princeton: Princeton UP, 1957.

Spinoza, Baruch. *Ethics.* Trans. Samuel Shirley. Indianapolis: Hackett, 1982.

On Linking Machinery and Show

A Revised Concept of Ideology

*I*n "Althusser's Dramaturgy and the Critique of Ideology,"
Étienne Balibar offers a "description of Althusser's quest for a critical concept of ideology" (2). The quest results in a reconstruction of "a *dramaturgic
model* of the political function and political transformation of ideology" (4).
Balibar's reading of Althusser is divided in two: first comes the "description of *theater as politics*"; it is followed by "an attempt at conceptualizing
politics as theater" (19). Theater receives careful attention but neither for
its own sake nor simply for the sake of its possible political *impact.* Following Althusser, Balibar is interested in theater as a privileged political *site.*
Theater is privileged due to its revelatory, that is, *theoretical* power, for it is
a site in which the ideological apparatus shows itself and hence can be better
grasped and criticized. The same goes for the theatrical nature of politics;
what is important about it in this context is that it helps us grasp the ideology at work. The point is not to politicize theater or dramatize politics, but
to understand that ideology—which certainly connects the two—is always
already a mise-en-scène and that it is from this perspective that it should
be analyzed.

Volume 26, Number 3   DOI 10.1215/10407391-3340360
© 2015 by Brown University and d i f f e r e n c e s : A Journal of Feminist Cultural Studies

In the past, Balibar devoted several texts to Althusser's concept of ideology, to which he kept returning and which he always revisited from new perspectives. Whereas these works were mostly concerned with a "macro theory" of ideology, that is, its place in the general typography of society, now Balibar seems to be looking for a "micro theory" of ideology. He is no longer interested in Althusser's distinctions between ideology and theory, philosophy, or science—and consequently reality—(as in, for example, "Althusser's Object," "Avant-propos," "Non-Contemporaneity," "Politics," and "Tais-toi") or with the political effects of this or that particular ideology (as in "Ambiguous"; and Balibar and Wallerstein, *Race*). Instead, Balibar tries to come to terms with ideology as an operation and a relation centered on the subject. And instead of distinguishing and reconstructing different stages in Althusser's writings ("Althusser's Object"), he tries to grasp a concept of ideology as it is taking shape through the very movement, shifts, and wandering of Althusser's thought. The hermeneutic insight that guides Balibar's argument in "Althusser's Dramaturgy" is that throughout his many years of ruminations about ideology, Althusser always conceived it as a "dramaturgy." Balibar thus underscores and develops Judith Butler's basic insight that a "rewriting of Althusser's model" (11) should be informed by a careful attention to "the structure of the 'scene'" of interpellation (12). Understanding that "ideology is always already a dramaturgy" is "an important key," if not "the key," according to Butler, for deciphering the enigma that blocked Althusser from finishing any of his texts on ideology.

Balibar speaks here about *aporias* in the model of ideology, "particularly when considered from the point of view of a revolutionary politics" (4), of which Althusser was aware and which the dramaturgic model is meant to resolve. What are these aporias? Two are explicitly identified in an earlier text Balibar devoted to Althusser's concept of ideology. These "enigmas" prevented Althusser from ever completing a coherent thesis on ideology. The first one relates to the possibility of revolution:

> [T]he "ideological class struggle" on which the effectivity of the political struggle itself depends, since it prepares the conditions for the political struggle and mobilizes its bearers (the "revolutionary class"), cannot itself be the historical "last instance" of the political. [. . .] Thus it is as if Althusser were trying to reinforce and accentuate the "totalitarian" image of bourgeois domination and the obscure power of the state, in order ultimately to arrive, by an oxymoron, at the possibility of overthrowing it. [. . .] And

the idea of an organization external to ideological forms of orga-
nization, which are obviously apparatus-forms in their turn, is,
it will be agreed, quite enigmatic. ("Foreword" xiv, xvi)

The second aporia relates to the possibility of resistance to interpellation
by "bad subjects," which is actually about the possibility of freedom. How
are subjects constituted through an ideological apparatus capable of acting
otherwise than programmed by that apparatus?

All indications would seem to be that Althusser refuses to iden-
tify the "real," as Lacan does, with the negative function of an
impossible or a traumatic event that is unrepresentable because
it cannot be symbolized. [. . .] What, then, constitutes the positiv-
ity of the real, the correlate of the materiality of the imaginary?
The suggestion is made on the text's horizon, but, here too, in
very enigmatic fashion, that this question can probably not be
divorced from the question of the "bad subject," the one who does
not manage to "go all by herself" or who resists interpellation.
("Foreword" xvii)

Althusser was no less aware of these aporias than were his critics. The seemingly deterministic nature of ideology (the subject has no way to resist; even
bad subjects are subjects of ideology) precludes revolutionary aspirations.
If ideology is so ubiquitous, how would Althusser account for the possibility
of valid critique and emancipatory politics?

In 2003, when the foreword was written,[1] Balibar felt that he
could offer his readers only a "vanishing point" of a perspective from which
the "combination" of "the two 'divorced halves'" of Althusser's aporias
could be grasped. The vanishing point is "the question of praxis, a common
name for an idea of 'organization without organization'" that would make
conceivable the revolution and also the idea of the "counterinterpellation
of the subject" (xviii). Balibar does not claim to resolve the two aporias, but
only to show how they were related in Althusser's thought and work and
thus to introduce a certain coherence to his theoretical quest. Yet even this,
he warns his readers, should be taken cautiously, for it smacks of a *soixant-*
huitardism in which Balibar fears he may still be caught. A decade later,
when the text was republished (as a foreword to a later edition of Althusser's
Sur la Reproduction [2011]), Balibar stressed the fact that it remained intact
("Foreword" vii). The questions it opened remained unanswered as well. I
believe that "Althusser's Dramaturgy" can be read as an attempt to resolve

the questions left open in the earlier essay—except that now, the enigma is not left to "the actual readers of Althusser's text, in one or another of its configurations," who are called upon to seek new keys for making sense of it (xviii). In the present essay, it is the *concept of ideology* itself, not only *Althusser's quest* for it, that becomes coherent. *Ideology* may now be proposed not merely as one of those concepts "signed" by Althusser and singularized under his name, that constituted "the object of his philosophy" ("Althusser's Object"), like "epistemological break" or "symptomatic reading"; rather, ideology appears now as a concept Balibar offers to share with us, his readers, as *our* possible concept of ideology.

The quest for and the concept of ideology make their appearance on the stage of "Althusser's Dramaturgy" in two separate scenes: First, ideology shows itself and exposes its machinery on some real theatrical stages (in those productions visited and discussed by Althusser). These concrete examples, and the potential they reveal for displaying the ideological apparatus on the theater stage, politicize the theater as a practice and an institution. Then, Balibar's renewed effort to revise Althusser's generic model of ideology, which he bases on the fifth chapter in the latter's posthumous book *Machiavelli and Us*, forces politics itself to reveal its theatrical dimension. In that fifth chapter, according to Balibar, the theatricality of power is systematically, albeit briefly, analyzed, and power is interpreted from the point of view of this theatricality in order to articulate its "politics of ideology" (10), which actually determines its effectivity as *political* power.

This is a "partially new" description of Althusser's quest, Balibar writes (2), and I believe it should be read as an attempt not only to make sense of Althusser's quest for a concept of ideology but also as a way to revise it, combining Althusser's own insights with those of some of his recent readers. As mentioned above, this revision is made by following the trajectory of Althusser's ruminations about politics and theater until a dramaturgic model of ideology appears. This model is then shown to resolve the major aporias mentioned above. Moreover, it does so without recourse to the Lacanian framework.

In the earlier essay, Balibar mentions Althusser's break with the Lacanian framework: "Althusser refused to identify the 'real,' *as Lacan does*, with the negative function of an impossibility" ("Foreword" xvii, emphasis added). "The positivity of the real," however, remained enigmatic for Althusser and also, I think, for Balibar. At the text's "horizon," there appears a clue: the real must be related to the question of the "bad subject" who resists interpellation. But how the "real" operating in interpellation can provide at one and the same time an explanation of ideology at work and a promise of possible liberation from its grip, Balibar did not say. In "Althusser's Dramaturgy," the dramaturgic model seems to resolve the difficulty. Balibar discounts without argumentation the Lacanian interpretation of ideology developed by Slavoj Žižek (*Plague* and *Sublime*, and recently again in *Absolute*) and turns instead to Spinoza and Machiavelli. He takes his insights from Spinoza's *Theological-Political Treatise*, which for Althusser (and for Balibar himself) was "a stronger inspiration" (15), and from Althusser's reading of *The Prince*. Remaining on the political stage as a privileged arena for thinking interpellation, Balibar gives a new role to the Prince; the major figure in the theater of politics appears as an "*interpellated* Legislator," and his role both substitutes for and transforms the Lacanian Subject (15).[2] The shift from Lacan to Spinoza is truer to the spirit of Althusser's thought (Balibar seems to believe) than is the Lacanian inversion of Althusser offered by Žižek, and the dramaturgic model should be understood (I believe) as an alternative to Žižek's concept of ideology.[3] The dramaturgic model performs in theory what some theatrical productions perform onstage, namely a "shift from psychology to structure" that makes 'visible' [. . .] ideology's grip on the consciousness of its subjects (*but also the limits of this grip* in certain situations of exception)" (6, emphasis added).

The shift hinges on the attention given here to Althusser's writing on theater. In addition to the obvious texts on ideology, "Ideology and Ideological State Apparatuses" and "On Ideology," and the posthumous book on Machiavelli, Balibar reads some "minor" essays on "*art*, particularly theater and painting" (2), which he presents as Althusser's reports from his visits to the theater and the museum.[4] More than abstract reflections on aesthetics or theatricality, and certainly not an application of a theory in the case of a particular work of art, these essays are "essentially descriptions of singular *experiences* resulting from an 'encounter' with a work or a group of works" (3). These descriptions serve Althusser as "theoretical *dispositifs* or *machines*" whose purpose is "to resolve theoretical problems and identify the object of a theory" (2)—the concept of ideology, in our case. Especially important in this context is to discover with Balibar that Althusser's early essays on theater and art are, in fact, early attempts to identify the plane on which ideology works "behind the backs" of its subjects and at the same time where this work can be exposed and put on display. This simultaneity is what Althusser's reflection on Giorgio Strehler's production of *El nost Milan* brings to light. Althusser looks for a realm where nonconsciousness or "the back of consciousness" (Hegel qtd. in Balibar, "Althusser's Dramaturgy" 8) would be forced to show itself, enabling us to explain how ideology works on its subjects' consciousness and reflect on possible ways to escape its reign. On the basis of this discovery, Balibar insists that Althusser was always looking for a *dramaturgic* model of ideology.

Balibar reconstructs the dramaturgic model by paying careful attention to the way theater and politics are interlinked in Althusser's writings. The model follows the reading and reflects it, placing the concept of ideology in between the concepts of theater and politics; the latter are necessary for the explication of the former. For politics, theater is not only one of its sites but also its performative model. Hence, while politics is always also a theater, theater, as a mode of art and a quasi-autonomous sphere, is always a specific site where politics takes place, and human relations appear—or disappear—in their "politicality." The concept of ideology is explicated through these two other concepts precisely because it links them. The theater is political because ideology is at work there and may still be put on display, becoming an object for its subjects' gaze; politics is theatrical because power interpellates its subject only when it is staged and performed in this or that show. Shows of power are still theatrical even when the show is reduced to a call, which must already be staged in order to interpellate, as Butler aptly observes: "[I]nterpellation is not an event but a certain way of staging the call" (107).

To understand ideology is to understand this linking of politics and theater, and Balibar's conceptual labor consists in demonstrating it. Linking a few selected concepts, let me note here in passing, is always crucial for conceptual labor. Concepts come in clusters, if not in hordes, and the craft of the philosopher is to let only a selected few enter his theater so he can orchestrate their exchange and movement onstage, lest no concept be able to show itself properly or at all. In this particular case, with respect to the concept of ideology, linking operates on two levels at once. On the one hand, at the level of the *énoncé*, in *the world described by the text* (in Althusser), ideology itself is shown to consist of a special link between theater and politics; it would not take place if its own theater were immune to politics and its own politics were devoid of theatricality. On the other hand, at the level of enunciation, *at the text's surface* (which Balibar's reading exposes), ideology links theater and politics as two spheres of activity; it is responsible for the theatricality of politics as well as for the political nature of the theater.[5]

This becomes clear in Balibar's reading of the last chapter from Althusser's book on Machiavelli, which he uses as a prism for revisiting

"Ideology and Ideological State Apparatuses," resolving the tension between the two parts that make up the essay. The first part analyzes the function of ideology in the reproduction of the social order, while the second presents the operation of ideology as a machine of subjection and subjectivation. In the first part of the essay, ideology appears as one dispositive among many, an integral part of and element in the system of (re)production, and no notice is taken of the show; in the second part, ideology itself combines "machinery and a show" (19), and the question of this combination comes to the fore. Ideology is not simply the show of power or its imaginary phantom; rather, it is the way this show is anchored in the machinery of power and how it interpellates its subjects to act and reiterate their roles in the show. If ideology is what links power's machinery and power's show, interpellation is what links the machinery and the show as two elements of ideology at work. The *show* here refers to the way the call is staged; *machinery* refers to the way this staging implicates the one addressed by the call as an actor in the play of power.

When read through the dramaturgy of ideology, political power appears to operate by "combining [. . .] a machinery and a show." Balibar uses this phrase to capture what interests Althusser in the discussion of political power and authority in Machiavelli, Montaigne, and Pascal, but the phrase captures as well, I believe, what is at stake for Balibar himself in this revised concept of ideology. Obviously, it is not only the "costuming of magistrates" (19) that one is concerned with here, but the many ways in which the show of power is rooted in, is backed by, or veils and dissimulates power's institutions, its legal and military apparatuses, and how the latter operate through the former. Power, one may add here, becomes political to the extent that it is capable of linking a machinery and a show, the pulling of strings behind the scene and a staged play consumed by large publics. This linking is the task of ideology; or, better put, if political power operates by combining machinery and show, ideology consists in the linking itself.

Recognizing One's Role

How does this work? Here is a possible description. On the stages of theater and politics, linking is achieved when an individual who finds herself addressed by a show or a call of power (of any authority, master, or law) recognizes the world as a show in which she has a role and herself as the one playing this role (if only by way of negation, that is, "This is not me," "We are not like that"). She associates this role and this show with certain elements in the machinery of power that runs the show, those with which she becomes acquainted as an actress playing a role, which she may also take as either legitimate or contestable (or both), something to work with or against. At the same time, there are other elements in the machinery of power that tend to become invisible, elements that she naturalizes or takes for granted and learns to ignore (ideology, after all, functions through reduction). Almost always, the call finds her after many rehearsals,[6] through numerous repetitions of a script, a lexicon, and a repertoire of possible responses, through more or less coordinated responses from her fellows who happen to be on the same stage with her. Once called, she recognizes the role assigned to her in the play, accepts and embraces it.

Note that in the dramaturgic model the question of recognition concerns not the identity of the interpellated self, but the role assigned to it. Interpellation does not open the question of who I am or what the other wants from me; rather, it states what role I should play now, in response to the other's call—but not necessarily because this is the role the other wants me to play. Assuming a role is a response to a situation created by a call, which may or may not be mediated by fantasies about the origin of the call and the law it implies or makes present (as will be demonstrated below). Sometimes the interpellated individual may believe—or somehow feel without articulating—that the role he or she is interpellated into concerns, reassures, or questions who he or she "really is"; but there is no need to presuppose that this is always, or even often, the case. The fantasy in which each and every subject identifies with the role he or she is assigned and plays it in a way that would allow the reproduction of power is the fantasy of power[7] and not that of interpellated subjects. But there are enough staged situations, at home and in the workplace, in the shopping mall, on the street, or in front of a television set, in which roles are assigned "properly" and effectively and individuals are hooked into a show. Ideology is at work when individuals "act in concert" but do nothing new[8] because they perform their roles in a well-orchestrated show, taking their cues from the roles played by others who share with them the same situation. Individuals show each other how to play; the machinery of power ensures that the roles offered seem inevitable and that counterproductive roles are rare.

Without presupposing the answer, we may still ask: Does the actress need to will her role, internalize it, and identify with the character she is playing? Isn't it enough that she play *as if* she has become one with it? The answer depends on the theater school and the directions of the playwright and the director and is open to the audience's interpretation.

From theory's point of view, and as far as the effect of ideology is concerned, many options are available. For successful interpellation, it is enough that the subject's role *seem* inevitable. At stake is not how deeply an actress has internalized her role, but how effectively she is performing it. A skilled performance may be interpreted as a sign that the actor herself has been *integrated into* the machinery of the show and become an integral part of the world presented through the show, whose (re-)creation depends on her very presence onstage. But is this necessarily so? A sign is not a proof; it may even be misleading precisely because she is such a good actress, as the pious man who moves his lips in the church may only pretend to believe in God while he secretly thinks of himself as an atheist, or does not think at all, acting as he does only to be left alone by parents, teachers, and pastors.[9] The question of self-recognition, together with the phantasmic boundary between how I appear and who I really am, may be pushed to the background. At the foreground, we now find proficiency in performance. The question would surface only in moments of crisis, when recognition and its phantasms become necessary for the performance. This is the case much less often than it may seem. More often, performance goes smoothly, questions of identity and recognition remain dormant,[10] and the show goes like clockwork, as the cliché has it, with no interruptions; the machinery of power merges with its show. Only when ideology functions properly can an observer watching the world from a bird's-eye view truly believe that the world is a stage.

The complex linking that forms individuals as subjects of power can happen only because (and to the extent that) ideology itself is already a combination of a machinery and a show that needs no public stage and that may be put onstage anywhere one finds oneself in the addressee position. An individual may be alone or at home among family and friends, and the address may come from any other. A howling dog, a blooming flower, a work of art, a gun, or a camera: anything can send the signal that brings the one who finds herself addressed to set the stage and take a subject position. Ideology is at work if, when addressed, one responds by staging this address as a call, remote as it may be, that originates in a show of power in which one has a preset role to play and a command to belong, that is, to take part in the show. The question, so important to many of Althusser's critics and followers,[11] is why one should ever respond in this way and turn when addressed: what is the desire that disposes one to find and found subjectivity in and through the way one is addressed by another? This question is not discussed here perhaps because it need not be posed in the first place. The address means that there will be a stage; the expectation for response has already been sown, and even a lack of response is doomed to be a form of staging (at least for the one who has heard the call).[12] A stage will be opened, delineated, but never closed by the address. The response is "a strange sort of middle ground (taking place, perhaps, in a strange sort of middle voice)" that neither party to the scene can determine unilaterally (Butler 107). Agency and responsibility for this staging, even its very articulation, can be decided only later, after the fact (there has been an address; someone has been addressed), as part of the response to the call (and it may always remain contested).

Ideology works when the interpellated subject finds herself or recognizes herself (or, better, finds herself recognizing herself) playing a role that precedes her, inscribed in the machinery of power. But this means that interpellation always involves more than staging, for at the very moment one recognizes oneself as an actor on that stage, that is, as the subject whose position one is supposed to take, one is already in the grip of the machinery of power. The reiterating phrase has already been performed, and the debt of subjectivity to power has already been incurred. But this is not guaranteed, for the address only determines that there will be staging. How to stage is the open question of the subject: how to link the staged show to the apparatus of power and guarantee the subjection of the subject is the *open* question of ideology.

Violence

"Combining thus a machinery and a show," a formula Balibar uses almost in passing, is the hallmark of ideology that lies, I believe, at the heart of this revised Althusserian, dramaturgic concept of ideology. Althusser speaks about power as the "*combination* of repression and ideology" ("On Ideology" 203). This may be the source of Balibar's metaphor, but it is also a clear example of the way his reading transforms Althusser's initial formulation. The combination of repression and ideology can only be achieved through the power of ideology to combine machinery and show. Combining machinery and show is a powerful formula describing a *form of relations* that *operates* at all levels involved in this theoretical quest. It is the form of interpellation, the skeleton of the ideological apparatus, but it is also a form that replicates itself through interpellation, from the isolated scenes where interpellation takes place to the most general frameworks and networks of power relations, as well as various specific spheres of activity, artistic (theater), intellectual (theory), and discursive (writing). *Interpellation is ideology's machinery and show; ideology is the linking of power's show and its machinery; and machinery is the very existence of a system of coordinate networks of multiple linkings that does not show, that seems to work by itself.*

Linking must be performed by a subject, or more precisely, by an individual who rearticulates, problematizes, and reasserts her subjectivity in taking or abandoning her subject position or role in the show. One takes and maintains a subject position by performing this linking and reiterating this performance; when delinking is performed, the subject position is vacated. Everything hinges on the linking. It cannot be mechanical, forced, or artificial. It belongs to the very constitution of the subject and must appear to be both voluntary and inevitable, or, as Butler magisterially puts it, "[T]he simultaneity of submission as mastery and mastery as submission is the condition of possibility for the emergence of the subject" (117). Linking's aim is to achieve this simultaneity. Let me dwell for a moment on this freely chosen, inevitable role.

If linking were not conceived as inevitable, that is, if the subject felt free to choose other roles or even other shows to play in, nothing would guarantee the reproduction of power relations, and the show of power might become a farce. In the first case, power might collapse at any moment into an order of sheer violence in which subjects could be killed but no stable, reproducible subject positions could be generated (not even that of the soldier). The suspension of violence and the display of its occasional eruptions in a well-demarcated space become an integral part of the apparatus. When the bracketing of violence during the regular operations of the apparatus no longer functions, an apparatus steeped with violence becomes part of the show. Thus the show of power and its machinery become indistinguishable (see Azoulay and Ophir). In the second case, power is hollowed out from within and is pushed to the verge of disintegration. What becomes inevitable is not the response of the subject, but the appearance of ruptures in the reproduction of order and power relations. The two extreme possibilities tend to generate each other: ruptures call for violence (this is how *power*—that is, subjects who play roles incarnating it—is often interpellated); the retreat to sheer violence calls for more ruptures (this is how some *bad subjects* are interpellated, although the inversion is not symmetrical). When one prefers to play a role so as not to die, one is usually already in the grip of some ideology presenting one's choice as inevitable. But if linking the show to power's machinery is experienced as a choice made at gunpoint, and submission (or the slave's position) is merely another role, power would be compelled to present its guns forever to achieve the same effect. Ideology does not thrive in states of extreme violence.[13] Its grip on subjects is significantly weakened, changing of sides becomes frequent, loyalty shrinks, and disrespect for any authority not accompanied by overt violence grows.

When machinery and show become indistinguishable, individuals play their roles in the show and the order of power as if glued to them by force. The linking that ideology performs without effacing the distinction between machinery and show turns now into fusion, as violence melts subjectivity into submission for as long as the effects of its terror last. Let's recall that the dissociation of ideology from violence is Althusser's point of departure in his essay on ideological state apparatuses. "Exploitation is not reducible to repression [. . .] the state apparatuses are not reducible to the repressive apparatus alone [. . .] individuals do not have their own personal 'cop' behind them or 'in their heads'" ("On Ideology" 179–80). Althusser insists on the distinction between exploitation and repression and argues that an economic system and social order based on exploitation (as they all are except for true communism) cannot be reproduced (and survive) if it relies on a repressive state apparatus alone (176).[14] It is easy to explain why. Even if the workers succumb to state violence, some of their managers and employers, and certainly the policemen and the soldiers who repress their resistance, must be good subjects of state ideology. And each one of them may function in relation to his employees and fellow workers as an incarnation of that "Other Subject" of ideology.

But when Althusser tries to keep ideology and repression clearly separated, things become messy. "In production, the functioning of the relations of production is ensured by a combination of repression and ideology, in which ideology plays a dominant role" ("On Ideology" 203). He identifies "agents of the productive process themselves (factory directors and all those under their orders [. . .] as well as most 'engineers' and upper-level technicians)" as "agents of exploitation and repression internal to the process of production itself." The means they use, however, are drawn from "the 'avant-garde' techniques of public relations or human relations" (202). This means that there is an ideological repression internal to the production process and a process of repression external to it, where techniques of public relations and human relations are replaced by techniques of violence. Are these then clearly separated from ideology? The dramaturgic model cannot sustain this distinction. How can repression, violent as it may be, be effective without a theater of repression, where violence is both shown, that is, exercised, *and at the same time* suspended? After all, the workers are needed as hands on the assembly line, not as dead bodies in the barracks. Sometimes the gun simply helps them understand what years of schooling failed to do; sometimes, as changes in the market turn such old habits into an obstacle for profit, the gun helps power to uproot them.

If repression has its own theater, it means that it, too, stages its own scenes of interpellation. Whereas in the nonrepressive apparatus it is the voice of the law incarnated in fatherly figures and subsidized by guilt,[15] here, in the theaters of repression, one is interpellated by the presence of the club and the gun, by images of firing squads and rumors about being fired. Ideology does not substitute for repression; it must inhere in it for repression to function. But it does substitute for and supplement *the means* of violence through which repression works. One may illustrate this by playing with the famous invertible formula: war is politics pursued by other means / politics is war pursued by other means (Clausewitz, bk. 1, ch. 1, no. 24; see also Foucault 15–16, 47–48). Here, ideology takes the place of politics in the formula: war is ideology pursued by other means / ideology is war pursued by other means. And precisely as there is politics of and in war, and the only thing that changes is the means through which politics is performed,[16] so there is ideology of and in war (or repression) and the only thing that changes is the means through which ideology is performed.

Violent repression is called for when nonrepressive ideology fails. One may always refuse the commanding voice (or spectacle or script) or try to evade it, changing the terms of the show and in one way or another delinking the show from the apparatus, threatening to render power's show into a mere show of power. But this may cost a fortune; it may also cost one's life. Delinking unto death, one may turn one's body into the ultimate proof of the failure of one ideological apparatus (of the colonial power, for example) and the success of another (of the liberation movement, for example) in the name of which a sacrifice has been made. On the other hand, when many become subjects of the same ideology, when it becomes hard to come across even a single example of deviating behavior, the very ability to imagine an alternative route of action, a different kind of performance in response to the call, becomes very limited, almost nonexistent. Ideology works like a telephone, an email network, or a Windows program. When only a few people have access to the technology, it is quite useless; when it becomes ubiquitous, you can hardly think of an alternative—until an alternative shows up and makes an impact by showing the possibility of another way to link.

Both the gun and the voice or apparition of the Other Subject may interpellate, and each needs the other. The gun interpellates by imposing the element of inevitability that the voice introduces as internal. Therefore, its recurring presence is needed unless it is supplemented by ideological identification (for example, "I will obey; it would be stupid to die now, for nothing; my family still needs me . . ."). Without the voice, the effect of the gun is short lived, and the investment in more violence soars. Without recourse to the gun, at least to its memories and threatening shadow, the voice may lose its lasting effects. Effects here should be understood as anything between a short-term *fusion* and the long-term *linking* of show and machinery, that is, free individuals taking proper subject positions and performing their roles voluntarily. The gun and the voice have opposite temporal effects, and none of them suffices alone. If ideology functions in the reproduction of an entire social order, it must be a result of a proper balance between these two major means for interpellating subjects and their different temporalities. The long-term *linking* of show and machinery achieved through the voice and spectacle of the law must be accompanied by the threat of their short-term *fusion* at gunpoint, when role-playing is reduced to the strict following of orders and the playfulness of acting is replaced by their tense execution. It is then that one is obsessed with knowing the will of the other, for any mistake might result in death. Since both the gun and the voice can interpellate, to maintain the distinction between violent and nonviolent interpellation is to maintain an unstable distinction between fusion and linking. There is a continuous line here stretched between the torture wheel and the tempting smile, and no real dichotomy; an opposition may be imagined only with respect to the two extremes: violence that does not care to speak and tender love that never threatens pain.

Linking

I have taken the metaphor of linking seriously, that is, literally, and applied it meticulously.[17] A good place to look for this literalization is in the theater itself, where several devices, machines, and instruments support the show, sometimes from behind the curtain or below the stage, sometimes onstage as part of the show. How is linking performed there? It is a matter of skill and practice, numerous rehearsals (reiterations, *répétitions*), and a sense of timing. Both actors and stagehands should know the right time for moving and speaking (in relation and in response to the movement of objects on- and offstage as well as to the movement of the stage itself), for putting a device into action or stopping its operation (timing, the temporality of *Kairos*, it should be noted in passing, was also the time of Machiavelli's Prince).

But even the most skillful crew makes mistakes, misses a gesture or a movement by a second or entirely; sometimes strings are broken; curtains rise ahead of time or refuse to fall. Due to mistakes and laziness, malfunctioning instruments, unfit actors, and ill will, delinking is always possible. Linking is therefore an ongoing and unfinished business till the last curtain falls. An actor or a stagehand may arrive drunk or sick or suddenly change his mind about taking part in the show. Anticipating such risks to production, that is, to the play's reproduction, the theater management tries to screen out rogue subjects. Usually, when something goes wrong, the management and the crew do their best to ensure that the show goes on, despite whatever hampers the reproduction process. At these moments in particular, the good guidance and leadership of an authoritative director or stage manager are crucial, as are a well-trained crew, capable of acting in concert while improvising without betraying the script. Once in a while, however, all this does not help; sometimes it so happens that the show is severely or completely interrupted, and "the show must go on" becomes no more than a cliché drawn from some repertoire of theater ideology.

This description presupposes that almost everyone involved is already a good subject of the theater company and that interpellation into subject positions well preceded the first rehearsal and continue incessantly throughout the production season. How can a model that presupposes ideology at work explain it? The dramaturgic model seems to be caught in a circle: it seeks to explain ideology by imagining a world in which everyone is always already ideologically interpellated and takes some subject position. But this is precisely the point. No rehearsal for a new show can begin when there are no subjects to man the technical crew and the actors' band. In the world of power, there is no premiere. Whatever individuals do and however they act, they are always *in medias res.* That ideology has no history means, in fact, that it has no prehistory within human history, that new ideologies and new ideological apparatuses are forged out of old ones. Newborns who are not yet subjects are born, as Althusser famously explained, into an ongoing show, having their names, roles, and scripts ready for them ("On Ideology" 192–93). Interpellation may be part of an ongoing show or a moment of its interruption, but there is always already a show, a stage, and a script in relation to which the one addressed responds. It is in this sense that one should understand Althusser when he says that "ideology has no outside" (192).[18]

If ideology is reduced to the linking of show and machinery, it means that the existence of the stage, the theater hall, the playhouse—theater as industry and cultural field, a work place, and a space of creativity—must all be imagined, projected, and partially articulated in various degrees of coherence, detail, and scope by the subjects involved in the (re)production of the show. It also means that the reproduction and coordination of these imaginary representations are part of the ideological apparatus that operates in the theater precisely before and after the show (when salaries are negotiated, a new crew is hired, new plays are chosen for the next season, and so on). The apparatus involved here is not the one that runs the show itself, but rather the one that runs the theater as an institution. Everything becomes more complicated now, more difficult to direct and orchestrate, and, for lack of surrounding walls and a demarcated stage, less secure and less stable. Linking in this larger space becomes all the more important but all the more open to change and variations, contestable, and harder to control. There are many reasons for this complexity and instability, but the most obvious one is that there are always many shows running in town at the same time, and neither mobility among subject positions nor modes of linking can be fully controlled. Actors and stagehands, the laborers of the theater industry, for example, must recognize themselves as loyal employees, no matter how underpaid they are, and must never go on strike at the season's height. But here, too, one can speak about linking show (the alarm clock, the arrival of a paycheck, the shout or shadow of a nervous director, and so on) and machinery (theater as institution and industry), except that now the relation between show and machinery has been inverted; the show has been allocated a role in the operation of the machine.[19]

The crucial point is that there are many other shows outside the theater hall, and the dramaturgic model tells us little about how they are related. The dramaturgic model helps us understand the conditions for successful, reproducible linking: it must be performed within the confines of a well-controlled space, or something that functions like it, with a relatively clear demarcation of the show's stage and times with an experienced, trained crew whose members act in concert without producing anything new. The model does not tell us how such conditions can be established outside the theater hall. Specifically, there is nothing in the dramaturgic model that guarantees that the state could function like the theater's management. The relative unity and coherence of the theatrical production,[20] the ability to grasp and capture at a glance the entire spectacle onstage and follow it as it is unfolding, the skillful, coordinated action of its crew, the relatively clear relations of authority on- and offstage—all these features have made the theater a desirable metaphor for an efficient power structure (along with other such metaphors of unity and coordinated action from Plato's ship through Hobbes's Leviathan to Althusser's own apparatus). But this metaphor belongs to a particular ideology of the state, of which Althusser himself was a subject (as the last three chapters of "Ideology and Ideological State Apparatuses" clearly demonstrate), according to which the state is a successful unifying set of apparatuses whose function is to guarantee the coordinated reproduction of the entire social order.[21] The dramaturgic model says nothing about the state, its structure and real power, or about any other institution, for that matter, that lacks the conditions of production and reproduction characteristic of the theater. It is solely a model for understanding the political function of ideology and the conditions for its successful operation. And it is precisely for this reason that it can resolve the aporias in Althusser's thinking about ideology.

Delinking, Threshold

In the dramaturgic model of ideology, freedom is presupposed and revolution is not precluded. Freedom is presupposed because interpellation is understood as a moment of linking, which always implies the possibility of delinking. An episode invented (or recounted and, in any case, staged) by Jean-François Lyotard in *The Differend* demonstrates this well: "[T]he officer cries *Avanti!* and leaps up out of the trench; moved, the soldiers cry *Bravo!* but don't budge" (para. 43). In this "little theatre" (one among many), Lyotard shows a case of linking two different regimens of discourse, an order and an evaluation. The purpose is to demonstrate that linking is never dictated by the addressing phrase, that is, by an interpellation. "It is necessary to link, but the mode of linkage is never necessary" (para. 41). Entering the addressee's position does not determine anything. Even a dog may enter a subject position (call out "Hey, dog," and he will stop running, turning his head); even a trained, docile soldier may abandon it. Even in wartime, even when everyone knows what is expected, an order can be followed by a comic gesture (evaluation) and not by the act that executes it.

The same goes for any interpellation into any subject position. When the link is "improper" enough, as is the case in Lyotard's little show, the subject delinks her show from the apparatus that has assigned her role. This delinking may always mean linking elsewhere, but it is not always clear where. The soldiers shouting *Bravo!* to their officer are no longer good subjects in the theater of war. But which subject position are they taking? The officer might not know. From now on they cannot be trusted. Having ruptured the chain of command and the order of power, they might fail any or all expectations. To maintain his own subject position, their officer must stage their act as a moment of rebellion. He must react, violently, if necessary. The other option is to accept their *Bravo!* as a joke, join the comical moment, and open the way for a disintegration of the power structure. The point is that there is always an option, usually many; roles may always be changed, stages abandoned, and scripts transformed.

Moreover, the interpellating voice may come from below, from the depths of the trench. No one exemplifies this better than the newborn baby, whose name precedes her birth. Long before they know it, babies have already used the scream and smile that interpellate the adults around them, calling them to take their various adult positions. Althusser was not always careful to take into account the fact that interpellation is not a one-way street, and this is precisely what Balibar is trying to revise. In line with what he did elsewhere (for example, in "Non-Contemporaneity" and *Spinoza* 71–75), he now turns to Althusser's reading of *The Prince*, where Althusser is concerned with the way the Prince is interpellated by the masses. From this perspective, "Power" appears as nothing but the existence of a more or less coordinated network of subject positions from which individuals are authorized to anticipate and respond to the behavior of bad subjects. If they cannot eliminate the emergence of bad subjects, they can at least turn them—what they have done and what is being done to them—into elements in their show of power. The Prince has more authority than the others, but this means that he has even less freedom than others to take a bad subject position. This is no less true in the case of the baby's parents or of theater management.

There is nothing obvious, nothing guaranteed about the efficiency of an ideological apparatus, let alone about the success of the initial call into a subject position. Delinking (and linking elsewhere) is always possible: the sense of inevitability that accompanies the voluntary responses to the call is not always properly instilled in the addressee; misrecognition can work in more than one direction, and, most importantly, one can always stay, for a short while or forever, at the play's threshold, standing on that imaginary line that separates one stage from another, exactly where the soldiers in Lyotard's episode stood upon hearing the command. Nothing illustrates this better than one of the most famous episodes Althusser used for demonstrating the power of interpellation. Let me conclude this tribute to Balibar's dramaturgic model of ideology by dwelling on the story of Moses and the burning bush (Exodus 3.1–4.17).

Althusser sketches the story of the burning bush quite hastily and in almost the same words in the two versions of his essay on ideology ("Ideology" 267–68 and "On Ideology" 195–96). He takes it to be a paradigmatic site for demonstrating how "religious ideology presupposes the 'existence' of a unique and central other Subject, in whose name religious ideology interpellates all individuals as subjects [*en sujets*]" ("On Ideology" 195). He takes the liberty of quoting the biblical scene "in a combined way, not literally, but 'in spirit and truth'" (195n28): "And it came to pass at that time that God the Lord (Yahweh) spoke to Moses in the cloud. And the Lord called out to Moses, 'Moses!' And Moses replied 'It (really) is me, Moses! I am Moses your servant, speak and I shall listen and obey!' And the Lord spoke to Moses and said to him, 'I am that I am.'" Althusser goes on to interpret the episode:

> *God thus defines Himself as the Subject* par excellence, *He who is through Himself and for Himself ("I am that I am"), and He who interpellates His subject, the individual subjected to Him by His very interpellation, that is the individual named Moses. And Moses, interpellated-called [*appelé*] by his name, having recognized that it "really" was he who was called by God, recognizes— yes indeed!—recognizes that he is a subject, a subject of God, a subject subjected to God, a subject by the Subject and subjected to the Subject. The proof is that he obeys Him, and makes his people obey God's Commandments. And we are on the way, Ladies and Gentlemen, to the Promised Land.* ("On Ideology" 195–96)

But as Eyal Dotan has noted, this is not the whole story, and Althusser interrupts it at the wrong moment, missing a crucial aspect of the scene (18–19). Between Moses's first encounter with the strange spectacle and the glorious march to the Promised Land, after Moses is called by his name and before he assumes the role assigned to him by God, there is a prolonged exchange between the two in which Moses asks questions and God provides answers (Exodus 3.11–15, 4.1–17).[22] Hastened by his "theoretical reduction," Althusser ignores the whole political dialogue and tense struggle that is taking place near the burning bush. Let me follow the scene in some detail.

Note first that the "great sight" (3.3) that draws Moses's attention is immediately abandoned for a speaking voice that calls Moses twice by his name. Moses answers, "Here I am." The only thing Moses's response ("*hineni* [here I am]") indicates is that he has recognized himself to be the subject of a call. God recognizes Moses, while Moses recognizes himself when called. At this first moment of recognition, no question is asked and no action is taken. God then gives Moses (stage) directions ("Come no closer here. Take off your sandals" [3.5]) and only then declares himself to be who he is, "the God of your father." He never claims to be "unique and central," as Althusser has it, but rather of a common kind, a god of a particular tribe, to which Moses happens to belong: "the God of Abraham [. . .] Isaac, and [. . .] Jacob" (3.6). Only after God establishes his own identity in a condensed narrative (3.6–9) comes the command: "And now, go that I may send you to Pharaoh" (3.10). Moses understands that the call comes from God and expresses this recognition by hiding his face (3.6). Up to this point, no doubt, question, desire, or misrecognition has been expressed or betrayed by the text. Poor as always in psychoanalytic insights, the biblical text sets the stage for a straightforward exchange between the Lord of the tribe and one of its members, a man who already acknowledges his authority and is only partly impressed by it. Indeed, Moses is afraid to look toward the speaking voice; perhaps he knows a thing or two about his Lord's violent, wrathful temper, but after God's story ends, he is not afraid to question his command. Once more, Moses raises questions and objections, insistent in his attempt to convince God that the command has been misdirected. This is the exchange that Althusser leaves out of his account of the episode as a result (and example) of his *theoretical reduction.*

Moses is not questioning God's authority to command—only his wisdom. Still, it is doubtful whether the Other Subject speaking to him can be ascribed with "self-identity," and even if Moses imagines or projects such identity on God, it is certainly not reassuring.[23] With each new question, the gap widens between the subject and the position he is supposed to assume. Moses is already placed in the theater of God, but he is not taking up the role assigned to him. Even after being interpellated into a subject position and even though he is entirely in the grip of the voice emanating from an Other Subject, it is not yet clear, and certainly not yet settled, what it all means for Moses (and for us).[24] God, Moses seems to argue through his repeated questions, misrecognizes his subject for what he really is. "Who am I that I should go to Pharoah?" (3.11). He is not made for the task. God offers him a sign to reassure the Israelites that Moses is indeed his messenger (3.12), which Moses ignores. He demands to know God's name, so when he comes back to the Israelites in Egypt as God's mediator, he would be able to name the One in whose name he is speaking. God calls himself by an enigmatic name, "I shall be that I shall be [אהיה אשר אהיה]," but then adds a whole speech that is meant to close the gap that the name has opened and gives Moses more detailed directions for action (3.13–22). But Moses is still not impressed. They will not believe me, he tells God (4.1). To assure the people's recognition, God teaches Moses sorcery, turning his staff into a magic wand (4.2–9). Moses sees the miracles, and he is still not convinced. He proposes a final excuse: he cannot perform his role because he has a speech impediment, which he bears from long ago (4.10). He seems to know well who he is, who he has been all along, and even what God may not like about him, but he doubts whether God knows him well enough. God knows his name, certainly, and may give him limitless power to perform miracles, but does he know what Moses is capable of doing on his own? Can he know this better than Moses?

Standing barefoot at the threshold of his new subject position, Moses turns it into a space of suspension. It is only a few years since he left Egypt, where he had grown up as a prince and from which he then escaped like a fugitive (2.11–15), finding shelter in the household of a Midianite priest (2.18–21). He is married now with a child (2.22) and has a family to care for. He has already been interpellated several times in ways that have radically changed him: by the suffering of his people, by violence (of people from all three nations he knew: Egyptians, Israelites, and Midianites), by rumors that made him fear death, and perhaps also by the Midianite girls and the generosity of his Midianite host. He was a prince and a fugitive who has become a family man; he has lived in the most civilized of places and in the most deserted ones. Clearly, he knows how to take subject positions but also how to leave them. And now he is called by God to take the position of supreme authority, second only to God, and lead the people of God from slavery to redemption. Only now, for the first time, does he resist a call. He forces God to perform miracles and make promises and go out of his way to convince his subject to take his leading role. Suspending his decision, Moses is stalling for time, and while trying to convince God that he is not the right man for the mission, he learns about the scope of the mission and the means at his disposal.

This is more than political negotiation; it is a real struggle between a servant and a master, an actor and a director, over the role the subject might play in a drama whose script has already been announced (3.15–22). Moses is not becoming a subject through the interpellation of the burning bush. He does not want to take part in the show. He has other roles to perform, a new world where he feels at home, or at least less alienated. God insists. When Moses runs out of questions and excuses, he keeps pleading: "And he said, 'Please, my Lord, send, pray, by the hand of him you would send'" (4.13). This makes God angry, and his wrath is well expressed. He refuses to listen and dismisses Moses's last plea. The show has already begun, he tells Moses; your brother Aaron is going to speak for you. He is already on his way to meet you. Your wand is ready, go and take it with you (4.14–17). No veiling effect, no withdrawal of the voice's origin is at work here.[25] Only now, when faced with God's wrath, when the voice from on high is supplemented with a clear and direct threat of violence does Moses obey. The text does not describe Moses's submission; the readers gather this when they follow Moses in the next act: "And Moses went and returned to Jether his father-in-law, and he said to him, 'Let me go'" (4.18–20).

Butler observes that the impact of Althusser's concept of ideology owes much to his choice of examples. Althusser draws many of his examples from theological contexts or models them after such theologically loaded episodes. These are situations in which "the divine power of naming" is set as a model and the force with which it is ascribed is "extended" (and hence secularized) to the social authorities (Butler 110, 114). My reading of the biblical passage should be understood not as an attempt to rid the theory of ideology of the theological straitjacket in which it finds itself, but rather to offer an alternative theological framework. In this framework, for which the Hebrew Bible provides ample examples, God is a "great and awful" other but not an ultimate or transcendental one. He is not necessarily imagined as both "unique and central," but rather struggles hard to become such, and this struggle is often spectacular and not always successful, as both his unity and his oneness are often questioned. He uses both voice and violence as means of interpellation, his commands are open to interpretation and—more importantly—negotiation, his decisions and stage directions may change in the middle of the play, and his scripts are constantly rewritten.[26] He is said to be the sovereign of the world but can hardly lead his own chosen people safely to their Promised Land. His is a figure of the interpellating-interpellated Other that fits the dramaturgic model of ideology and helps it avoid its theoretical impasses.

Thinking about the other in this way, it becomes clear that what is split at the moment of interpellation is not only the subject but the ideological apparatus itself, whose cracks might break open at any minute because the responsibility for the show—and hence for linking the show to the apparatus—is always shared by the interpellated subject and subsequently by all those readers interpellated by the story. These readers now share with the text's narrator (another candidate for taking the position of a transcendent other) the responsibility for integrating the tense episode near the burning bush into the national narrative. They can either imagine, pretend to believe, or actually perform the coordination of this episode with numerous others, conflictual and conflicting, so as to form or disrupt the march from slavery to redemption.

Finally, one must face the question this essay has tried to avoid: if ideology is so precarious, if so much may happen in the gap between a call and a "proper" response, between the position of the addressee and the subject position she is called to take; if ideology must always be in the plural and no ideological apparatus is capable of totalizing the multiple "local" ideologies and their numerous subject positions, coordinating and orchestrating their effects, then how can ideology explain the reproduction of the social order? The straightforward, short answer should be that it cannot. Within the dramaturgic model proposed by Balibar, ideology cannot play the role assigned to it in the two canonical texts where Althusser presents his theoretical show ("Ideology" and "On Ideology"). No single apparatus can fill this role. A solution for the enigma of reproduction must be sought elsewhere.[27] The first step might be to ask what, if anything, is reproduced exactly. The dramaturgic model ensures only the reproductions of multiple theatrical productions, and these may last only as long as the public likes the show.

I would like to thank Dikla Bytner for excellent comments on a previous draft of this essay.

ADI OPHIR is Professor Emeritus at Tel Aviv University. He is currently a visiting professor at the Cogut Center for the Humanities at Brown University. His most recent book (in Hebrew) is *Divine Violence: Two Essays on God and Disaster* (Van Leer Jerusalem Institute, 2013).

Notes

1   As Balibar explains in his introduction, the text was first published as the preface to the Hebrew translation of Althusser's "On Ideology." Balibar wrote it in 2003 in response to an invitation by the Hebrew translator Ariella Azoulay.

2   See Balibar's presentation of Spinoza's critique of monarchy in *Spinoza and Politics* 71–75.

3   At the outset of his latest take on Althusser's concept of ideology (*Absolute* 51–64), Žižek, following Mladen Dolar, does invoke the theater, only to reiterate his Lacanian presuppositions. Comedy, Žižek argues, is "an intermediate space or passage" between "the two levels of the ideological process," the one external, material, and practical and the other internal, where interpellation operates and generates (mis)recognition and (dis)belief. The passage takes place when "a *character* in comedy" (my emphasis) enacts an internal belief precisely when "he acts as if he believes" or "just believes that he acts" (51). For Balibar, we shall see, the passage is not from an external to an internal level (their separation is not assumed), but back and

forth from machinery (the world behind the scene) to show (the world onstage), and the focus is not on the *character* but on the *actor*.

4   Of special importance for Balibar is Carlo Bertolazzi's play *El nost Milan*, produced by Giorgio Strehler's Il Piccolo Teatro di Milano and performed in Paris in 1962.

5   Althusser's writing may be responsible for the world represented in the text, while Balibar's reading is responsible for the way the text's surface takes shape and appears to us. But as the text (and my reading) proceeds, it becomes more difficult (and unnecessary) to maintain the distinction between these two layers.

6   The French *répétition*, Balibar reminds us ("Althusser's Dramaturgy" 12), means both the rehearsal on the theater stage and the reiteration of everyday practice.

7   That is, of those—politicians and philosophers alike—who imagine themselves at power's origin, capable of possessing it.

8   This understanding of ideology uses and inverts Hannah Arendt's concept of action and its relation to power and the new beginning (see ch. 24–28). Much more can be said about this inversion but must be left for another occasion.

9   Note that the possible estrangement of the actress with respect to the role she is playing is different from the belief of the good subject that is not entirely identical with the subject position (e.g., he is a humanist, not only a soldier; he is a capitalist but also cares for the poor, etc.). When Žižek argues that "an ideological identification exerts a true hold on us precisely when we maintain an awareness that we are not fully identical to it" (*Plague* 27), he precludes the possibility of theatrical acting. Ideological identification with a role one acts is exerted only as long as the show goes on.

10 Unless such questions are imposed by this or that "politics of identity."

11 See, for example, Butler; Dotan; Žižek, *Plague* and *Sublime*.

12 As Derrida says (without invoking Althusser's concept of ideology): "I can only answer this call, I have already answered it, even if I said no [in fact, even if I said nothing]" (103). See also Dotan 27. This is a point made by many; I prefer to follow here Lyotard's version.

13 It is worth noting that in Balibar's writings on forms of extreme violence (e.g., "Outline" and "Violence"), the concept of ideology receives little attention.

14 But Althusser recognizes that violence is needed even when the ideological apparatus functions generally well. Sometimes, "as need sorts," when it is truly impossible to deal otherwise with the "bad sorts," one should call upon the "carefully deliberated assistance, the intervention of the detachments specialized in repression, namely, the magistrates of the Inquisition or, when it is a question of ideologies other than religious ideology, of other specialized magistrates and police officials" ("On Ideology" 197).

15 Althusser tries to associate the distinction with the division of the social into public and private realms ("Ideology" 243), but this division is untenable, for both the gun and the new media through which the law is mediated tend to blur the distinction between the two realms.

16   "We see, therefore, that War is not merely a political act, but also a real political instrument, *a continuation of political commerce, a carrying out of the same* by other means" (Clausewitz, bk. 1, ch. 1, no. 24, emphasis added).

17   I owe my use and emphasis on linking, as well as my understanding of the moment of hailing, to Lyotard's analysis in *The Differend* (see especially paras. 40–41, 102–5, 135–40).

18   The full quote reads: "[I]deology has no outside (for itself), but at the same time it is nothing but outside (for science and reality)" ("On Ideology" 192), and as such the claim seems naive and must be rejected. Ideology is not outside of science as it is not outside of any other cultural sphere. Science has its theater halls, and sometimes what is shown there is presented as "real." To imagine a situation in which no interpellation is at work is a thought experiment not very different from that involved in theorizing "the state of nature," and it would be no less problematic.

19   The dramaturgic metaphor seems to give excessive weight to the show over the apparatus. The most important things in the life of power (or of the "social order" or the "relation of production"), one may object, take place offstage behind the scenes, and the show of power is merely an auxiliary in the service of the winning forces. In the theater, on the other hand, the show is of the essence; the machinery is merely an auxiliary. This argument may be wrong on both counts, as a description of power as well as of the theater, but even if it were true, it is still beside the point, for what it challenges is the relation and hierarchy between machinery and show, not their necessary (and essential) linking. No apparatus

of power can work without a show of power, even if the show takes place behind the curtain, as a recent television series, *House of Cards*, illustrates, in fact, in great detail. And even if the real essence of power shows itself behind the scene, power, political power at least, still needs the show, and linking is necessary.

20   This should not be confused with the imagined unity of space, time, and plot prescribed by Aristotle.

21   Since the relations of production are a key element in a system of production that comprises the entire social order, "the reproduction of relations of production" means maintaining the outlines and structural features of the system intact. Althusser's innovation, and what he is especially concerned with in "Ideology and Ideological State Apparatuses," is the distinction between repressive and ideological state apparatus. This duality is further complicated by the plurality of existing and rival ideological apparatuses, but the existence of one dominant apparatus, the ideological apparatus of the ruling class (245), is announced *ex cathedra* and is assigned the role of orchestrating the multiplicity and ensuring that the "concert is dominated by a single score" (251; see also "On Ideology" 199–200). Since the repressive apparatus is unified anyway (247)—this is what the classic theory of the state is about, after all—and the unity of the ideological apparatuses under the dominant one is ensured, nothing can disturb the unity of the state. Althusser, at any rate, has never questioned it. To say (correctly) that this unity is "merely" an imaginary effect of ideology cannot be a counterargument here. Althusser's point, reiterated numerous times, is that ideology is effective indeed!

22   All quotes from the Bible are from Robert Alter's translation. References are by chapter and verse number.

23   This is one of the points in Althusser's description of the scene that Butler emphasizes (108).

24   This is not the first time such dialogue with God takes place, and it is not the only time Moses questions God's plans. See Genesis 18.17–32 and Exodus 32.7–14.

25   Emphasizing the staging of the voice in Althusser, Balibar refers to the same episode: "[I]t is the veiling effect that produces an effect of transcendence, the effect of *withdrawing the origin* of the interpellation, removing the possibility of identifying an author,

except through the tautologies asserting his authority. *I am who I am*, says the voice that interpellates Moses from behind the Burning Bush" ("Althusser's Dramaturgy" 14).

26   Recently, this image of God in the Hebrew Bible has become popular among scholars and theologians. See, for example, Muffs; Ophir, *Divine*; Sommer.

27   The solution must be sought elsewhere, but neither outside of ideology (for ideology would inhere in any other apparatus involved in the reproduction of social order) nor inside it (for the question is always how to achieve a coherent effect of multiple, conflicting ideologies).

Works Cited

Alter, Robert. *The Five Books of Moses: A Translation with Commentary.* New York: Norton, 2004.

Althusser, Louis. "Ideology and Ideological State Apparatuses." *On the Reproduction* 232–72.

——————. *Machiavelli and Us (Radical Thinkers).* Ed. François Matheron. Trans. Gregory Elliot. London: Verso, 1999.

——————. "On Ideology." *On the Reproduction* 171–207.

——————. *On the Reproduction of Capitalism: Ideology and Ideological State Apparatuses.* Trans. G. M. Goshgarian. London: Verso, 2014.

Arendt, Hannah. *The Human Condition.* Chicago: U of Chicago P, 1958.

Azoulay, Ariella, and Adi Ophir. "The Order of Violence." *The Power of Inclusive Exclusion: Anatomy of Israeli Rule in the Occupied Palestinian Territories.* Ed. Adi Ophir, Michal Givoni, and Sari Hanafi. New York: Zone, 2009. 99–140.

Balibar, Étienne. "Althusser's Dramaturgy and the Critique of Ideology." *differences* 26.3 (2015): 1–22.

——————. "Althusser's Object." Trans. Margaret Cohen and Bruce Robbins. *Social Text* 39 (1994): 157–88.

——————. "Ambiguous Universality." *Politics and the Other Scene.* London: Verso, 2002: 56–75.

——————. "Avant-propos pour la réédition de 1996." *Pour Marx.* Ed. Louis Althusser. Paris: La Découverte, 1996. i–xiii.

——————. "Foreword: Althusser and the 'Ideological State Apparatuses.'" Althusser, *On the Reproduction* vii–xviii.

—————. "The Non-Contemporaneity of Althusser." *The Althusserian Legacy*. Ed. Ann Kaplan and Michael Sprinker. London: Verso, 1993. 1–16.

—————. "Outlines of a Topography of Cruelty: Citizenship and Civility in the Era of Global Violence." *We, the People of Europe? Reflections on Transnational Citizenship*. Trans. James Swenson. Princeton: Princeton UP, 2004. 115–32.

—————. "Politics and Truth: The Vacillation of Ideology II." *Masses, Classes, Ideas: Studies on Politics and Philosophy before and after Marx*. Trans. James Swenson. New York: Routledge, 1994: 151–75.

—————. *Spinoza and Politics*. Trans. Peter Snowdon. London: Verso, 1998.

—————. "Tais-toi encore, Althusser!" *Les Temps modernes* 44.509 (1988): 1–29.

—————. "Violence, Ideality, and Cruelty." *Politics and the Other Scene*. London: Verso, 2002. 129–45.

Balibar, Étienne, and Immanuel Wallerstein. *Race, Nation, Class: Ambiguous Identities*. Trans. Chris Turner. London: Verso, 1991.

Butler, Judith. *The Psychic Life of Power*. Stanford: Stanford UP, 1997.

Clausewitz, Carl von. *On War*. Ed. and trans. Michael Eliot Howard and Peter Paret. Princeton: Princeton UP, 1984.

Derrida, Jacques. "'Eating Well,' or the Calculation of the Subject." *Who Comes after the Subject?* Ed. Eduardo Cadava, Peter Connor, and Jean-Luc Nancy. New York: Routledge, 1991. 96–119.

Dotan, Eyal. "Kol Korē Ba'Midbar: Interpellatzia, Ideologia and Mikrē ['Vox Clamans in Deserto': Interpellation, Ideology, and Chance]". *Theory and Criticism* 22 (2003): 9–34.

Foucault, Michel. *Society Must Be Defended: Lectures at the Collège de France, 1975–76*. Ed. Mauro Bertani and Alessandro Fontana. Trans. David Macey. New York: Picador, 2003.

Lyotard, Jean-François. *The Differend: Phrases in Dispute*. Minneapolis: U of Minnesota P, 1988.

Muffs, Yochanan. *Personhood of God: Biblical Theology, Human Faith, and the Divine Image*. Woodstock: Jewish Lights, 2005.

Ophir, Adi. *Alimut Elohit: Shnei Khiburim al Elohim ve-Asson* [*Divine Violence: Two Essays on God and Disaster*]. Jerusalem: Van Leer Jerusalem Institute, 2013.

Sommer, Benjamin D. *The Bodies of God and the World of Ancient Israel*. Cambridge: Cambridge UP, 2009.

Žižek, Slavoj. *Absolute Recoil: Towards a New Foundation of Dialectical Materialism*. London: Verso, 2014.

—————. *The Plague of Fantasies*. London: Verso, 1997.

—————. *The Sublime Object of Ideology*. London: Verso, 1989.

Althusser's Materialist Theater: Ideology and Its Aporias

*I*ntroducing how individual contributions make up the collective project of *Reading Capital*, Althusser writes: "The studies that emerged from this project are no more than the various individual protocols of reading: each having cut the peculiar oblique path that suited him through the immense forest of this Book" (14). He alludes to these contributions as an "adventure," one whose "risks and advantages" are preserved in their unaltered publication, which, by instilling the novel "experience of a reading," will incite the reader to conduct his own—"so that he in turn will be dragged in the wake of this first reading into a second one which will take us still further" (14). Althusser refers to Marx's magisterial work, *Capital*, as an "immense forest," and this is not a metaphor to be taken lightly. This is a forest into which different paths need to be cut, as intellectual forays into a complex whole, each of which can only be slanted, partial, somewhat arbitrary, if not completely contingent, conditional on the goals of the reader, and productive of unforeseeable effects. What connects the different paths, however, is revealed by way of a confession: they constitute a *philosophical* reading, which defends the necessary partiality of its approach while

Volume 26, Number 3 DOI 10.1215/10407391-3340372

© 2015 by Brown University and d i f f e r e n c e s : A Journal of Feminist Cultural Studies

also asserting that at stake in every reading pretending to be innocent is the unconfessed "guilt" of not having problematized what it is to read (15).

Étienne Balibar's essay "Althusser's Dramaturgy and the Critique of Ideology" presents us with a spirit of reading similar to the one Althusser identifies in the contributions that make up *Reading Capital*, but now the "oblique path" is cut through the forest of Althusser's own oeuvre. Balibar's *philosophical* reading offers a new foray into Althusser's theory of ideology, which, rather than a straight and predictable path that would lead us directly to "Ideology and Ideological State Apparatuses," takes us on an "adventure" that begins with "The 'Piccolo Teatro'" and extends toward Althusser's reflections on Machiavelli, passing en route through the essay on the ideological state apparatuses (ISAs), which thereby assumes a different significance, no longer being the primary or sole destination. Moving us from the materialist practice of theater to the theatrical practice of political agency, by way of the "theoretical theater" of interpellation that stages the dual process of subjection-subjectivation in the exemplary hail of the police, Balibar takes us into the depths of the Althusserian forest in which, beyond the existence of the trees, there lies another world to be discovered.

This foray is no more innocent than the readings of *Capital*: it confesses its "guilt" by stating its aim—to provide "a partially new description of Althusser's quest for a critical concept of *ideology*" (Balibar, "Althusser's Dramaturgy" 2). But inscribed in this deceptively simple goal is nothing less than a new way of reading Althusser: for Althusser, against Althusser. Balibar reminds us of Althusser's most significant theoretical contributions on the question of ideology, suggesting in particular how he transformed the way we pose questions about ideology, and gives us the opportunity to reassess Althusser's legacy while also taking into consideration the limits of his thought. At stake in Balibar's iteration of Althusser's reading "for Marx, against Marx" (2) is more than a philosophical reconstruction, an intellectual history, or an exegesis of Althusser or, through Althusser's mediation, of Marx. Balibar reopens a question that has lost nothing of its philosophical and political importance, even though it has receded in our theoretical conjuncture: the question of a revolutionary politics and the possibility of thinking revolutionary politics from within a problematic of ideology.

Such a move designates subjectivity as a critical site of political contestation and radical transformation. An emancipatory politics, according to Balibar, should involve the "action of the masses (or the people) *upon their own imaginary* that would use the artifices of visualization and representation in order to orient it toward actions that are in their own interest, following ideals in which they believe—without believing 'blindly,' as it were, or in which they believe *with a distance*" (19). The point is not simply to think the ways in which one mass ideology can be substituted for another, however revolutionary it might be, but to understand the processes and forms in which political subjects are constituted so that the conditions of possibility of their transformation can be delineated. This understanding, or a critical theory of ideology, is necessary precisely in order not to believe "blindly," but to pave the way for obtaining a distance from ideology, even if the reconfiguration of subjectivity still takes place within the terrain of ideology. The production of that theory is not carried out in the absence of ideological influences, nor is a theoretical critique of ideology without ideological and political consequences. Perhaps a certain circularity is not altogether avoidable in the effort of explicating a theory of ideology, leaving us with constitutive aporias to which Balibar asks us to attend. Our knowledge of these aporias has a direct bearing on emancipatory politics, both in terms of our ability to theorize the subjects of revolutionary transformation and insofar as our theorization is informed by and becomes part of political struggle itself. Without understanding how ideology works to produce subjects, Balibar tells us, we cannot theorize how subjection is reproduced or how it can be disrupted. At the same time, without having a critical concept of ideology, it appears, we can hardly become different subjects.

Althusserian Décalages

The question of the relationship between philosophy and politics, or theory and practice, permeates Althusser's contributions to a theory of ideology, and perhaps even his oeuvre as a whole. Balibar's compelling reconstruction throws light on this intricate nexus between philosophy and politics while offering us the powerful metaphor of *theater* and its multiple connotations to explore it further. Indeed, Balibar's essay also avows this connection by the very protocol of reading he follows.

Balibar delineates the trajectory of Althusser's problematic of ideology by connecting three different sites of Althusser's oeuvre, moving from "The 'Piccolo Teatro'" (1962) to "Ideology and Ideological State Apparatuses" (1970) and, finally, to the manuscript of *Machiavelli and Us* (1972–76). It would be wrong to assume, however, that the temporal progression in the composition of these texts corresponds to a linear development in Althusser's thought. Instead, Balibar characterizes this movement as one of successive dislocations that form an "aporetic trajectory" (3). Formally,

Balibar's reading proceeds through the identification of a series of *décal-ages*, invoking Althusser's impressive reading of Rousseau's *Social Contract*. This is a procedure of reading that analyzes how the central "philosophical object" of a discourse is made to function by tracing how it "solves" a problem (Althusser, "Rousseau" 113–14): each articulation of the problem involves a theoretical solution that has its internal limits, which are displaced to the next register, where these limits become problematized and the new problem, thus posed, meets a new theoretical solution but which poses, in turn, new limits that are displaced to the next. Balibar ostensibly adopts this protocol; however, his artful execution renders it something other than a straightforward repetition.

Althusser looks at the limits of Rousseau's conceptual innova-tions and how their "play" sustains the central object of his discourse, the social contract, which also imprisons his thought in a problematic inher-ited from Hobbes. Balibar, on the other hand, calls attention to Althusser's "aporias," showing how their transposition onto different registers works not simply to sustain the functioning of a central object, in this case ideol-ogy, but restlessly drives the movement of his thought, chasing, as it were, after a central object that is reconfigured each time. Thus, in contrast to Rousseau's *social contract*—a problematic from which he cannot free him-self—Althusser's *ideology* is a problematic that he considerably transforms, injecting novel conceptual elements to those he inherited from Marx, shift-ing their configuration, and ultimately, if still aporetically, producing a philosophical object that is only nominally the same as the one with which he began. Most importantly, unlike the chain of discrepancies that Althusser identifies as internal to Rousseau's *Social Contract*, as necessary constitu-ents of Rousseau's philosophical system that enable it to cohere and function in an ultimately "ideological" way—"flight forward in ideology or regression in the economy" (155–57)—the chain of *décalages* Balibar identifies in his longitudinal view of Althusser's theoretical production points in the opposite direction: the discrepancies that drive the development of Althusser's prob-lematic of ideology refuse the *ideological* closure of his thought, presenting us rather with a series of reformulations—"philosophical detour[s]" (4)—that, ultimately, opens it up to the indeterminacy of politics.

What are these reformulations? At the most abstract level, the chain of discrepancies indicates an overall movement from a focus on the politics in theater to the theatrical in politics, in which the thread of continu-ity, according to Balibar, is established by the *dramaturgical* nature of ideol-ogy (19). This movement takes us from one register to another, transversing the aesthetic, through the materialist theater of Carlo Bertolazzi's *El nost Milan* as directed by Giorgio Strehler and Leonardo Cremonini's "antihumanist and materialist" paintings ("Cremonini" 239), to the register of the social—in the complex mechanisms of the reproduction of the relations of production that delineate the family, the school, the media, the trade union, the church, the sports club, and the political party as so many different institutions that make up the ISAs—and, subsequently, to the explicitly political register by way of the analysis of the figure of the Machiavellian Prince. In each register, different thinkers gain prominence; however, whether it is Brecht, Spinoza, or Machiavelli, with Freud and Lacan, it is always Marx whose thought is at stake.

But these reformulations of the problematic of ideology suggest a transformation more profound than the difference among registers would seem to imply. In "The 'Piccolo Teatro,'" the problem of ideology is initially posed in terms that are not altogether different from a *camera obscura*, to recall Marx, positing an antithetical relation between reality and its consciousness. Althusser finds the plot of the play to enact a confrontation between "a world without illusions" and "the wretched illusions of the 'heart,'" a confrontation in which reality triumphs over the "myths" of consciousness that takes a particularly "melodramatic" form ("'Piccolo'" 134). Despite this juxtaposition, which would seem to locate the critique of ideology either in the Hegelian dialectic of consciousness that takes place among the characters in the play, specifically in Nina's rejection of her father's values, or in the negation of this consciousness by the real conditions of Nina's existence—poverty and misery that define the life of the Italian subproletariat—Althusser's innovation is that he places the critique of ideology in the ability of the Bertolazzi play to show the very dissociation between reality and its consciousness (140–41; Balibar, "Althusser's Dramaturgy" 3–5). Materialist theatrical practice is marked by the capacity *to stage* this dissociation for the spectators in terms that are not simply internal to the plot. Because the performance as a whole actively enacts the critique of ideology by way of distanciation, Althusser contends, it enables the spectators to become aware of how ideology works, as it were, behind the backs of the actors onstage and, by extension, of the spectators themselves (Statkiewicz 46).

The mechanism of distanciation that Althusser identifies in Bertolazzi's *El nost Milan* does not achieve its critical effect by means of a dissociation between the play and the spectators, a dissociation that would disrupt the spectators' identification with the characters in the play in terms

akin to Brecht's V-effect (*Verfremdungseffekt*). The mechanism of distanciation, or what I have elsewhere called overdistanciation (*surdistanciation*)
to distinguish it from the Brechtian V-effect as an *overdetermined* form of
distanciation (Bargu 98–102), instead works by putting the dissociation on
display. "It is not a question of changing the place of some small elements
in the play of the actors," Althusser maintains, but "a question of a displacement that affects the whole of the theater's conditions" ("On Brecht" 142).
Althusser's theoretical solution to the problem of ideology, then, resides in
the latent structure of the play, a structure of dissociation that juxtaposes
different temporalities and spaces in an uneven way. The event, with its
melodramatic consciousness, is displaced to the wings and cast against the
noneventful, atemporal void of the masses, which is radically separated
from and largely indifferent to it. This latent structure reveals itself only
to the spectator, "making paradoxically 'visible' [. . .] what is in principle
invisible, namely, ideology's grip on the consciousnesses of its subjects," as
Balibar puts it ("Althusser's Dramaturgy" 6), by offering a play of mirrors
that destabilizes their process of recognition, urging them to action. It thus
offers, according to Balibar, a critique of ideology that depicts a materialist theater as "destitute of ideology" (6) or theorizes "interpellation *out of
ideology*" (9).[1]

    This solution is encumbered, however, by its aporetic character.
Does Althusser not return to a dialectics of consciousness in precisely the
Hegelian sense he wants to reject when he expects the transformation of
spectator-consciousness as a result of the critique of ideology enacted by
the materialist practice of theater? Does he not admit to the limits of his
own solution when he emphasizes the "unresolved alterity" of the play, an
alterity that he anticipates will have transformative effects on the spectator
("'Piccolo'" 142)? Does he not relapse into a model of subjectivation through
identification even as he rejects the identification of the spectators with the
actors of the play as a psychologistic model and suggests instead the "play"
of recognition and misrecognition, which refuses a subjectivity that is completely transparent to itself (149)? Balibar perceptively suggests that the very
effect of Althusser's theoretical solution is ultimately based on the implicit
relationship established between the spectators and the characters in the
play as "antithetic 'others' who nevertheless appear the same as oneself" (10).
Althusser thus attempts to theorize an exit from ideology within ideology, or
within the critique of ideology, providing a solution of whose incompletion
he, too, is aware ("'Piccolo'" 151). As a result, although Althusser's problematic of ideology has shifted the terms in which the problem was initially

posed, that is, as the discrepancy between reality and its consciousness, it nonetheless lacks a definitive closure: it leaves us with the indeterminate effects of a playful constitution of spectator-consciousness.

The "unresolved alterity" that goes into the making of a "new spectator, an actor who starts where the performance ends" ("'Piccolo'" 151) is transposed to the social register when Althusser attempts to work out, with respect to the masses, the possibility of transformation that he has discerned in the spectator's subjectivity. As the aporias of subjectivation now become articulated in the form of a central problem, Althusser offers a new theoretical solution with the concept of *interpellation*, emphasizing the unconscious determinants of subjectivity, on the one hand, and subjection as the inevitable, dark side of subjectivation, on the other. As Balibar remarks, the voice in the "theater" of interpellation, as if coming from behind a mask or a curtain, does not reveal its origin, which "produces an effect of transcendence" ("Althusser's Dramaturgy" 14) while it also induces the subjects who hear the voice to fill the distance between themselves and the veiled origin with their imaginary (15). This symbolic theater enables Althusser to highlight the effects of the "absent cause" of the social whole in the constitution of subjects and their structural assignment to social positions determined, in the last instance, by the demands of reproducing the capitalist relations of production. These demands are such that the masses must necessarily act "all by themselves" while they follow the rules of comportment expected of them in line with the social roles to which they are assigned, without continuous supervision or coercion. The state, now naming a social imaginary in which it assumes the position of the transcendent, interpellating Subject, becomes pervasive and generic. Balibar provocatively suggests how this theater positions the state as God, as the hidden "'force' acting behind the scene or, rather, behind the theater itself" (16).

Interpellation may be the theoretical solution of the problem of subjectivation, but its own aporia is formidable, almost disabling, since it renders exiting the state machinery of ideological reproduction impossible. Althusser's discovery thus imparts an "utterly deterministic and for that reason also fatalistic character" to the account of subjectivation (Balibar, "Althusser's Dramaturgy" 11). Having moved from the performance of ideological recognition onstage to the multiplicity of social practices in which interpellation renders theater into a "*general model* for the staging of discourse" (13), Althusser's novel solution leads to a conception of subjectivation that offers no possibility of emancipation, since it is always coupled with subjection. "Even the 'bad subjects' are trapped," writes Balibar, "perhaps more than the others" (13). Althusser's brief indications regarding the possibility of different interpellations, for example, by the "Revolution," remain questionable, according to Balibar, for even if we were to acknowledge that they may produce divergent political effects, it is dubious whether they would still not necessitate the structural role of the Subject—the State—as part of the theater of interpellation to be filled (13, 14).

If Balibar thus points to the "deep pessimism" of the text whose theoretical effects come to contradict its political goals, he also shows how the aporia of interpellation is in turn transposed onto another register, the register of political practice. In Althusser's reading of Machiavelli, there is the discovery of a new solution: a "politics of ideology" (Balibar, "Althusser's Dramaturgy" 18). Here, Balibar finds not the functionalist impasse of the ISAs essay, but the formulation of mechanisms by which ideology can be politically instrumentalized, involving an agential capacity to control the effects of one's subjectivity and, through that capacity, to shape popular opinion. Machiavelli, of course, attributes this creative capacity to the lonely figure of the Prince, noting how a skillful combination of dissimulation, force, and lawful conduct can help the Prince stage himself for the people in order to gain their friendship. Only with this support can the Prince create the conditions of his rule, to found a national-popular state and secure its endurance (*Machiavelli* 89–101). For Althusser, by contrast, the problem is not the subjectivity of a singular founder but that of collective subject formation, for which the model of the Machiavellian Prince can be productively adapted to the demands of revolutionary transformation in the present.

One way to interpret Althusser's turn to the model of the Prince is to see it as the expression of the communist strategy of acquiring state power in order to transform its apparatuses, thereby channeling its interpellations toward a proletarian politics. Such an interpretation can be derived, on the one hand, from viewing Machiavelli as the theorist of originary "political accumulation" that gives rise to the modern state ("Machiavelli's Solitude" 125) and, on the other, from the identification of the instruments available to the Prince to achieve the task of founding and maintaining that state as strategic tools. Either way, for Althusser, Machiavelli becomes the means to think the formation of the proletarian state and its ideological politics, precisely because he finds Machiavelli's thought to contain, in advance, the outline of a Marxist theory of the state (*Machiavelli* 82).

Balibar's reading entails a different interpretation, one in which the emphasis is on the way in which Althusser's turn to the political practice of the Prince and its effectivity in molding popular opinion offers a solution to the impossibility of an emancipatory subjectivation. This politics of ideology, understood to operate at a mass level, posits a greater space for the agency of subjects over their own subjectivity through their active participation in struggle and a greater role for indeterminacy, since the effects of struggle can hardly be foreseen. Accordingly, Althusser's theoretical solution to the aporia of interpellation now seems less about working out how a subjectivity could be free from the subjection in interpellation than about the espousal of the active struggle over the direction of the effects of subjection, having conceded the constancy of subjection. Politics must work with and within dominant ideology, rendering popular opinion or the masses' achievement of mastery over their own subjectivation the real theater of struggle. Does this solution not substitute for the all-encompassing State the collective agency of the masses without, however, eliminating its interpellating role? Does it not assume the masses to be a more or less unitary force that is in command of its own subjectivity, even as it struggles over its subjection effects? The aporias do not disappear, Balibar implies, but they, too, have been transformed, along with the transformation of the problematic of ideology.

From the perspective of the aporias of ideology, then, the successive displacements in Althusser take us from a theorization of a possible exit from ideology to the recognition of its impossibility and, then, to the immanent potentialities within ideology with an awareness of its specific limits and risks. Balibar's protocol of reading draws us out of the loggias from which spectators watch a play, however actively, first, to the stage itself, the scene of interpellation, only to entice us further into the backstage of political power, as it were, to the vast field of mass struggles over their imaginary. As such, his text skillfully lays bare the structural edifice of Althusser's theater of ideology. The overall effect of the chain of dislocations, of the movement that Balibar traces in Althusser's different formulations, which are connected to one another with the thread of dramaturgy, amounts to nothing less than a reversal of the problematic of ideology, or, to use Balibar's terms, a shift from "*theater as politics*" to "*politics as theater*" ("Althusser's Dramaturgy" 19). This theoretical reversal is important because, avoiding the imposition of a false resolution of Althusser's aporias, it shows how they are relegated, in the last instance, to *politics*, stressing both the performative dimension of Althusser's philosophy and its corresponding theoretical limits, limits that he sought to overcome by the hopeful indeterminacy of a politics in which he could locate and enact the agency he called for.

An Aleatory Althusser

One of the effects of Balibar's argument, which pinpoints a reversal in the terms that compose Althusser's problematic of ideology, is that it
reveals a rather unfamiliar Althusser, whose thought opens to performativity, theatricality, stagings, agential interventions, and the uncertainty of
politics. Indeed, from the reader of the "latent structure" of *El nost Milan*
to the theorist of the "conjuncture" in Machiavelli, we seem to have come a
long way. Perhaps, however, there is even more distance to be traveled. If,
in fact, *Machiavelli and Us* is considered together with "The Underground
Current of the Materialism of the Encounter," another posthumously published manuscript that dates from the early 1980s, it is possible to make the
case that the transformation in Althusser's thought is even more extensive
than Balibar's reconstruction admits.[2] Despite the problems the status
of the manuscript poses, as the "a posteriori construction" of the frag-
mentary, unfinished, and palimpsestic manuscript Althusser left behind
(Matheron and Corpet 164), it nonetheless presents us with a radically
different Althusser. In Althusser's late work, we witness the irruption of a
new problematic, that of aleatory materialism, or what Althusser also calls
the "materialism of the encounter."[3] With this new problematic come new
insights but also new aporias.[4]

Althusser turns to the history of political philosophy to excavate
an alternative tradition that has been there since Epicurus, even though this
tradition has been repressed, distorted, and marginalized by its opponents
and by posterity. This tradition is one that passes through figures such as
Lucretius, Machiavelli, Spinoza, Hobbes, Rousseau, Heidegger, and Deleuze
and one that includes Marx only with a significant reworking. More point-
edly, Althusser posits this tradition as antithetical not only to traditions of
idealism but also to all forms of materialism, which, through their rational-
ism and formalism, their teleological orientation and necessitarian logic,
constitute "transformed, disguised form[s] of idealism" ("Underground" 168).
This is an Althusser who points to the "absolute limits" of Marx's thought
and attempts to overcome them by putting forth a novel interpretation of
materialism that turns away from a preoccupation with determinacy toward
the analysis of singular conjunctures, chance encounters, and unpredictable transformations. We thus arrive at a new *scene* in Althusser's work, in
which contingency takes center stage along with a cast of concepts such as
the encounter, the void, and the swerve, concepts that though not completely
absent from Althusser's earlier writings nonetheless now take on new roles.

Aleatory materialism entails a veritable *break* in Althusser's oeuvre, dramatically modifying the existing elements and entailing retroactive effects on how we read Althusser as a whole.[5]

Balibar refers to the aleatory while discussing Althusser's reading of Machiavelli, but only in passing. The "politics of ideology," he argues, is "a politics without guarantee, hence without certainty" ("Althusser's Dramaturgy" 19), both in its conditions and in its effects. His account, however, stops short of tracing the impact that the advent of the aleatory holds in store for the question of ideology. It is from the lens of Althusser's work on aleatory materialism that I want to revisit his theory of ideology in dialogue with Balibar's reading but ultimately pursuing another "oblique path" into the Althusserian "forest." In so doing, I propose to revisit the broader manuscript on social reproduction, originally written in 1969 but only posthumously published in France in 1995, from which the widely read and critically acclaimed essay "Ideology and Ideological State Apparatuses" was extracted (by Althusser himself). In other words, I want to open a path between two posthumously published texts: *On the Reproduction of Capitalism* and "The Underground Current of the Materialism of the Encounter." These manuscripts ostensibly present us with two faces of Althusser: the structuralist and the conjuncturalist, the determinist and the contingent, the historical materialist and the aleatory materialist. Recognizing how these polarities cohabit Althusser's thought can move us toward a new appreciation of the complexity of his oeuvre.

On the Reproduction of Capitalism, in a form more accentuated than the short essay on the ISAs, reveals an orthodox commitment to Marxism-Leninism that permeates Althusser's arguments, a commitment that might seem almost archaic to contemporary readers. The manuscript proceeds didactically from the basic definitions of Marxist concepts to the central theses of Marxist theory on social formations, namely, the primacy of the base over the superstructure and the primacy of the relations of production over productive forces. The text also puts forth a complex theory of ideology, however, that according to Warren Montag presents an "irreversible break with all preceding theories of ideology" (*Althusser* 143). Straddled between the two commitments, the text presents us with a fecund site of exploration.

I am proposing another *décalage*, then, one that begins where Balibar ends. This *décalage* moves us in the opposite historical direction, however, taking off from Althusser's writings on the materialism of the encounter, composed in the aftermath of the "politics of ideology" thesis, and returning to the work on the ISAs, which is temporally situated between

"The 'Piccolo Teatro'" and *Machiavelli and Us*. Reading Althusser from the viewpoint afforded by the aleatory materialist problematic, I submit, not only allows us to see deeper layers of the manuscript on reproduction, layers that are otherwise buried under Althusser's overt preoccupation with the reproduction of structures, but it also provides the opportunity to further explore the role of disobedience and struggle within his theory of ideology by carving out the space for theorizing the disruption of those structures. I propose this *décalage* in reverse not in order to rewrite the development of Althusser's thought in the "future anterior" ("On the Young" 75), based on the erroneous assumption that we can find the later Althusser already present in embryonic form from the beginning—an assumption that Althusser himself had submitted to fierce criticism in relation to Marx's work. I suggest it, rather, to magnify and liberate those elements that are occluded in his earlier work, precisely because they are submerged beneath the dominant elements dictated by a different problematic. After all, it is Althusser who teaches us that sometimes we can open a new path that will help us advance only by moving backward, by a retreat (76–79).

A Path in Reverse?

Viewing *On the Reproduction of Capitalism* from the aleatory materialist problematic, one is immediately struck by the dual conception of materiality that inhabits the manuscript. Althusser's text opens with a conventional sense of materiality that views a social formation through the prism of the base-superstructure metaphor, in which the material basis comprises the relations of production and productive forces, in turn composed by the combination of the objects and instruments of labor and labor-power. This material basis is the anchor of the social formation, which determines, in the last instance, the superstructure and its different levels of effectivity. Althusser then moves to complicate this conception of materiality that dominates the Marxist perspective by shifting the viewpoint to that of social reproduction. Because the reproduction of the conditions of production necessitates the reproduction of the skills and comportment of laborers, his argument goes, we need to attend to the mechanisms by which submission to the existing order is reproduced. In a class society, it is ideology ("State Ideology") that does the work of ensuring submission. This ideology, he contends, is concretized in ideological state apparatuses.

Here we encounter one of the most innovative features of Althusser's theory of ideology, namely, his assertion of its materiality (*On the*

Reproduction 184). Counterposed to the predominant conception of ideology as a system of representations that come from ideas, which are then translated into beliefs and actions that conform to these beliefs, Althusser's approach eliminates the independent "ideality" of ideology, making it materially immanent to practices and apparatuses.[6] Following Pascal's critical injunction, "Kneel down, move your lips in prayer, *and you will believe*," Althusser substitutes comportment in place of consciousness, or comportment *as* consciousness, refusing a mind-body dualism (186). Althusser argues that ideas are "material acts inserted into material practices regulated by material rituals which are themselves defined by the material ideological apparatus from which [. . .] [they] derive."

The immediate ramification of this statement is the move from ideas to practices, but Althusser's shift further involves the qualification of materiality into different modalities represented by the proliferating use of *material* as adjective. Althusser continues: "[T]he materiality of a walk to church to attend mass, of kneeling, of making the sign of the cross or penance, a gaze, a handshake, an outer verbal discourse or 'inner' verbal discourse (consciousness) is not one and the same materiality" (186). The conception of materiality thus developed stands in strong tension with the one that refers to the "base" or the "infrastructure," connected only by the successive mediations introduced to articulate them, the mediations of apparatuses, rituals, practices, actions, and discourses.

The problematic of aleatory materialism accentuates the conception of materiality inhabiting Althusser's thesis that "ideology has a material existence" (*On the Reproduction* 184) and augments its complexity. It continues to think the specific modalities of materiality beyond the relations of production and productive forces. It proliferates the kinds of materiality to encompass practices, experiments, experiences, discourses, gestures, and traces ("Philosophy" 263), ultimately leading toward the singularity of each. This singular or *singularizing* materialism is built on a nominalism that recognizes the irreducible plurality of the world, in which "there exists nothing but cases, situations, things that befall us without warning" (265). In a Wittgensteinian statement, Althusser writes, "[T]he world is everything that 'falls,' everything that 'comes about [*advient*],' 'everything that is the case,'—by *case*, let us understand *casus: at once occurrence and chance*, that which comes about in the mode of the unforeseeable, and yet of being" ("Underground" 190).

On the other hand, this conception of materiality, when taken up in connection with the centrality of contingency, calls into question

Althusser's necessitarian account of social reproduction and destabilizes the machinic reproduction of existing structures by implying that they are open to the effects of what is unforeseeable, unexpected, least probable. It urges us to move away from a determinism that proceeds by tracing "ordered successions [*conséquences*] deduced from an Origin that is the foundation of all Meaning, or from an absolute First Principle of Cause" ("Only" 11). Putting contingency at the center entails focusing on the "sequences [*séquences*] of aleatory encounters," which, if they take hold, produce contingent structures that become necessary as a consequence of their reproduction ("Underground" 193–94). Such a view does not deny determinacy, but it does question its *iron* laws. As Althusser writes, "[T]he necessity of the laws that issue from the taking-hold induced by the encounter is, even at its most stable, haunted by a *radical instability*" ("The Underground Current" 195). Revisiting Althusser's theory of ideology in this light, we begin to see not only the specific histories of different state apparatuses, which helps to denaturalize them, but also the volatility that permeates the state apparatuses and their material practices, which helps to demystify them. In light of the contradictory nature of reality, everything can change "at the drop of a hat, revealing the aleatory basis that sustains them, and can change without reason, that is, without an intelligible end" ("Underground" 195–96).

Aleatory materialism also throws into sharp relief the many instances in the manuscript where class struggle, acting out the contingency in history, constantly disables or counteracts the general functionality of apparatuses and the smoothness of the process of social reproduction. It imparts a heightened significance to the delineation of ISAs not only as the material concretization of dominant ideology with a crucial role in social reproduction but also as relatively "fragile" institutions (in comparison to the repressive core of the state) that are prone to the "grating" effects of popular struggles (*On the Reproduction* 89). From this perspective, the historical discussion in the broader manuscript gains critical importance. Throughout Althusser's discussion of history, which is for the most part left out of "Ideology and Ideological State Apparatuses," class struggle takes place both outside and within the apparatuses, affecting these apparatuses in ways that are neither identical nor predictable. For example, Althusser demonstrates how the struggle between the bourgeoisie and the feudal aristocracy benefited the workers' political organizations but not the workers' economic organizations (*On the Reproduction* 117, 125), displaying the aleatory effects of class struggle on the political ISA and the associative ISA. Similarly, Althusser's analysis of Bonapartism positions it as an aleatory response within the political ISA, even a contradictory one in conflict with the dominant ideology of liberalism, developed in order to quell the threat of class struggle from below, as a solution to put the masses back in their place after they helped the bourgeoisie acquire power (119). Moreover, Althusser considers contemporary working-class organizations, trade unions, and parties as the precarious triumphs of the working class or as concessions that the dominant classes had to make—once again, as the aleatory effects of class struggle, this time between the bourgeoisie and the working class. He thus stresses the different degrees of autonomy these institutions have from "State Ideology," drawing attention to the constant threat of reformism that haunts them insofar as they are part of the state.

Looking at the aleatory in Althusser's historical discussion brings to light the ways in which ISAs are both the result and the site of struggles that not only disrupt the smooth and machine-like workings of the apparatuses that materialize dominant ideology but also embody alternative ideologies and their practices. The emphasis on the aleatory therefore lends greater credence to Althusser's assertion that the ISAs are the "object and *theatre* of the class struggle" (*On the Reproduction* 177, my emphasis). While the historical examples Althusser discusses can be considered tangential to an approach that emphasizes the reproduction of dominant ideology, they are central to the aleatory materialist reading of the ISAs. Dominant ideology appears much less homogeneous and total; it is rife with internal contentions, antagonisms, and struggles. Furthermore, institutions appear much more provisional as the contingent outcome of ongoing struggles and their recurrent site. Such a reading does not completely eliminate the aporia of interpellation, namely, the impossibility of exiting the circle of ideological reproduction, but it nonetheless gives prominence to struggles outside, within, and over the apparatuses of reproduction, implying a much more brittle circle.

The aleatory reading brings the dynamism of class struggle to the fore; however, it entails a new limit: it cannot explain how struggle arises in the first place. Indeed, as Balibar also highlights, it is difficult to account for disobedience or the constitution of "bad subjects" who disobey the rules of comportment in Althusser's work. Althusser's thesis on the materiality of ideology displaces the idealist construction of the Enlightenment subject as the source of ideas and the author of actions into a subject whose comportment is, rather, the effect of structures and the material practices associated with them (Lock 85). Since there is no outside of the social whole that molds us into subjects, subjectivity partakes of the "omni-historical" structure of ideology, modeled after the "unconscious" (Althusser, *On the Reproduction* 175). This implies an atemporal subjectivity, or a timeless universality: not only is every subject interpellated in the same way, but each is "always-already" a subject (187–88). With these theses that attribute a teleological certainty of subjection-subjectivation to interpellation, Althusser pushes ideology into the unconscious and renders subjects captive to ideological reproduction. In this vein, Balibar notes how Althusser seems to offer "no line of escape—except for a tragic notation in passing, where Althusser refers to the fact that there are 'bad subjects' who refuse to turn around, to answer the call of the subjecting authority, at the risk, in fact, of their lives or their mental integrity" ("Althusser's Dramaturgy" 11). Similarly, Judith Butler insightfully detects in Althusser's scarcity of references to "bad subjects" the contradictory nature of the very expression of "bad subject," as one who is not yet subject, "not yet to have acquitted oneself of the allegation of guilt" (*Psychic* 119). Without a theory of the "bad subject," however, we are left simply to assume the continuous presence of class struggle, springing up automatically, as it were, from the relations of production, independent of the constitution of the subjects that partake in it. Bringing the perspective of aleatory materialism to bear on Althusser's theory of ideology, I contend, is most helpful here, as it provides a new solution to the aporia of interpellation.

Bad Subjects

Before turning to how the aleatory materialist reading might alter Althusser's conception of subjectivity to make room for disobedience, let me briefly revisit the paradoxical scene in which exceptionality is introduced within interpellation. In this "mise-en-scène of interpellation" (*On the Reproduction* 194), Althusser describes the constitution of the subject by the act of turning around to the police hail "Hey, you there!," writing: "With this simple 180-degree physical conversion, he becomes a *subject*. Why? Because he has recognized that the hail 'really' was addressed to him and that 'it really was he who was hailed' (not someone else)" (191). The police hail plays a central role in this drama of subjection-subjectivation. Even while Althusser identifies hailing as an everyday ritual, one that may be issued "*by (or not by) the police*" (190), even while he insists that the "formal structure" of ideological interpellation is the same, he also notes that with the police hail, it "takes *spectacular* form" (190n24, my emphasis), thereby standing as a limit case for every interpellation. What is this limit? Let us read Althusser more closely:

*Hailing as an everyday practice governed by a precise ritual takes spectacular form in the police practice of hailing: "Hey, you there!" (It functions in very similar forms in interpellating or summoning at school.) Police hailing, however, unlike other kinds of hailing, is repressive: "Your papers!" [. . .] Identity, concentrated in first and last names, and so on, makes it possible to identify the subject (presumed in police hailing to be more or less suspect; initially presumed, that is, to be a "bad sort"), thus to identify him without confusing him with another subject, and either "let him go" ("It's all right") or "take him in" ("Follow me!"), with consequences familiar to all who have been "taken in" at a popular demonstration: a shift to casual forms of address or a casual beating, a night at the police station, and the whole terribly material ritual that ensues when a policeman recognizes a "bad sort" [*mauvais sujet*]. (190–91n24)*

The interpellation is spectacular not only because it issues from the repressive state apparatus but also because it is accusatory, as it involves the presumption or suspicion of guilt on the part of the one hailed, the implication, as Althusser puts it, of being a "bad sort" (*mauvais sujet*), which assigns the one hailed the task of proving her "innocence" so that she can be "let go." Insofar as the accusatory nature is constitutive of interpellation as such, we can conclude with Butler that subjection-subjectivation requires being constantly "in the process of acquitting oneself of the accusation of guilt" (*Psychic* 118). At stake also is always a reward, since exculpation from accusation—the proof of innocence—produces freedom: one is "let go" rather than "taken in"; one is thus constituted as a "free" subject that does not need to be subjected to violent repercussions, ranging from a "casual beating" to a "night at the police station." In other words, one is set free on the very condition that one is captured by the state. In all hails, Althusser seems to suggest, the guarantee of subjectivation is the confirmation that the subject is a "good" subject, subjected, that is, to the "good" ideology, ideology apposite for social reproduction—"State Ideology." "Nine times out of ten," Althusser writes, individuals respond to the hail that was meant for them, proving themselves good subjects (*On the Reproduction* 191). This means that in one out of ten cases, interpellation fails; for those, the repressive apparatus of the state is always ready.

In reference to these limit situations, Butler writes, "the one who is hailed may fail to hear, misread the call, turn the other way, answer to another name, insist on not being addressed that way" (*Psychic* 95). The failure of an interpellation due to misrecognition, however, cannot be taken as the automatic equivalent of resistance or refusal, even though it may provide its conditions of possibility. In this sense, it would be more accurate to distinguish the one who "fail[s] to hear" and "misread[s] the call" from one who "turn[s] the other way," "answer[s] to another name," or "insist[s] on not being addressed that way." It is more likely that a "bad subject" in the former sense is a failed subject, a not-yet subject, a nonsubject—not captured by that particular hail—whereas the latter is a "bad subject" understood in the sense of a *countersubject*, a subject of disobedience and resistance.

How, then, can we account for those subjects who act outside the script of ideological reproduction, even against it? One way to address this question and to develop a theory of the "bad subject" is by *retemporalizing* the (timeless) structure of interpellation. In Butler's reading, we find two solutions (or two moments of one solution). The first is the assertion that there is a prior desire in the subject to turn to the hail, thereby introducing an interiority (a "conscience") that may provide the resource with which the subject can interrupt, shift, or reverse her subjectivation. Butler writes, "Although there would be no turning around without first having been hailed, neither would there be a turning around without some readiness to turn" (*Psychic* 107). This founding submission is based on guilt, or a "passionate expectation of the law" (129).[7] The implication is that the same passion, or conscience, can be generative of a different subjectivation, in Butler's words, a "different kind of turn, one that, enabled by the law, turns away from the law, resisting its lure of identity, an agency that outruns and counters the conditions of its emergence. Such a turn demands a willingness *not* 'to be'—a critical desubjectivation—in order to expose the law as less powerful than it seems" (130). The second, related solution is to invest the performance of subjectivity with instability, variability, and disruption by pointing to how interpellation can produce an excess effect that undermines its disciplinary mechanism, which thereby opens up the reenactments of subjectivation to contestation. "This repetition or, better, iterability thus becomes the non-place of subversion," contends Butler, "the possibility of a re-embodying of the subjectivating norm that can redirect its normativity" (99). Hence, the interpellation can result in a refusal that interrupts dominant ideology through the "parodic inhabiting of conformity that subtly calls into question the legitimacy of the command, a repetition of the law into hyperbole, a rearticulation of the law against the authority of the one who delivers it" ("Gender" 382). In this innovative interpretation, the circularity of interpellation that entails the atemporal subjectivity posited by Althusser's theory of ideology is complicated by a retemporalizing move that nonetheless remains, as Butler cautions us, "tropological."[8]

Building on Althusser's late work on the aleatory, I want to propose a different way to think about disobedience within the problematic of ideology. Even though Althusser himself does not articulate this solution, it can plausibly be attained, I contend, by developing the theoretical innovations of the "materialism of the encounter" to address the aporias of ideological interpellation. In my view, the challenge that aleatory materialism presents to a formal determinism that emanates from an origin or originary cause and that is burdened by a teleological movement is its proposal of viewing history as the result of an aleatory sequence of encounters. This principle can be fruitfully utilized to address the problem of the "bad subject" in ideological reproduction by privileging the idea of an aleatory *sequence* of interpellations over the timeless *structure* of interpellation, or thinking them together. Accordingly, while the structure of each interpellation is constant, the sequence of particular interpellations for each subject is historical, variable, and contingent—based on the encounters that are shaped by and that in turn shape one's circumstances and biography. These interpellating encounters subjectivate in successive, shifting, contradictory, and cumulative ways, creating an *overdetermined* process of multiple subjectivations whose structuration can be retrospectively studied but whose specific configuration cannot be directly derived from an originary principle (in this case, dominant ideology).

Aleatory materialism thus implies a *layered* subjectivity, one that is based on the cumulative effect of contingently sequenced subjectivations. While there are common patterns among these sequences for different subjects (as encounters with different ISAs are not wholly indeterminate), the specific configuration of subjectivations—the relationship among different layers of subjectivation and which layers achieve dominance—is unique to each subject, making up a contradictory unity that each subject must negotiate on her own. Such an account does not temporalize the structure of interpellation, but it casts into view multiple interpellations, which are differentially sedimented over time. Furthermore, in keeping with Althusser's insight of the rarity of an incomplete interpellation, the possibility of disobedience comes not from any residual interiority of the subject, a part untouched by the colonization of subjectivation, but from the countersubjectivations that result from the encounter with oppositional discourses, practices, and institutions that are embodiments of oppositional ideologies, in other words, from the *becoming-dominant of countersubjectivations* within the contradictory unity that is each singular subjectivity.[9]

It is when viewed in this light that the following statement by Althusser becomes more meaningful: "Ideologies never stop interpellating subjects as subjects, never stop 'recruiting' individuals who are always-already subjects. The play of ideologies is superposed, criss-crossed, contradicts itself on the same subject: the same individual always-already (*several times*) subject" (*On the Reproduction* 193–94, my emphasis). Aleatory materialism thus brings to the fore what remains latent and underdeveloped in the manuscript on reproduction, namely, that each subject is an overdetermined effect of the sedimentation of multiple and contingent subjectivations that result from encounters with different ideologies, either as rivals that combat one another as they are materialized in institutions and practices or as differential internal fractions of dominant ideology. These ideologies may reinforce one another; they can coexist in tension or openly contradict each other (205). Insofar as these ideologies are at odds with one another, they can lead to "conflicts of conscience" (200), pulling the subject in different directions at once. Consequently, disobedience or resistance to authority must arise, if it does, as a result of the conflict between different subjectivations that arise from multiple encounters (some of which are fleeting, others more sustained and recurrent) that interpellate the subject. The resistance of the subject, then, must be sought in the encounters that provide the conditions of possibility of the activation of the layers of countersubjectivation, catapulting them to dominance in the complex and stratified unity of the subject, thereby enabling both individual and collective resistances and refusals. Developing aleatory materialism in this direction thus renders subjectivity the site of fierce struggles. With the conception of stratified subjectivity, aleatory materialism enacts a new shift in the problematic of ideology, a new *décalage*, in which subjectivity more than state apparatuses becomes the theater of revolutionary politics.

In his "Note on the ISAs" (written in 1976), Althusser will "correct" his earlier overstatement of the internal unity and homogeneity of dominant ideology and be more attentive to the fissures within it: "[T]he dominant ideology is never a *fait accompli of class struggle* that is itself exempt from class struggle" (*On the Reproduction* 218). In response to critics, Althusser writes that class struggle has been "at the heart of [his] concerns" all along (218). An increased emphasis on the instability of existing structures is already visible in Althusser's insistence on how struggles between the dominant and the dominated classes but also within the dominant class present a constant challenge for the reproduction of relations of production (219). While Althusser allows room for resistance to dominant ideology, however, he still understands it as a *derivative* form of class struggle, a "direct or indirect echo of the class struggle" (220), whose existence must in turn be assumed. Proletarian ideology, which, in Althusser's view, is at times present within the state apparatuses in the form of parties and trade unions but is mostly outside them, embedded in the conflictual practices of class struggle itself, interpellates subjects as "militant-subjects": "bad subjects" not as *nonsubjects* but as *countersubjects* (227). Althusser seems to propose that militant-subjectivation is simply the effect of interpellation by a different ideology, that is, neither a lack of subjection nor an incomplete subjectivation. Nonetheless, it is the *scientific* character of proletarian ideology (228), according to Althusser, that enables it to "decenter" the structure of ideological interpellation, even if it cannot overcome it completely. It thereby makes room for a critical subjectivity *within* ideology (since there is no outside) by enabling an internal distance, so to speak, that is built on the knowledge of history and historical practice of critique offered by Marxism.

Even if we were to adopt a more capacious understanding of emancipatory ideologies that can subjectivate in critical and oppositional forms, questioning the privileged role Althusser grants to Marxism by way of its scientificity and systematicity, Althusserian "freedom," as Balibar writes, would perhaps not amount to much more than "*shifting from one identification, one interpellation,* to another" ("Althusser's Dramaturgy" 13). Aleatory materialism, however, proposes to think this "freedom" not simply as a matter of arbitrary choice or voluntary power over one's subjectivity or as the consequence of Marxism's scientificity but, rather, as a partly unconscious process of the becoming-dominant of a countersubjectivation among many subjectivations that are sedimented in the layered subject, activated, on one hand, by different interpellating encounters, experiences, practices of struggle and, on the other, by a partly conscious internal struggle with the contradictions in the whole of each subjective formation.[10] Overall, then, in the midst of the largely static, unchangeable construction of society that permeates the functionalism of Althusser's discourse, we find the space for a multiplicity of subjects, each with their unique constitution of layers of subjectivation-subjection, that deposit the contingent history of contradictory interpellations, holding in store their unpredictable effects.[11]

A Rejoinder to Balibar: Theater within the Theater

Balibar's *philosophical* reading of Althusser revisits the problematic of ideology in order to raise the question of revolutionary politics today. In his reconstruction of Althusser's thought, Balibar alludes to the "indeterminate" political effects of different ideologies, but he locates the presence of the aleatory in Althusser's silences: "[H]e doesn't say (and in fact nothing in his text says) that different interpellations, which *have the same ideological structure, the structure of 'ideology in general,'* produce the same historical and political effects" (14). I hope to have shown that the aleatory can be read not only in the explicit omissions of Althusser's manuscript but also in the presence of latent elements that remain tangential to his preoccupation with the reproduction of capitalist relations of production. When accessed from the path opened by aleatory materialism, these elements obtain a new visibility and role, allowing us a different reading and a different Althusser.

Balibar's exposition of the dramaturgical nature of ideology in Althusser's thought ends by suggesting a reconceptualization of history as a series of "productions" in a "theater without an author" (20). Balibar's formulation evokes Althusser's conception of history as a "process without a subject," taken up in turn from Hegel, where the process itself becomes the subject of history (Althusser, "Reply" 51). For Balibar, too, it seems to me, theater itself becomes a subject, but one whose ultimate direction is aleatory, or, at the very least, conditioned by the performances in it. These productions are not the rehearsals for the final play to come; on the contrary, it is the indeterminacy of the future that makes the stage all the more open to improvisations.

With the Althusser known to readers of the ISAs essay, ideology seems akin to the director of this theater, assigning actors to their roles and ensuring that they play according to script. Only a counterideology embodied in collective practices of struggle and mass institutions can redirect the play. Hence, revolutionary politics largely plays out as a struggle in and over the ideological apparatuses of the state. If the last *décalage* in the problematic of ideology I have suggested is on the mark, however, we encounter an aleatory Althusser for whom, while ideology has lost nothing of its importance, the actors and their performances constitute the new sites and stakes of revolutionary struggle. Althusser can thus be considered to have introduced another play on the stage, the play of/in subjectivity, bringing into view a theater within the theater or, better, an infinite multiplication of plays within the same theater.

Have we not come full circle? We are, once again, before the stage where different plays are juxtaposed. A materialist practice of theater, if we follow Althusser, means that the juxtaposition of different plays, with their singular temporalities, reveals a latent structure of their contradictory and uneven encounter, which, by way of its overdistanciating effects, interpellates the spectator as a new actor. Balibar teaches us that this is no longer the theater of Brecht or Bertolazzi; it is Althusser's *materialist* theater. Only now *we* are the ones being hailed, and perhaps we always were.

BANU BARGU is associate professor of politics at the New School for Social Research. Her main area of specialization is political theory, especially modern and contemporary political thought and critical theory. The thematic focus of her work spans theories of sovereignty, biopolitics, and resistance, as well as aesthetics and materialism. She is the author of the award-winning *Starve and Immolate: The Politics of Human Weapons* (Columbia University Press, 2014). Her essays have appeared in such venues as *Angelaki, diacritics, Contemporary Political Theory, theory & event, South Atlantic Quarterly, qui parle,* and *Constellations.* Bargu is currently working on a book-length manuscript on Althusser's political thought and aleatory materialism.

Notes

1   The significance of "The 'Piccolo Teatro': Bertolazzi and Brecht" in Althusser's oeuvre cannot be emphasized enough, although it has received relatively scant attention. Balibar has alluded to it before in "The Non-Contemporaneity of Althusser" (16n13). For detailed discussions of the essay, see, for example, Bargu; Carmichael; Kowsar; Matheron, esp. 513; Montag, *Louis* 23–37; Sprinker 267–95; Statkiewicz.

2   On Althusser's analysis of Machiavelli, see Emmanuel Terray's excellent essay "An Encounter: Althusser and Machiavelli"; and the in-depth exposition in connection to aleatory materialism by Mikko Lahtinen, *Politics and Philosophy.*

3   Althusser also refers to this materialism as the materialism of the "rain," the "swerve," "the take [*prise*]" ("Underground" 168).

4   I refer the interested reader to "Althusser's Late Thinking about Materialism," Wal Suchting's

unsurpassed exegesis of aleatory materialism and its aporias. His essay provides suggestive answers to very important questions borne by Althusser's "The Underground Current of the Materialism of the Encounter." See also Morfino, "Althusserian."

5   Althusser's work can be periodized in a number of different ways. Gregory Elliott, for example, has divided Althusser's work into a pre-Althusserian moment of transition from Catholicism to communism in 1945–51, a structural Marxist phase of 1960–67, the period of self-critique in 1967–75, a period of autodeconstruction in 1976–78, and, finally, the materialism of the encounter in the 1980s (74–75). A slightly different periodization is suggested by Balibar from the angle of the different meanings and effects of the "epistemological break" taken as the object of Althusser's discourse: the "break before the break," referring to the 1959 Montesquieu book, the construction and naming of

the "break as break" in *For Marx*, the generalization of the break in *Reading Capital*, the critique of the break in 1968–76, and the "break after the break" in his last writings (Balibar, "Althusser's Object" 161–74). In terms of aleatory materialism, however, Goshgarian locates a definitive turn as early as 1973 ("Translator's Introduction" xlvi–xlvii), whereas Negri situates the break in 1977 (51, 58).

6 See Montag, *Althusser* 143–44 and "Beyond" 102.

7 I do not have the space to discuss the religious paradigm that informs the guilt-confession model of subjectivation that Althusser puts forth, a model whose theological quality Butler rightly emphasizes (*Psychic* 109–11, 114). See also Pierre Macherey's critical engagement in "Judith Butler."

8 Butler differentiates this from a historical temporalization (*Psychic* 3–4, 201–2). On this point, see also Choi 33.

9 A contrasting view can be found in the following statement: "I do not see from where we could borrow the forces to resist the apparatus if not from the depths of a subject having claims that are not infected by this supposed submissive constitution. How else will someone produce a break in the seemingly closed shell of ideology?" (Ricoeur 66).

10 I agree with Panagiotis Sotiris, who contends that the reference to Marxism as a science does not convincingly eliminate "the gap separating radical political action and subjectivity as ideological subjection" in a way that accounts for the "emergence of collective 'bad subjects'" (402). Sotiris points to the production of mass forms of intellectuality through collective political militancy instead. I, on the other hand, think it is still necessary to explain the subjective conditions that give rise to collective militancy in the first place.

11 The layered subjectivity that I am proposing can be read in productive conversation with Vittorio Morfino's interpretation of aleatory materialism, in which the emphasis is on the layers of time. See Morfino, *Plural*.

Works Cited

Althusser, Louis. "Cremonini, Painter of the Abstract." *Lenin* 229–42.

——————. "Ideology and Ideological State Apparatuses (Notes towards an Investigation)." *Lenin* 127–86.

——————. *Lenin and Philosophy and Other Essays*. Trans. Ben Brewster. New York: Monthly Review P, 1971.

——————. *Machiavelli and Us*. Trans. Gregory Elliott. Ed. François Matheron. New York: Verso, 1999.

——————. "Machiavelli's Solitude." *Machiavelli and Us* 115–30.

——————. "Note on the ISAS." *On the Reproduction* 218–31.

——————. "On Brecht and Marx." Trans. Warren Montag. *Louis Althusser*. By Warren Montag. New York: Palgrave Macmillan, 2003. 136–39.

——————. *On the Reproduction of Capitalism: Ideology and Ideological State Apparatuses*. Trans. G. M. Goshgarian. London: Verso, 2014.

——————. "On the Young Marx." *For Marx*. Trans. Ben Brewster. London: Verso, 1969. 49–86.

——————. "The Only Materialist Tradition, Part 1: Spinoza." Trans. Ted Stolze. *The New Spinoza*. Ed. Warren Montag and Ted Stolze. Minneapolis: U of Minnesota P, 1997. 3–19.

——————. "Philosophy and Marxism: Interviews with Fernanda Navarro, 1984–87." *Philosophy* 251–89.

——————. *Philosophy of the Encounter: Later Writings, 1978–1987*. Ed. François Matheron and Olivier Corpet. New York: Verso, 2006.

——————. "The 'Piccolo Teatro': Bertolazzi and Brecht." *For Marx*. Trans. Ben Brewster. London: Verso, 1969. 129–51.

——————. "Reply to John Lewis." *Essays in Self-Criticism*. Trans. Grahame Lock. London: New Left, 1976. 33–100.

——————. "Rousseau: *The Social Contract* (The Discrepancies)." *Politics and History: Montesquieu, Rousseau, Hegel, and Marx*. Trans. Ben Brewster. London: New Left, 1972. 113–60.

——————. "The Underground Current of the Materialism of the Encounter." Trans. G. M. Goshgarian. *Philosophy* 163–207.

Althusser, Louis, and Étienne Balibar. *Reading Capital*. Trans. Ben Brewster. London: New Left, 1970.

Balibar, Étienne. "Althusser's Dramaturgy and the Critique of Ideology." *differences* 26.3 (2015): 1–22.

——————. "Althusser's Object." Trans. Margaret Cohen and Bruce Robbins. *Social Text* 39 (1994): 157–88.

——————. "The Non-Contemporaneity of Althusser." *The Althusserian Legacy*. Ed. E. Ann Kaplan and Michael Sprinker. New York: Verso, 1993. 1–16.

Bargu, Banu. "In the Theater of Politics: Althusser's Aleatory Materialism and Aesthetics." *diacritics* 40.3 (2012): 86–111.

Butler, Judith. "Gender Is Burning: Questions of Appropriation and Subversion." *Dangerous Liaisons: Gender, Nation, and Postcolonial Perspectives*. Ed. Anne McClintock, Aamir Mufti, and Ella Shohat. Minneapolis: U of Minnesota P, 1997. 381–95.

——————. *The Psychic Life of Power: Theories in Subjection*. Stanford: Stanford UP, 1997.

Callari, Antonio, and David F. Ruccio, eds. *Postmodern Materialism and the Future of Marxist Theory: Essays in the Althusserian Tradition*. Hanover: Wesleyan UP, 1996.

Carmichael, Thomas. "Structure and Conjuncture: Literary Study and the Return to Althusser." *E-rea* 3.1 (2005). http://erea.revues.org/618.

Choi, Won. "Inception or Interpellation? The Slovenian School, Butler, and Althusser." *Rethinking Marxism* 25.1 (2013): 23–27.

Elliott, Gregory. "The Necessity of Contingency: Some Notes." *Rethinking Marxism* 10.3 (1998): 74–79.

Goshgarian, G. M. "Translator's Introduction: In Memory of Constance Coiner 1948–96." Althusser, *Philosophy* xiii–l.

Kowsar, Mohammad. "Althusser on Theatre." *Theatre Journal* 35.4 (1983): 461–74.

Lahtinen, Mikko. *Politics and Philosophy: Niccolo Machiavelli and Louis Althusser's Aleatory Materialism*. Trans. Gareth Griffiths and Kristina Kölhi. Leiden: Brill, 2009.

Lock, Grahame. "Subject, Interpellation, and Ideology." Callari and Ruccio 69–90.

Macherey, Pierre. "Judith Butler and the Althusserian Theory of Subjection." Trans. Stephanie Bundy. *Décalages* 1.2 (2012). http://scholar.oxy.edu/decalages/vol1/iss2/13.

Matheron, François. "Louis Althusser, or the Impure Purity of the Concept." *Critical Companion to Contemporary Marxism*. Ed. Jacques Bidet and Stathis Kouvelakis. Leiden: Brill, 2008. 503–27.

Matheron, François, and Olivier Corpet. "The Underground Current of the Materialism of the Encounter." Althusser, *Philosophy* 163–67.

Montag, Warren. *Althusser and His Contemporaries: Philosophy's Perpetual War*. Durham: Duke UP, 2013.

——————. "Beyond Force and Consent: Althusser, Spinoza, Hobbes." Callari and Ruccio 91–106.

——————. *Louis Althusser*. New York: Palgrave Macmillan, 2003.

Morfino, Vittorio. "An Althusserian Lexicon." Trans. Jason Smith. *borderlands* 4.2 (2005). http://www.borderlands.net.au/vol4no2_2005/morfino_lexicon.htm.

——————. *Plural Temporality: Transindividuality and the Aleatory between Spinoza and Althusser*. Leiden: Brill, 2014.

Negri, Antonio. "Notes on the Evolution of the Thought of the Later Althusser." Callari and Ruccio 51–68.

Ricoeur, Paul. "Althusser's Theory of Ideology." *Althusser: A Critical Reader*. Ed. Gregory Elliott. Oxford: Blackwell, 1994. 44–72.

Sotiris, Panagiotis. "How to Make Lasting Encounters: Althusser and Political Subjectivity." *Rethinking Marxism* 26.3 (2014): 398–413.

Sprinker, Michael. *Imaginary Relations: Aesthetics and Ideology in the Theory of Historical Materialism*. New York: Verso, 1987.

Statkiewicz, Max. "Theater and/of Ideology: The Notion of *Spostamento* in Althusser's Theory of Theoretical Praxis." *Rethinking Marxism* 10.3 (1998): 38–50.

Suchting, Wal. "Althusser's Late Thinking about Materialism." *Historical Materialism* 12.1 (2004): 3–70.

Terray, Emmanuel. "An Encounter: Althusser and Machiavelli." Callari and Ruccio 257–77.

The Performance of Poverty:
On "Althusser's Dramaturgy and the Critique of Ideology"

*I*s ideology a kind of theater? If so, we would seem freer than we suspected to perform ideas other than those of the ruling class. Are we? Is it possible that revolution is as near at hand as a triumphant performance that (so to speak) brings down the house? And if not, then what follows? Politically speaking, what sorts of action should we be rehearsing for?

I take these questions to lie at the heart of Étienne Balibar's characteristically dazzling essay on Althusser's dramaturgy. They are important questions. Like so much of Balibar's writing, this essay starts with micro scopic attention to one or two minor texts and then pulls back to reveal that, in fact, it has been investigating the building blocks out of which the social universe is composed, trying to figure out, more precisely, why the social universe has so much injustice built into it and how much freedom we have to take it apart and put it together differently.[1]

Althusser's thinking on theater and art was not intended for readers primarily concerned with theater and art. It was intended as an indirect way of solving other problems, in particular the problem of ideology. Like mourning as interpreted by Freud, theater offers a behind-the-scenes

Volume 26, Number 3   DOI 10.1215/10407391-3340384
© 2015 by Brown University and d i f f e r e n c e s : A Journal of Feminist Cultural Studies

glimpse into how subjects are constituted. This is the premise of Balibar's essay, which seems both correct and valuable, even if cultural critics have been more likely to value Althusser's insistence on the capacity of art (here, individual experiences of art rather than art in general, though the distinction doesn't seem entirely convincing) to take or create critical distance from ideology. There is, in fact, a general theory of theater here and not merely an account of the experience of one or two specific works: "[T]heater forces a subject to identify in a contradictory manner, simultaneously, with antithetic 'others' who nevertheless appear the same as oneself" (10). One can imagine exceptions, but this is a quite persuasive account of what many of us continue to ask our students to perceive and discuss in our literature classrooms.

The issue brought front and center here, however, is ideology itself. Ideology is one of the materials out of which society is constructed. The concept of ideology, as opposed to (say) culture, has the virtue of keeping the focus on injustice. And unlike the economy (or the relations of production), which, of course, has often been taken as the material base on which the social edifice rises, it has the virtue of indicating aspects of social life that are more rather than less open to change. The metaphor of dramaturgy underlines this relative openness or, as Balibar would say, contingency. What has been staged can be restaged otherwise.

These points may seem too obvious to need restating. What is less obvious is how carefully and creatively Balibar is trying, as he explores Althusser's moments of thinking theatrically about ideology, to capture the inescapable constraint without which the term *ideology* would be meaningless or insignificant. Constraint is crucial here. If ideology were merely false consciousness, as so many have assumed, the truth would be enough to set us free. The light bulb would go off and that would be that. The whole line of modern thinking about ideology, to which Althusser belongs but which he did not of course initiate, has been devoted to explaining why things aren't so easy.

It sometimes looks as if the model of ideology as false consciousness fell into disfavor because it was suddenly judged to be impolite—arrogant, insulting, elitist. How dare we assume that ordinary people are so dumb as to let themselves be fooled? But the real problem was never the concept's arrogance or condescension. The problem was that false consciousness could not account for why ideology is so much more tenacious than one might have expected. Subsequent thinking about ideology has adopted some version of the premise that people are up against a much more formidable opponent, something more deeply entrenched in their identities, in how they are "constituted as subjects." This is why so many, including Althusser, have turned to Freud. It is also why gender and sexual identity continue to be taken as crucial and even paradigmatic cases. Gender and sexual identity cannot be transformed or abolished with a wave of enlightenment's magic wand. They are dark and stubborn. They go deep.

But how deep? If you assert that they go very, very deep, you are of course making it very, very hard to imagine what Balibar calls a politics of ideology, or any politics at all. Injustice, built into the deep structure of identity, would become coterminous with human life itself. As an account of selfhood as such, ideology can no longer be a measure dividing less desirable from more desirable modes of life. This is a hole that thinkers about ideology routinely dig for themselves. As I read him, Balibar sees that many of us find ourselves in this hole, and he is trying to help us climb out of it. Here is his account:

> It is not, in fact, recognition, *whether as acceptation of a belief or authority or as mimetic association with others, that is built on the basis of some "misrecognition" of reality, but just the reverse: misrecognition is made possible by the deep structure of recognition, the "specular" process taking place in the back of consciousness that is consciousness itself. Therefore, to break with the contents of the dominant ideology, or to liberate oneself from its power, from the "stories" that it tells us and has us tell ourselves permanently, always presupposes a capacity to disrupt recognition, in other words one's identity. (8–9)*

That is, "misrecognition is made possible by the deep structure of recognition." What gives me an identity in the first place makes it inevitable that I will also misrecognize myself, the world, and my place in the world.

As the word *recognition* suggests, this is a rewrite of the dialectic of recognition that Hegel inscribed in his famous fable of the Lord and the Bondsman in chapter 4 of the *Phenomenology of Spirit*. Filtered through the Lacan of the mirror stage essay, and perhaps Sartre's "look" as well, that fable in Althusser comes out missing its ongoing dynamic; the process seems permanently blocked. It is this fatal blockage that Althusser seems to have in mind in the Piccolo Teatro essay when he cites Hegel on consciousness of oneself as consciousness of an enemy.

Judith Butler's *Psychic Life of Power*, which Balibar engages at some length in "Althusser's Dramaturgy," illustrates the way Hegel's dialectic can be reread as liable to get stuck forever in a state of miserable self-antagonism. Chapter 2 of that book, "Stubborn Attachment, Bodily Sub-jection," refers to that state of tortured stuckness as *unhappy consciousness*. Readers of Hegel's *Phenomenology*, Butler argues, have usually stressed the reversal by which the Lord, having come into existence by winning out in a life-and-death struggle, is then surpassed or transcended by the vanquished Bondsman, who carries the story of self-consciousness forward. But this emancipatory reading neglects the section that follows, which ends less happily with the Bondsman, having left the Lord behind, now identifying with an imaginary Lord and thus punishing his own body. The sacrifice of bodily pleasure to a newly invented God of norms and laws, which Hegel associated with the period of medieval Catholicism, here escapes its peri-odization and becomes a permanent fixture of the subject as such. Atheism becomes impossible; from the moment we learn to see ourselves as divided into body and soul, God is within us, and we can't get rid of him even though he makes us unhappy. There is no alternative to self-alienation.

Or one might say, putting this a bit differently, that unhappy consciousness offers no alternative in or to the world of embodied subjects. Those who seek a way out (and who would not want one?) will be obliged to seek it at the level and by means of the disembodied imagination, the sole faculty of freedom in an unfree world. The imagination tells us that "X is only a construct." Constructionism, or the stoic freedom to reimagine oneself freely while one's body remains enslaved, will thus become a mainstream temptation, at least in the humanities. The prevalence of "everything is X" where X is like language, narrative, rhetoric, theatricality, or performance is arguably a sign that this temptation has proved unavoidable.

As Balibar observes, Hegel is omnipresent in Althusser's Piccolo Teatro text, and he serves there not merely as object to be critiqued but also, more surprisingly, as an instrument of critique. "Althusser's essay is an astonishing counter-Hegelian reformulation of Hegel himself" (8). I take this to suggest that floating somewhere in the background of the Piccolo Teatro essay, and of Balibar's as well, is the almost unspeakable and apparently un-Althusserian idea of a desirable telos, analogous to the psychoanalytic cure, in which consciousness would be reconciled with the world of bodies that seems to oppose it—a world where bodies would free themselves.

It is this almost unspeakable idea that I see Balibar turning toward when he comments on *The Psychic Life of Power*. Balibar agrees with Butler about the circularity of "Ideology and Ideological State Appa-ratuses," where individuals exist only as already constituted subjects. He applauds her discovery that this circularity need not lead to determinism or fatalism. If ideology or discourse cannot exist without being enacted or reiterated, as Butler suggests, that leaves open the possibility that it can be rejected or troubled, that one can become a "bad subject." But Balibar pauses to note that, for Butler, reproduction (of discourse or ideology) does not depend on "*production* in the Marxist sense" (12). His own essay is not in any obvious way about production in the Marxist sense either. Indeed, it has more to say about "the production" in the theatrical, "show-must-go-on" sense. If he mentions production, it is not because he is going to fall back on a predictable, buck-stopping materialism. It is because he cannot give much positive value to a freedom that does not properly recognize the relevant forms of constraint, including bodily or material constraint. It seems to me that Balibar is struggling not to embrace the too easily available freedom suggested by the terms *theatricality* and *imagination*—more generally, the common sense of "*X* is a construct." Instead, he is trying to specify a zone of political freedom that, as far as possible recognizing and overcoming constraint rather than evading it, would be a more significant desideratum.

In a direct, if also appreciative, response to Butler, Balibar says that "there is no way out" of interpellation. "Even the 'bad subjects' are trapped—perhaps more than the others" (13). Like Freud, he leaves no room (other than madness) for a subjectivity that would be liberated from identification. You cannot not identify just as you cannot not be interpellated. So what follows? Balibar's way out of the dilemma or aporia, which is bolder than it sounds, is to assert that some identifications are better than others—much, much better. This is the crucial step in his argument.

He lists some identifications: Revolution, the State, the Nation, the Market, God (13). The sequence here suggests that only the first of these is even worth considering. But that is not finally the case in this essay or in Balibar's work in general. It is the state that will come back, later in the essay, when Balibar talks about Althusser's ISAs essay. The state is that obscure something that Althusser senses acting behind the scenes, exerting power only by withdrawing into invisibility. But Balibar is clearly taking some distance from the Althusser of that classic essay, and he does so, it seems to me, in part by rehabilitating the state—that is, politics in the traditional sense, carried on by citizen-subjects—as a zone of constrained and therefore significant action.

Balibar and Butler have always shared a fascination with the semantic and conceptual duplicity of subjecthood: in Butler's words (from "Stubborn Attachment, Bodily Subjection: Rereading Hegel on the Unhappy Consciousness"), subjecthood is "the simultaneous forming and regulating of the subject" (32). Balibar refers to "subjection" and "subjectivation," or "the conjunction of self-reference, or identification of the subject, and subjection to power or authority, therefore a phenomenon of constitutive domination" (10). The point seems to be roughly the same for each: becoming a self-conscious individual means becoming a dominated self, subject to power. But the slight difference in emphasis between regulation and domination indicates a greater willingness on Balibar's part to consider the subject as a citizen, a political subject whose actions relate to and make claims on the state but are not entirely dominated or regulated by it.

To put this difference more crudely: for Balibar, becoming a subject (in the identity sense) need not mean subjecting oneself absolutely to domination. It cannot be taken for granted that subjects in the political or citizenly sense are totally subjected. Balibar has not always spelled out fully his reasoning on this point, perhaps because it might seem to entail a more reformist politics than he is comfortable with and/or imply too little sympathy for the sufferings and injustices involved in racial, gender, and sexual subjecthood. But one might also argue that proper attention to the injustices built into racial, sexual, and gender identities would itself require a politics that assumes, as he does, that the play of political subjecthood leaves room for something other than domination. In any event, that has been his consistent assumption.

In the last pages, Balibar takes a further step. Combining the section of the ISAs essay on social reproduction with the more famous scene of interpellation, he draws the polemical conclusion that the state is not imaginary. He distinguishes his point from the "banal" Marxist critique of the state as an instrument of class domination. But perhaps more can be said about the distinction. By making it, Balibar could, for example, be offering an allegory of neoliberalism. In the 1970s, as Althusser was writing about Machiavelli, his former friend Foucault was lecturing on neoliberalism and suggesting (or so Foucault's followers Pierre Dardot and Christian Laval have argued) that the neoliberal state colludes in its own disappearance.[2] The state is not an innocent victim of privatization, downsizing, and defunding. Though the market seems to be attacking it, the state is not worth defending.

Is that what Balibar is saying as well? I don't think so. He jumps from his insight about the state's more-than-imaginary nature to "the *political* problem of liberation *from ideology* as such" (16)—that is, to the question (he calls it a "Marxist" question, in quotation marks) of whether we must seek an *interpellation without a State*. There follows a list of further provocative questions, including the question of whether

"Revolution" and "Communist Party" might be "other names" (and "other forms of organization") that are comparable in function to the State. The question should, I think, be read as a statement: there is a parallel between State and Revolution, both of them discredited, one might say, and both of them nonetheless necessary. And there is a further statement, or exhortation: what we wish for in the utopian, infinitely postponed term *Revolution* must be sought in the area of what we already have in front of us, in the State, and in politics at the level of the state. This is what it means to be properly dialectical.

This is the same point that Balibar makes from another angle when he moves, in conclusion, to Althusser's posthumous book *Machiavelli and Us.* The new Prince is not an agent of the State, Balibar says, but an actor on the stage. Yes, but notice the huge difference from the ISAs essay. In the ISAs essay, the voice of the State comes from behind; the source of the interpellation is necessarily withdrawn, invisible. The actor on the stage, however, stands in front of his audience. He is visible as well as audible. This changes the power dynamic. It changes everything.

Althusser took from Spinoza, Balibar notes, the idea that the Prophet or Legislator can enunciate the law only on condition of adapting his imaginary to the dominant imaginary of the majority. In the Machiavelli book as Balibar reads it, the new Prince, like the old Prince, is an actor. And his staging of his passions for an audience is similarly dependent on the audience's passions. This dependence is crucial to the shift in focus that I mentioned at the outset and that defines the direction in which Balibar's thought is going: from performance itself to the conditions that have to be in place in order for a performance to be felicitous—that is, to that by which the performance is constrained. Which is also that which makes it significant.

Ideology, Balibar writes, "*is always already a dramaturgy*" (19). This sentence could lend itself to misinterpretation. Balibar is here defending the autonomy of politics, but he does not present dramaturgy as autonomous and still less as if it enjoyed the blithe freedom of the other "everything is X" terms. The new Prince is an actor on the stage. That means, as Balibar reads Althusser reading Machiavelli, that the Prince is constrained by the opinions of the majority. As Balibar again notes very carefully, the majority is made up mainly of the poor (18). In other words, the Prince's performance is constrained by poverty—poverty as a defining condition of the world in which he acts, in both senses of that word. Poverty is decisive. We have returned to "production in the Marxist sense," which has much to do with why the majority is poor and stays poor.

Poverty has already made a more than casual appearance in the early part of Balibar's essay, where it defines the collective experience of the characters in Carlo Bertolazzi's *El nost Milan* and presumably is crucial to the mystery of Nina's final gesture and how Giorgio Strehler staged it. There must be a logic in the lives of the poor, we are led to speculate, that outsiders cannot grasp—and that may be indeterminate even for insiders. What does it mean to choose money over ideals? Is this melodrama or antimelodrama? When Nina *se retourne*, or turns around, turning her back on her father, she looks like she is acting out the process of interpellation, but we cannot be sure whether she is in fact being interpellated by ideology or, on the contrary, turning away from it—that is, being interpellated by something else. It cannot have been wholly inconvenient for Althusser to glimpse in her the working class's refusal to become the ideal revolutionary subject, as prophesied by Georg Lukács and other Marxist humanists. She makes it more plausible to rescue Marxism from the heavy burden of having failed to realize that prophecy.

One of Balibar's intended points here is, no doubt, that for Althusser, ideology is not necessarily located behind one's back or, for that matter, below or beyond what we see, as certain recent polemics have suggested.[3] The model of the theater allows for ideology and its subjects to confront each other directly. In doing so, it also encourages us to visualize the underlying comparability of State and Revolution as objects of identification, the common ground between "bad" and "good" ideology. In other words, it breaks apart that too easy opposition. (A quietist opposition, since under inspection what ideology is really "good" enough to sustain political commitment?) Compared to an active, ideal citizenry, a theatrical audience is, of course, more passive—no doubt much too passive. Yet Balibar sees the Prince's audience as exercising a good deal more agency than the subject of interpellation. He goes so far as to reimagine the Prince himself as a sort of vanishing mediator in a dialectic where the real action belongs to the masses, who transform their own imaginary, interposing the Prince so as to create distance between that imaginary and some other possible version of themselves.

Constrained as he is by the opinions of the impoverished majority, Althusser's Prince acts politically. One would like to say that he is also constrained to act on the forces that create and maintain poverty: on "production in the Marxist sense." Balibar does not take that step in this essay, which is not to say that he might not want to take it elsewhere. What he does here, with a certain zest for paradox, is to use the analogy between ideology and theatrical performance to defend the significance of politics as a performance that is anything but free—that is, rather, informed and invested with meaning by its constraints. In this, he is true to that connotation of the word *ideology* that, for all its problems, has kept it in such constant circulation: the fact that it points to unacceptable injustice.

BRUCE ROBBINS is Old Dominion Foundation Professor in the Humanities at Columbia University. His latest book is *Perpetual War: Cosmopolitanism from the Viewpoint of Violence* (Duke University Press, 2012). He is also the director of the documentary film *Some of My Best Friends Are Zionists* (2013).

Notes

1   I discuss Balibar's work at greater length in "Balibarism!"

2   See Dardot and Laval. I question this premise in "The Monster of Governmentality."

3   This error is forcefully corrected in Rooney; Bewes.

Works Cited

Balibar, Étienne. "Althusser's Dramaturgy and the Critique of Ideology." *differences* 26.3 (2015): 1–22.

Bewes, Timothy. "Reading with the Grain: A New World in Literary Criticism." *differences* 21.3 (2010): 1–33.

Butler, Judith. *The Psychic Life of Power: Theories in Subjection.* Stanford: Stanford UP, 1997.

Dardot, Pierre, and Christian Laval. *The New Way of the World: On Neo-Liberal Society.* Trans. Gregory Elliott. London: Verso, 2013.

Hegel, G. W. F. *The Phenomenology of Spirit.* Trans. A. V. Miller. Oxford: Oxford UP, 1977.

Robbins, Bruce. "Balibarism!" *n+1* 16 (2013): 160–72.

—————. "The Monster of Governmentality." *Los Angeles Review of Books* 10 June 2014. http://lareviewofbooks.org/review/monster-governmentality.

Rooney, Ellen. "Live Free or Describe: The Reading Effect and the Persistence of Form." *differences* 21.3 (2010): 112–39.

Red Detachment of Women: Revolutionary Melodrama and Alternative Socialist Imaginations

Set in Hainan, an island in south China, the 1961 film *Red Detachment of Women* [*Hongse niangzi jun*] depicts the transformation of the female protagonist, Qionghua, from a maid in a landlord's household to a revolutionary heroine. Upon her father's fatal persecution by the landlord and her own enslavement to him, Qionghua is determined to avenge her family. Saved and freed by a Chinese Community Party (ccp) cadre named Changqing, she joins the Red Army and finally turns her personal pathos into the revolutionary action of fighting for the proletariat.

Driven by polarized conflicts between good and evil, virtue and villainy, and visually characterized by a strong contrast between dark-toned and bright-colored settings on the screen, the film is a typical revolutionary melodrama that portrays nonnegotiable class conflicts and reenacts the official history of a ccp-led revolution that liberated the oppressed and led them to the new China. The film is also an emblematic text of "women's liberation," with Qionghua and other women soldiers representative of socialist women who are freed from the bondage of feudalism and gender inequality. *Women hold up half the sky. Whatever men can accomplish, women*

Volume 26, Number 3 DOI 10.1215/10407391-3340396
© 2015 by Brown University and d i f f e r e n c e s : A Journal of Feminist Cultural Studies

can too. These were widely circulated sayings in Mao's China. As Xueping Zhong, Zheng Wang, and other women who grew up in Mao's era wrote in their memoirs, empowered by these discourses of women's liberation and the gender practices in Mao's China, many women endeavored to take up unconventional roles and enter traditionally male domains.

Since the late 1970s, however, in the era of Opening and Reforms and in the political climate of "farewell to revolution," this state-sponsored "women's liberation" has come under severe criticism.[1] One of the many charges leveled at Mao, in both official discourse and feminist discourse arguing for "natural" gender differences, is that the privileging of class over gender during Mao's era denied women's identification of their own needs. Once valorized as "iron women," women soldiers such as Qionghua and other images of new socialist women, who appeared in traditionally male professions and showed strength, determination, and strong will, became in post-Mao discourse objects of mockery (Dai; Dong). Advocating *women* as an autonomous category not dependent upon the notion of *class*, Li Xiaojiang, a feminist literary scholar, proposed in the 1980s a biologically essentialized notion of "women" as a "human ontological category" (32). In the particular context of 1980s China, Li's influential argument, though obviously problematic because of its unexamined essentialism, "helped to dislodge Maoist class analysis and enable the emergence of 'woman' as a legitimate subject of research," as Gail Hershatter and Zheng Wang have noted (416).

Li's argument reflected a general trend in post-Mao China to question the discourse and practices of state-sponsored feminism of the Mao era. Many post-1980s studies in both Chinese and English effectively reveal the discrepancy between socialist gender discourses and women's real life conditions in Mao's era. Scholarly works in the English-speaking world often center upon the neglect of the specificities of women's bodies and the suppression of gender differences by the dominant discourse of class.[2] Perceived as "desexualized and androgynous" (Dong 95), "iron women" came to exemplify the elimination of gender differences during Mao's era; women's participation in collective labor and public realms was also criticized as an instrumental exploitation of women's labor by the socialist state. However, this type of argument in English scholarship, as Hershatter points out, "is necessarily limited by its sources, juxtaposing government rhetoric from the Mao years extolling gender equality with 1980s memoirs and fiction in which women turn a critical eye on the Maoist past" (*Women* 44). In other words, these arguments should be historicized in the context of the post-Mao and post–Cold War political environment, specifically, the rise of the market economy, the commodification of bodies, and the shifting labor markets in post-Mao China, as well as the failure of state socialism on the global stage.

To offer a more critical examination of these discourses regarding gender politics in Mao's China is not to deny their effectiveness by exposing the discrepancy between official discourse and real practices, but to advance a more complicated understanding of gender imaginations and practices in relation to the power of the Party-State. Refusing a totalizing picture, recent scholarship urges a reconsideration of socialist gender practices, especially the indispensable role of women's participation in public realms and collective labor in redefining femininity and reshuffling the gendered order.[3] In other words, the appearance of women in traditionally male-dominated professions, such as women pilots and tractor drivers who had become role models for many women in Mao's era, enabled the reconstruction of femininity in relation to the reorganization of labor.[4] Moreover, given the experimental nature of various policies at the earlier stage of the new socialist country and varied practices in different areas and periods, it would be overly simplistic to reduce the variety of socialist gender practices and imaginations to one version. The Party-State was never a uniform power, but always in negotiation with varied agencies. For example, studies on topics such as the 1950 marriage law and the Women's Federation show that women demonstrated more agency than previously believed in navigating different layers of state and local power.[5] The variances and shifts at the local level and in each individual case suggest the impossibility of a totalizing picture of socialist gender practices. I argue that it becomes crucial to recover the heterogeneity of the socialist imagination and its gender practices in order to salvage an unrealized potential that might renew our understanding of socialism and provide new theoretical resources for the practice of differences today.

According to Zheng Wang, the state's mobilization of women to participate in public affairs was accompanied by the popularization of Friedrich Engels's classic text *The Origin of the Family, Private Property and the State* ("Call Me"). It was a shared belief that women's rights were not merely a gender issue but interrelated with the issue of private property and the structure of social production. Wang reminisces about her own experience of growing up in socialist China: "I seldom thought of myself as a girl, a less meaningful category when the prevailing slogans encouraged us to be a 'socialist new person'" (19). To her, this "nongendered" category meant freedom that would allow her to "go in any direction" because of her "conviction in the official ideology 'male comrades and female comrades are the same'" (19). She also admits that her ambition to be a "socialist constructor" coexisted with her eagerness to establish her "femaleness." But the definition of "femaleness" became more fluid when interspersed with the subject formation of a socialist new person. "Nongendered" in this sense, instead of simply denying gender differences, means not sticking to conventional characterizations of femininity, and thus it implies more flexibility in negotiating and constituting a person's multiple social identities.

This openness in gender imagination is also reflected in renewed gender representations in the films of the Mao era. In focusing on *Red Detachment of Women*, this essay asks how gender representation in revolutionary melodrama might lead to alternative imaginations of gender differences. Of course, cinematic representation cannot be equated with the actual practices in Mao's China. As Yomi Braester and Tina Mai Chen suggest, films made in the Mao era should be examined as "part of larger practices of modernity" that participated in the articulation of socialism, rather than just "as a mirror to reflect political circumstances" (9). The politically turbulent years were also years of experimentation, leaving inconclusive the questions of what socialism is and what socialist China can be. Films are not merely reflections of political campaigns but, more importantly, material forces that register and generate competing imaginations. The fluctuating fate of many films produced in the Seventeen Years period (1949–66, from the founding of the People's Republic of China [PRC] to the official launch of the Cultural Revolution) suggests the coexistence of heterogeneous imaginations and understandings of socialism and socialist modernity, which cannot be subsumed under one totalizing ideology.

The heterogeneity of socialist imaginations with regard to gender can be detected in the hybridity of the film texts. On the one hand, the images of new socialist women as represented in *Red Detachment of Women* were directly related to gender policies adopted by the new socialist state, such as the "equal work, equal pay" policy and the 1950 new marriage law.[6] On the other hand, they also appropriated images of women warriors, such as Hua Mulan, from folklore and popular literature and of the new women in Soviet films, which were popular in the PRC (see Chen). Furthermore, Kristine Harris tells us that *Red Detachment* is based on a reportage about the stories of a group of revolutionary women soldiers active in the Hainan area from 1930 to 1932, and a local dialect opera that derived from this reportage. This complicated process of appropriating and remediating heterogeneous resources implies multilayered authorship and the continuous redefinition of *women*. An examination of the layers of gender representation in the film will help to reanimate the complexity of socialist imaginations.

I focus on the cinematic form of revolutionary melodrama, or, more specifically, on alterations made to family melodrama in the construction of the *socialist family* as an imagined social space, which, I argue, can function as a powerful critique of the forced separations of the domestic and the public, and of production and reproduction, the twin divisions that Western Marxist-feminist critics have long revealed as underlying the gender politics of industrial capitalism.[7] These forced separations, or binaries, also impact the representation of domestic space in Hollywood family melodrama. Thomas Elsaesser, for example, discerns the iconographic fixation on the "claustrophobic atmosphere of the bourgeois home" in the 1940s and 1950s Hollywood family melodrama (72). This space defines the ways in which female subjectivities are constructed—"women waiting at home, standing by the window" (72). Domestic space is a common setting in "women's film," often depicted in opposition to the social arenas of men's activities. This type of "women's film" ultimately reaffirms the role of women as wives and mothers who "naturally" belong to the domestic domain and the belief that "a woman's true job is that of just being a woman, a job she can't very well escape no matter what else she does, with the repression disguised as *love*" (Basinger 26). Elsaesser argues that the suffocating interiors in Hollywood family melodrama are connected to "the victimisation and enforced passivity of women" (84). While the heroine's perils and pathos may best expose patriarchal repression and social conflicts reflected in the bourgeois home, these films' melodramatic effects nevertheless "shift explicit political themes onto a personal plane" (72). This is to say, the conventions of family melodrama often provide an imagined solution to social conflicts on the personal level, as of revenge and redemption, leaving unquestioned the social conditions that lead to the suffocating interior of the bourgeois home and, ultimately, the separation of production and reproduction imposed by capitalist industrialization and its wage system.

In Chinese film history, family melodrama was a favorite genre of leftist filmmakers in the 1930s. Social crises brought about by colonial modernity in early twentieth-century China are rendered, as Paul Pickowicz writes, into "a dramatically heightened and sensationalized presentation of ordinary family life" (308). *Red Detachment of Women* continues this tradition of family melodrama by highlighting the suffering of Qionghua's family and its shattering into pieces under the evil hand of the landlord. But it also significantly transforms the genre and conjures up an alternative socialist space, which also provides room for more fluid gender formations that radically redefine such notions as *women* and *femininity*. The way it transforms the conventions of family melodrama can be read in line with the critique of the separation between production and reproduction in the Marxist feminist tradition. This essay focuses on the rewriting of family melodrama in *Red Detachment* and the gender politics it entails. I aim here to recapture the potential of an alternative socialist imagination that was conditioned by socialist practices in the early years of the PRC but that was not necessarily congruent with the socialist state's officially endorsed ideology. In the course of the essay, I also uncover flows of affect that blur the boundary between the fictive world of the mise-en-scène and the space occupied by audiences, an effect of affectivity that is neither confined within an individuated subject nor fully aligned with state power.

Joining the Revolutionary Family

Hollywood family melodrama and pre-PRC Shanghai leftist films typically turned the sufferings of victimized women into a visceral accusation of a corrupted society. *Red Detachment of Women* shares this practice. As Robert Chi observes, the melodramatic mode of deploying pathos and innocent victimhood fits squarely into the Maoist practice of "publicly airing grievances" that encouraged peasants to speak out about their experiences of "tears and blood" inflicted by the "old society" (154). One scene of such public grievance-airing in *Red Detachment* takes the form of a family melodrama: with tears running down her face, Qionghua tells the story of her father, who was cruelly tortured to death by the landlord Nan Batian, the villain who, at this point in the film, has been captured and is being paraded around the town by women soldiers. The melodramatic plot—the suffering of an innocent family and the identification of the villain—is condensed in this sequence to stage deep-rooted class opposition.

Given that the director, Xie Jin, was trained in the Shanghai film industry before the establishment of the PRC, it is not surprising that *Red Detachment* shows a close affinity with the family melodrama tradition of 1930s Shanghai leftist filmmaking. Film critic Cai Shiyong writes:

> *In fact, most of the artists devoted to the progressive film in the thirties and the forties later became, to different degrees, the major producers of the film of the people. Promoted by them, the fine tradition of Chinese progressive film was not interrupted.*

> *[. . .] [I]n 1957, a "Conference on the Tradition of Chinese Film" was held in Shanghai; even during the years of the "Great Leap Forward," when the past was systematically repudiated for the present, over a dozen articles on the topic of progressive film, among them Tian Han's "Memoir" and Hong Shen's "Chinese Film in 1933," were published in the journal* Chinese Cinema *[. . .]. In 1963, China Film Archive sponsored a retrospective of "Chinese Film in the 1930s," showing thirteen films in Beijing and Chang-chun [. . .]. It is groundless to assert that the filmmakers of socialist China knew little about the great heritage made in the previous two decades. (Qtd. and trans. by Xudong Zhang 406)*

The 1930s leftist films often infuse progressive political messages into popular melodramatic forms. As Zhen Zhang (*Amorous*) and Emilie Yueh-Yu Yeh, among others, remark, the formation of melodramatic films in early twentieth-century Shanghai drew intensively, for example, on the notion of retribution from Buddhist tradition that was already widely accepted among Chinese audiences before the emergence of cinema culture; from the cultural capital of popular fiction through the adaptation of the novels by the Mandarin Ducks and Butterfly School; from sensational crime stories published in newspapers and popular readings; and from the discourse of *Wenyi* (literally, "letters and arts") associated with literary works and translations in the late nineteenth and early twentieth centuries. Chinese melodramatic films thus become emblematic of what Miriam Hansen refers to as "vernacular modernism," where local traditions and exigencies are continually negotiated with and contested by the idioms and conventions of Hollywood.

The impact of Soviet cinema can also be detected in both the 1930s leftist tradition and in Mao-era filmmaking. The translation of Soviet film theory dates back to the 1930s. Although Sergei Eisenstein was a frequently mentioned name in Chinese film circles, it was Vsevolod Pudovkin's montage theory that gained popularity among Chinese film theorists and filmmakers, especially in the context of the early PRC years, when the principle of accessibility and comprehensibility to an ordinary audience became a high priority over the "formalist" pursuit of Eisenstein (see Chan). This made the reception of Soviet montage theory more compatible with continuity editing and other conventions of Hollywood. Stephanie Donald discerns that the most obvious formal influence of Soviet films is the use of the "socialist realist gaze," shots in which the character stares "exultantly off screen" to a horizon beyond the diegetic world (59–63). Shots of the socialist realist gaze do appear in *Red Detachment*, as, for example, in the scene where the CCP cadre Changqing is captured and soon to be executed by the landlord. The hero stares offscreen and sees a flag of the CCP that transports the character to a transcendental realm of revolutionary Truth. Jason McGrath further observes that in revolutionary model operas produced during the Cultural Revolution, the socialist realist gaze is combined with a *liangxiang* pose from the Peking Opera tradition (365).[8] Indeed, in *Red Detachment* and other films by Xie Jin in this period, the influence of Chinese traditional opera can be detected in the highly stylized gestures of characters and in the use of an orchestra to punctuate moments of intense drama (see Marchetti). Formal features of traditional opera performance were appropriated to reinforce melodramatic effects, thus underlining the mixture of international and local elements in revolutionary melodrama.

The 1930s Shanghai family melodramas, like their Hollywood counterparts, often end with a climax of female victims' emotional outbursts and a call for the rectification of justice. For example, in the final sequence of the 1933 film *Playthings*, directed by Sun Yu, after a merciless chain of events that leads to the dissolution of her family, the protagonist Sister Ye "bursts" into hysterical shouting, or, in Andrew Jones's words, "an almost unbearably visceral frenzy of madness and terror" (138). This emotional outburst is not the climax of revolutionary melodrama, however. In *Red Detachment*, the pathos-ridden story of Qionghua's family ends a third of the way into the film. The call for justice and the eventual punishment of the villain is delayed unusually long, with the action of revenge repeatedly impeded. The melodramatic plot thus suspended, the rest of the film shifts to the transformation of the female protagonist and her life at the revolutionary Red base. I would argue that this delay and *deviation* is a significant modification to family melodrama conventions and a key point for revolutionary melodrama in establishing a "new regime of morality," a phrase borrowed from Peter Brooks and Linda Williams (*Playing*), respectively. Both critics argue that the sufferings of the victims and a strong demand for the redemption of their sufferings are key to melodrama's function in attesting to moral legibility. In the new regime of morality outlined by *Red Detachment*, however, suffering alone is not sufficient to constitute virtue; suffering must be transformed into a consciousness of class—in this case, an identification with the revolutionary family.

To examine this point further, it might be helpful to start with Qionghua's relationship with her double, Honglian. On her way to the Red base, Qionghua stumbles upon a country house and gets to know Honglian, the daughter-in-law of the household. As Honglian tells her own miserable story of being sold to the household as a child bride, "married" to a wooden "man," and exploited as a slave by her so-called parents-in-law for ten years, the two women cry out, "There is no way to live like this any longer!" In the next moment, we see the two walk out of the dark suffocating house, arm in arm, to the Red base.

Earlier in this scene, the camera follows Honglian, with her cautious movements and almost neurotic alertness, into the dark interior space of her "home," which is divided and visually blocked by numerous doors and curtains. The suffocating domestic interior often associated with family melodrama is displayed here only to be discarded and supplanted by a different form of kinship. The two women's identification with each other's suffering soon makes them bonded sisters, even though they were strangers only a moment before. Yet this sisterhood is not ritualized until they join the Red Army: the moment that Qionghua is accepted as a woman soldier, she immediately declares, "I have a sister who wants to join too." With this declaration of sisterhood at the ritualized moment of joining the army, their shared pathos is transformed into their common political goal, by which their sisterhood is elevated beyond a simply individual relationship: they are bonded by their proletarian identity. Interestingly, their identification with the proletariat is rendered into a small drama of translation. When the head of the platoon examining Qionghua's background asks her, "Are you proletarian?," Qionghua is confused at first by the word *proletarian*, as it is obviously a neologism. But as other women soldiers help translate the question as "Do you own any land?," she soon identifies herself as proletarian by declaring herself to own no land or property. This suggests that official ideology has to go through a process of "vernacularization" and must adopt the language of common people in order to address varied local traditions and realities and thus never remain an immutable unity. Even the word *proletariat* may carry hybrid connotations as it proliferates in everyday language, not to mention the dissemination of such notions as "socialism" and "new women" among common people.

Worth notice here is the new correlation between kinship and class. Compare it with other similar sisterhood-motif melodramas made in the 1930s. In the 1933 family melodrama *Sister Flowers*, twin sisters named Dabao and Erbao are split into different social strata, cut off from each other for many years. Erbao, who was taken away as a child into the city by her gun-smuggler father, becomes a high official's concubine; Dabao, who remained in the countryside, is later forced by poverty to work as a nanny in the city, and coincidentally, in Erbao's household, without knowing that Erbao is her lost sister. Desperate for money to save her sick husband, Dabao attempts to steal a silver necklace from Erbao's baby but is caught red-handed and sent to prison. The film ends with their mother coming to rescue Dabao by revealing their sisterhood. Erbao, finally recognizing their kinship and determined to save her sister, takes Dabao to see her powerful husband.

In her reading of phantom sisters in Chinese cinema, Zhen Zhang argues that doubleness reflects the longing for sorority and companionship in a fragmented modern world. Referring to Hillel Schwartz's argument that "the vanishing (or disappeared) twin in the industrializing society serves as 'mute testimony to vanishing kin' in an epoch of massive social dislocation and 'fading networks of blood relations,'" Zhang relates this motif of twin sisters to the social disparity in a drastically changed Chinese society ("Urban" 351). In *Sister Flowers*, the dislocation of blood relations is dramatically embodied in the two socially severed sisters. While the contrast in their social situations provides a critique of social inequality, the end of the film also speaks of a utopian wish to reconcile social conflicts and fractures by "returning" to a society with a morality based on blood relations. In other words, in this typical family melodrama, the severed kinship becomes a most palpable indicator of drastic social conflicts, its repair an imagined, even fantastic solution to the alienation of modern society.

It is therefore reasonable to argue that the role of "family" in 1930s Shanghai melodrama films is ambivalent: on the one hand, the disintegration and alienation of kinship becomes the most pathetic accusation against social disparity; but on the other hand, the proposal of kinship as the resolution to social conflicts is problematic. Elsaesser's words regarding 1940s and 1950s Hollywood family melodrama also apply here because such a formation of family melodrama has "resolutely refused to understand social change in other than private contexts and emotional terms" (72). The family becomes a self-autonomous entity that is expected not only to contain but also to resolve social conflicts within itself. This imaginary of the family as paradoxically both contiguous to and cut off from social conflicts reveals the tension arising from the forced division of domestic space and work space, of production and reproduction.

The goal of women's liberation in Mao's China, to a certain degree, addressed these problematic separations by bringing women into the public domain and encouraging their participation in public labor.

Dong Limin argues that women's participation in public labor should not be regarded as the result simply of the state's top-down policy and the instrumentalization of women. Rather, collective labor earned women recognition among communities and enabled the formation of new subjectivities of socialist women, different from the kind of autonomous individuals that were idealized by white, middle-class Western feminism.

The reorganization of social labor inevitably entails changes in gender relations and familial order. Admittedly, in practice, these changes might not have fully unfolded for various reasons. Nevertheless, unrealized potential can be detected in films and other artworks. In *Red Detachment*, the disintegration of Qionghua's family is not redeemed by the formation of a bourgeois nuclear family. Instead, a new *revolutionary family* based on collective labor emerges as a new regime of morality and human relations. This imaginary of a *revolutionary family* is best manifested in the nonkinship-based sisterhood between Qionghua and Honglian but also in the scenes of Honglian's marriage. Before the ceremony, we see Honglian, in men's clothes, performing with Qionghua in a revolutionary drama. In this play-within-a-play, a melodramatic reenactment of revolution, Honglian, who of the two has a more delicate face and who has, in previous scenes, been Qionghua's demure counterpart, now acts as Qionghua's male counterpart, mysteriously and ambiguously invoking the scene of the two meeting for the first time, when Honglian was also dressed as a man. Although cross-dressing performance may be traced back to the Chinese opera tradition, it is important to acknowledge that these scenes of gender flexibility are contextualized within the sequences that feature the communal life and collective labor of these women soldiers. In the next scene, we see Qionghua training a group of kids, which is often regarded as women's work, relegated to the separated realm of reproduction in the structure of the bourgeois nuclear family. The ambiguous performance of gender roles invokes a fluid subjectivity that cannot be confined within any essentialized gender conceptions and raises the question as to what new socialist women can be. They are soldiers but also students who diligently absorb new knowledge, producers who happily plant seeds and harvest grains, educators who shoulder the responsibility of raising the next generation, and sisters to each other in this big family. Labor is no longer an oppressive activity imposed on them, but what connects them to others. Their varied activities and intersubjective connections allow an openness for molding and remolding the self. In this sense, family also takes on a different meaning. Honglian's marriage ceremony becomes a festive celebration of the Red base, with Honglian and her husband warmly surrounded by their comrades. Unfolding in joyful folk opera music, the wedding ceremony is also a harvest celebration, and the tropical landscape of Hainan Island becomes an imagined haven in which personal life and communal life are organically integrated. I am arguing that the replacement of the nuclear family by the *revolutionary family* here reflects precisely the socialist critique of the forced separation of production and reproduction, the premise on which the separation of bourgeois domestic space from work space is based.

The Understatement of Revolutionary Melodrama

Xie Jin's images of a big revolutionary family and his integration of domestic space into communal space can be regarded, to some degree, as his response to the critique of his earlier film *Woman Basketball Player No. 5*, made in 1957. Three months after the public screening of the film, Xia Yan, a top filmmaker and critic, declared the film flawed because of an inappropriate setting that showed the female protagonist, Lin Jie, a single mother, living in a fancy home that she would not likely have been able to afford. Xia Yan believed that this implausible setting represented an unhealthy trend in filmmaking, along with the convention in other films of the same period of depicting poor peasant girls made to awkwardly wear colorful new clothing. Mao Jian sees Xia's disapproval of fancy domestic space as "an outright criticism of the Shanghai cinema tradition" (78). According to Mao, Xia Yan clearly detected the danger of obvious references in *Woman Basketball Player* to earlier Shanghai films, such as scenes of the Bund—a waterfront area in Shanghai with modern buildings that once housed foreign banks and trading companies in the early twentieth century, often considered a symbol of imperial power and colonial modernity—and of the elegantly decorated interior space occupied by the female protagonist. Indeed, throughout the early years of the PRC, ornate interior space gradually accumulated negative meanings. In counterespionage films, well-furnished, wallpapered homes that demonstrate suspicious nontransparency often turn out to be the dens of surreptitious spies and "enemies of people," whereas a worker's home is always contiguous to open spaces such as the village square or busy streets, its door never shut (see Qi Wang).

Obviously cognizant of this politics of space by the time he made *Red Detachment*, Xie Jin supplanted the interior domestic space common in pre-1949 Shanghai films with an imagined, preindustrial paradise, which invokes the dream of a small ideal society of agricultural civilization that might date back to ancient times, such as Laozi's political idea valorizing a "small country" as a land of harmony and happiness.[9] But the porous boundary between the domestic and the public also registers the transformations of social spaces in the early PRC years. The collectivization of property and the mushrooming of people's communes challenged the family as a disparate unit of production. Moreover, housewives, particularly those in urban areas, were mobilized by the Women's Federation to participate in neighborhood work. Wang Zheng astutely comments that this "led to redrawing gendered social spaces in socialist state formation" because "[h]istorically, the local administrative system—*baojia*—had been run by men." Once women stepped into this traditionally male space and became managers of local communities, they were "extending their domesticity into the management of the 'socialist big family'" ("'State'" 541), thus reorganizing domestic and social spaces. The negotiations in *Red Detachment* between the real and the imagined, between premodern and socialist ideals bring forth this imagined space of utopia that conforms neither to the power of a monolithic socialist state nor to any existing demarcation of domestic and public spaces.

This imagined space can also be understood as "a space of innocence," which Williams identifies as an important feature of melodrama (*Playing* 28), a space soon to be invaded by the villain—the Kuomintang (KMT) troops, in this case.[10] The shattering of this paradisiac space reinforces the Manichean world of melodrama and accumulates pathos that will eventually lead to action. As Williams puts it, "[M]elodrama's recognition of virtue involves a dialectic of pathos and action—a give and take of 'too late' and 'in the nick of time'" (30). In her formulation, action is always driven by the outburst of private emotions and personal pathos. In *Red Detachment*, however, the loss of the innocent space occurs through not only individual but also collective pathos. Qionghua's personal expression of pathos at the beginning of the film has to be withheld until the latter half of the film, made to wait for the right timing for a collective action.

Such unexpected withholding of emotional expression creates not only an understatement of melodramatic emotions but also control of narrative temporality and of the orchestrated rising and falling of emotion. In *Red Detachment* this understatement of melodrama reaches its peak—or nadir—when Changqing is captured and killed by the enemy. Qionghua, who is hiding in the forest, witnesses him being burned to death. Remarkably, such a moment of immense pathos is not followed by efforts to rescue him "in the nick of time." We see tears in her eyes, her mouth suddenly opens as if to cry out, but no sound comes out; the sound and fury seem muffled. In the next moment, she falls over a tree, her shoulders shaking, yet her mouth is tightly shut, preventing her from bursting out. This moment of almost unbearable withholding is prolonged further by the power of self-control she exerts over her comrades. As she brings back the news of Changqing's death, they immediately take up their guns, determined to avenge him. But Qionghua stops them. "Wipe away your tears!" As she calls out to her comrades, tears trickling down her own face, her hands clench into fists: "Comrades, we should seek revenge, but not in an impulsive way!" Here immediate individual revenge becomes an "impulsive" and imprudent action that can ruin the overall strategy of the Red Army, a higher authority whose presence remains invisible throughout the film. In a volume collectively edited in 1964, some critics questioned the realism of the scene: how could Qionghua witness the death of her most admired comrade without doing anything? They argue that the scene not only is emotionally almost unacceptable but also that it blunts the sharp personality of Qionghua (*Yuan Wenshu* 429). In my view, this understatement is, however, even more powerful than any excessive expression: as Qionghua shuts her mouth tightly and clenches her fists, we can almost viscerally feel the immense pressure of her curbed emotions, which are withheld for an unusually long time and not released until the end of the film, when the landlord is executed. The withheld feelings and the melodramatic understatement justify even more powerfully the execution of the villain.

I should clarify my notion of *understatement*, which seems counterintuitive to our understanding of melodrama. Peter Brooks defines melodrama as "a mode of excess," "a dramaturgy of hyperbole, excess, excitement, and 'acting out'" (viii). It is "a form for a post-sacred era," "a measure of the personalization and inwardness of post-sacred ethics, the difficulty of their location and expression" (16). Elsaesser traces the birth of melodrama in the Western world back to eighteenth-century sentimental novels and, crucially, the interiorization of ideological conflicts as private feelings (70). The "sublimity" of melodramatic rhetoric, the emphatic articulation and gesture, as Brooks argues, is the effort to heighten the importance of everyday life and lay bare the morality in "ordinary" private life (13–14). No doubt, Brooks's notion of the lost "sacred" world is closely tied to the Christian tradition. But it is also relevant to a modern world, in which traditional values, communities, and kinship are swept away. The very paradox of melodrama lies in its reliance on an outburst of individual expression to overcome the pathos of alienated individuals who are confronted with the loss of communal life and values. It is exactly the moment of excessive individual protest that makes visible, or even turns into a spectacle, the desire for communication and recognition as well as the appeal for moral legibility in a modern world where every existing value is reestimated and reshuffled.

This moment of individual outburst as an imagined solution to the conflicts of the modern world cannot be adopted uncritically in revolutionary melodrama. Qionghua's personal hatred has to be transformed into class consciousness. In fact, the film reenacts the conventions of Hollywood and pre-PRC Shanghai melodrama by letting Qionghua experience a moment of uncontrolled individual effusion in a scene in which she is sent on a spy mission. The moment she sees the landlord, she is overwhelmed with bitter feelings and pulls out her gun to shoot him. Her uncontrolled outburst ruins her mission but also leads to her transformation, as well as to the transformation of revolutionary melodrama on the level of cinematic narrative and conventions. The *excessive* mode of individual expression is reenacted in the film so that it can be surpassed later by a more powerful collective outburst—that is, a revolution. The collective expression also makes legible a new regime of morality. In other words, the renewed form of revolutionary melodrama, with its rhetoric of understatement, proposes a different solution to the conflicts that previous melodramatic traditions imaginatively resolve, where the action is driven by individual pathos.

This emphasis on a collectivity that supersedes but does not trample individual interest can be read, to a degree, as the interpellation and disciplining of individuals by the nation-state. Two objects in the film synecdochically point to the presence of the state: one is a map of China on which Qionghua fails to locate Yelin county, a place too small, even, to be displayed on the map. The other is a pocket watch, which is passed down from Changqing to Qionghua after his death. It plays the role of orchestrating individual actions into the shared temporality of a larger imagined community. But the presence of the state should not be read simply as an oppressing power. Zheng Wang, in her study of the Women's Federation, shows that, while making women into state subjects, the socialist state also empowered women, especially by enabling housewives to participate in the management of public affairs. She admits that the process of empowerment involved complicated contestations between the feminist agenda and state power, but instead of seeing the state as a monolithic whole, she asks: "Can a feminist theory of state critical of all dimensions of state power also account for sites and effects of feminist negotiation and intervention in dispersed state processes?" ("'State'" 520). Similarly, we may ask: can a revolutionary melodrama in its negotiation with dispersed state and local processes generate an alternative socialist imagination that overcomes the dilemma of individualism and the forced separation of production and reproduction that is manifested in the form of suffocating domestic interiors in family melodrama? In other words, while the imagination of the collective in the film might be shadowed by the arms of state power, could it also gesture toward an alternative imagination of socialist collectivity?

The Unstable Understatement

The imagination of communal life and collective labor, while functioning as a critique of the capitalist separation of the domestic and the public, of production and reproduction, leaves unanswered the question of what kind of new gender relations could be established under socialist conditions. The undecided gender relations are best captured in the underplayed love scenes in *Red Detachment.* According to the scriptwriter, Liang Xin, there was a love plot between Qionghua and Changqing in the original script, but their confessions to each other were eliminated in the final version of the film. The disappearance of the love plot shows the ways in which state power may delimit the imaginary registers of the film. It is not coincidental that while *Red Detachment* was in production, another film, titled *The Story of Liubao Village* (1957), caused much controversy because of its love story between a People's Liberation Army soldier and a country girl.

State censorship, however, was just half of the story. A Tianjin-region moviegoer wrote a letter to scriptwriter Liang, which goes like this:

> *I have been thinking about writing this letter for a long time. Otherwise, I would feel uncomfortable (not telling you my thoughts).* Red Detachment of Women *is a good film. [. . .] Yet when I saw the scene in which Qionghua encounters Changqing at the Border Hill again when she comes out from the hospital, I thought to myself: "How awful! The scriptwriter is going to force on his audience another vulgar and silly love story." But fortunately, the scriptwriter successfully avoids the clichéd love plot. If the plot went on in that direction, how cloying that would be. (Liang 242)*

The problematic scene referred to in the letter occurs in the middle of the film: Qionghua leaves the hospital after she recovers from a gunshot wound. She encounters Changqing at the Border Hill, the same place where Changqing freed her from the landlord's house a year earlier. Reunited at the same place, the two seem to have a lot to say to each other. Qionghua, looking up at Changqing admiringly, starts talking about her feelings toward him. On the screen, we get a close-up of Qionghua's face as she shyly casts her eyes on Changqing, a shot immediately followed by a countershot of Changqing smiling back at her. The shot–reverse shot indicates the intimacy between the two, but the scene is immediately cut off to a distant shot, featuring the two talking about strategies of capturing the landlord, leaving their previous conversation abruptly interrupted. The moviegoer's intuition is correct. According to Liang, in the original script, there was another group of shot–reverse shots between the two that revealed their feelings toward each other.

It is worth asking why the audience member had the feeling that it was going to be a love scene even though what she saw was already a *clean* version with no explicit love plot. Why did she feel repulsed by the notion of "another silly love story"? Her immediate association of the scene with a love plot indicates that film audiences were familiar with the conventions of onscreen love scenes, which had already become a fixed set of cinematic idioms fully developed by both Hollywood movies and pre-PRC Shanghai films. The plots are typical in that a man rescues a victimized woman and the savior ends up becoming her lover. Marcia Landy summarizes the narrative convention of this type of melodrama: "The victims are most often females threatened in their sexuality, their property, their very identity. Often orphaned, subjected to cruel and arbitrary treatment at the hands of the domineering paternal and maternal figures or their surrogates, they experience a number of trials, until, if they are fortunate, they are rescued by a gentle and understanding lover, the 'happy, unhappy ending' in Douglas Sirk's terms" (14). This is the typical plot of "women's film," the type of film that provides women-centered narratives and centers around romance, domestic life, and other issues presumably appealing to female audiences. The clichéd savior-turning-into-a-lover convention would certainly be familiar to the sophisticated audience of *Red Detachment*.

Liang, upset by the letter, argued for the validity of the love plot in revolutionary films. But first he had to address the audience's repulsion. "When we talk about 'love,' we certainly refer to the love of the proletariat. Bourgeois types of love can only appear in films as negative examples. In some films, however, there are scenes that claim to be about proletarian love, but the images on the screen turn out to be about vulgar individual desire" (243). Liang was trying to make a distinction between "bourgeois love" and "proletarian love." If bourgeois love scenes are repulsive to audiences, scenes of proletarian love should differentiate themselves from previous conventions.

Such painstaking efforts to distinguish between revolutionary love scenes and earlier romantic conventions were partly driven by the film criticism of this period. Film critic Xing Zuwen, in a 1958 article about the "corruption" of Chinese films by Hollywood, accuses some domestic films of directly appropriating love scenes from Hollywood films (208–9). He gives as an example the script of a 1957 film, *The Footsteps of Youth* (*Qingchun de jiaobu*), which depicted love scenes thus: "Sometimes they stand at the peak of the mountains appreciating the beauty of the landscape, sometimes they sit side by side confiding secretly to each other. They are seen hand in hand in bustling streets, shoulder by shoulder on quiet roads [. . .]" (209). Xing criticizes the filmmakers for indulging in bourgeois self-appreciation. He continues to list scenes that he believes to be directly transplanted from Hollywood films and argues that love scenes do not have to involve kissing given that social customs vary in different societies. To him, a good love scene should be an expression of the characters' sophisticated emotions and noble sentiments.

This prohibitively severe critique virtually eliminated any existing cinematic idiom for love scenes. What, then, should a "proletarian love scene" look like? Liang Xin remarked about the difficulty:

> *The problem is how, rather than whether it is allowed, to cast love scenes. This "how" question becomes a real problem. Audiences may get impatient once they see nothing new added to the conventions (of love scenes). The Tianjin moviegoer got disappointed even before seeing any actual love scenes, as she thought that she could predict the plot. Because of this difficulty, every one either is unwilling to touch upon the issue, or has no intention of pursuing any further discussion. (243–44)*

This "how" question is crucial. With the love scene conventions so exposed and criticized, it was very difficult to achieve a clearly differentiated set of conventions. The above-mentioned Changqing and Qionghua scene with the ambiguous shot–reverse shots, which the Tianjin moviegoer regarded as an unbearable flirtation, fails to differentiate itself from "bourgeois love scenes" as the scriptwriter had ambitiously intended. I argue, however, that these very traces of the underdeveloped relationship between Changqing and Qionghua themselves become ambiguous and unstable understatements and, as I will suggest, create a field of openness for interpretation.

The Tactile Traces

Though explicit love scenes between Qionghua and Changqing are deleted from the movie, there are traces of their relationship left in the film, which provide multiple possibilities of interpretation. As scriptwriter Liang tells us, the four silver coins that Changqing gives to Qionghua are important clues about their relationship. The four silver coins appear four times in the film.

The first time occurs when Changqing takes Qionghua from the landlord's house and frees her at Border Hill. A medium shot of the two suddenly cuts to a close-up on Qionghua's face in soft focus; it is the first time that we see her smile, a moment signifying the change in her attitude toward Changqing. He takes out four silver coins for her to buy food on her way to the Red base. A close-up on Qionghua's palm reveals the four slightly dirt-tinted coins. Her palm fills up the whole screen. For the moment, the palm is dissociated from a particular person, inviting the audience to identify with it and to feel the warmth left on the coins.

The second silver coin scene happens when Qionghua is left on her own to examine her mistakes after she spoils her spy mission. She is soon joined by Honglian. As they start talking about Changqing as a model to emulate, Qinghua, in the foreground, turns her back to Honglian and faces the camera with a secret smile on her face. As she takes out the coins and gently strokes them one by one with her fingers, the lingering camera invites the audience to feel the texture of the coins and to share the intimacy with Qionghua.

The third scene is on the battlefield, when Changqing tells Qionghua that her application to join the Communist Party has been approved. She gives him back the coins as her membership fee to the party: a close-up on the four coins again, this time in Changqing's palm. As he clenches the coins tightly, we can almost feel the strength of his fist and the emotions that resonate and almost burst out between the two.

The last scene immediately follows Changqing's death. In Changqing's bag, Qionghua finds the four coins. She clenches them in her fist as the extradiegetic music of "The International" arises. An extreme close-up on her tight fist, held upright, fills the screen. Here the pathos from Changqing's death and the emotional bond of the two conveyed by the coins are mingled with her feelings of belonging to the Party.

Robert Chi characterizes the coins as a "calculus of debts" to the Party (155). Insightful as his comment is, his symbolic reading of the coins misses the ambiguity and tactility of the images. The power of the coins comes precisely from the fluid movement between the private and the public, the concrete and the abstract. The indeterminate relationship between Changqing and Qionghua leaves the significance of the four coins open throughout these scenes: they could be a token of their love or of the "emotional currency" that binds together an individual and the Party. The latter does not contradict the former. The sublimation of private desires in revolutionary melodrama does not negate interpersonal attachment, but constitutes fluid flows of affectivity and subjectivity that problematize the separation of the domestic and the public, the individual and the collective. The intertwining of personal feelings and devotion to the Party not only renders money—the most abstract, impersonal currency—into powerful, tactile traces but also makes the four coins a palpable medium between personal life and political cause. The physical gestures associated with the coins also become a ritual of this bond. The gestures invite the audience to join, to use Williams's description of body genres, as "an almost involuntary mimicry of the emotion or the sensation of the body on the screen" ("Film" 4). With such bodily enervation, revolutionary melodrama becomes a most powerful medium that helps reshape socialist morality and subjectivity.

    Red Detachment of Women was not the only the film of this period to transform underdeveloped love stories into an affective space renegotiating the personal and the political, the private and the public. The 1959 film *The Song of the Youth* (*Qingchun zhi ge*), adapted from a popular eponymous work of fiction, presents a similar underdeveloped love plot. It skillfully tackles the problem of love plots by including within itself two types of love: beginning with scenes of Lin Daojing's family life with her petit bourgeois intellectual husband, the film soon reveals the confines of this bourgeois family space when the husband claims her as his own property and forbids her from participating in revolutionary activities. The love plot between Lin and her intellectual husband displayed at the beginning of the film, in fact, is a typical love story prevalent in early twentieth-century China about young women who, inspired by Western-style women and the New Cultural Movement led by new intellectuals, rebel against arranged marriage and find their own love. Once regarded as a gesture of antifeudalism, free love per se falls short in defining new women in the socialist era. Instead of ending up becoming a bourgeois housewife, Lin has to negate her past again in order to become a new socialist woman. As Lin leaves this bourgeois household and gets closer to her revolutionary guide, Lu Jiachuan, the embryonic love story between her and Lu is abruptly cut off with Lu's persecution by the

KMT government. Long after Lu's death, Lin recites a poem to her intimate girlfriend confessing her passion for Lu. Ban Wang notices the energy and intensity conveyed by the kinetic camera movement, despite the absence of any explicit description of heterosexual love in the scene: "The love, though for a dead person, is not neutralized and rendered bloodless by politics; it parades its ecstatic intensity and passionate flamboyance. The failure to see this is an inability to see love and pleasure beyond the heterosexual relation, an inability to discern the sublimated forms that private desire can take in public, political, and apparently nonsexual guises" (135–36). Wang is insightful in discerning the presence of private desire contiguous with the enthusiasm for public and political causes. Heterosexual desire is not individuated and interiorized as the personal, but transformed into sisterly intimacy for common belief and cause in this scene. Moreover, the highly mediated confession keeps its targeted audience ambiguous: is it addressing Lin's secret lover Lu, or the invisible Party, or the film audience who is listening to her confession? This ambiguity leaves room for the coexistence of private desire and political enthusiasm and generates fluid flows of affectivity that are not confined within an individuated subject. This affective space contiguous with both the private and the public also indicates a sort of collectivity that neither presumes autonomous individuals nor is subsumed to a unitary state power.

■

Red Detachment of Women was adapted into a ballet performance and a Peking opera in the mid-1960s. Madam Mao Jiang Qing was closely involved in the production of the ballet version. Having run away from an arranged marriage and become a film actress in 1930s Shanghai, Jiang allegedly saw her younger self in the character Qionghua and the ballerina who played Qionghua (see Harris 326). The opera version was also repeatedly performed by amateur troupes for local audiences as a way for them to learn from the heroine and refashion themselves as revolutionary subjects. Jiang's supposed identification with the character and the way women across the country saw the character as a model suggest that the definition of *new socialist women* was never sealed off during the process of continuous reenaction and performance.

It may not be a coincidence that Xie Jin, the director of *Red Detachment of Women*, who played a key role in transforming family melodrama into revolutionary melodrama, returned to the conventions of family melodrama in his post–Cultural Revolution works as a way to critique the radical politics of Mao's era after his own ordeal during the turbulent years. Starting from his 1979 film *Cradle* and continuing to *Legend of Tianyun Mountain* (1980) and *The Herdsman* (1982), women characters increasingly resume the role of tender mothers and good wives. Zhu Dake, a sharp critic of Xie Jin films, characterizes these women characters as "complacent, docile, hard-working, the standard old-fashioned women, and the products of patriarchal culture" (237). Zhu's description of these female characters is congruent with Hershatter's observation that emerging notions of femininity in post-Mao China emphasized motherhood and sexual appeal to men ("Women" 46). Zhu continued to denounce Xie's use of excessive emotion to manipulate the audience into accepting the morality and ethics implicit in his films. Indeed, the morality that Xie promotes in his post-Mao films is a far cry from that of *Red Detachment*. Echoing the shifting political climate in Deng's China, Xie reverses his valorization of the emergent socialist regime of morality in Mao's era and uses family melodrama to render visceral the pathos and sufferings caused by the Cultural Revolution. In his 1987 film *Hibiscus Town*, we see that a victimized woman's dream of private, happy family life is repeatedly annihilated in political upheavals. Here two nuclear families (which come with the female protagonist's two marriages) become a counterspace to the collective space in *Red Detachment*, and the villain that brings suffering to the families now becomes a CCP female cadre, who is depicted as an androgynous devil.[11]

The overturned relations of gender, family, and politics in Xie Jin's melodramatic films mark the end of the Mao era and the collapse of its moral regime. Yet the gender practices and imaginations in the Mao era were neither a homogeneous unity nor subject to a monolithic state power. These imaginations didn't die with the end of the Cold War and the global setbacks in twentieth-century socialist movement, but continued to inspire us to rethink the relations between the public and the private, the political and the personal. The innovations of revolutionary melodrama examined in this essay remind us not only of the resilient political life of melodrama but also of socialist gender practices and imaginations that gesture toward the potentialities for alternative approaches to differences. The affective space around the cinematic screen also raises a powerful critique of liberal politics based on the assumption of autonomous individuals and indicates a collectivity not subsumed under a uniform state power but one of political potential for imagining an alternative socialism.

The author would like to thank Andrew F. Jones, Linda Williams, and two anonymous readers for their invaluable feedback and insight at different stages of writing.

XIAO LIU is an assistant professor in the Department of East Asian Studies at McGill University. She works in the areas of Chinese cinema, media history, and media theory. She is currently completing a book that examines the transformations in media practices and aesthetics in relation to the cybernetic and information discourses in post-Mao China.

Notes

1   Continuous revolution from the 1911 Revolution to the May Fourth Movement (1915–1923) and on to the CCP-led communist revolution has been the major narrative line of Chinese history in the textbooks of the PRC. With the end of the Mao era, however, this narrative of continuous revolution came under question. By the mid-1990s, Li Zehou and Liu Zaifu's call for "bidding farewell to revolution"—a call to stop using revolution as a theme to interpret modern Chinese history—became emblematic of the transformations of China's political climate with the country's accelerated marketization. See Li and Liu.

2   See Croll; Honig; Honig and Hershatter.

3   See Dong; Hershatter, *Gender* and *Women*; Lingzhen Wang, "Other Genders"; Zheng Wang, "'State'"; Xueping Zhong and Wang Zheng, et al.

4   The first female tractor driver, named Liang Jun, recalled that she was the only female attending the driver's training class. For an account of these socialist new women and their relation to the international circulation of images of Soviet female stars, see Chen.

5   See Diamant; Wang Zheng, "'State.'"

6   See Hershatter, *Gender* and *Women.*

7   See Vogel; Weeks.

8   *Liangxian* literally means "striking a pose." In Peking opera, the leading actors are supposed to make a statue-like pose before they appear on or leave the stage.

9   Laozi was an ancient philosopher of circa sixth-century BCE China and the putative author of the Daoist classic *Dao De Jing* (*Tao Te Ching*). The text raises the well-known concepts of "naturalness" (*ziran*) and "nonaction" (*wuwei*). There is a long tradition of commentaries on the text from various perspectives and periods. The reading of *Dao De Jing* as a text about the art of ruling and political philosophy is an important aspect of this commentary tradition.

10   Kuomintang (KMT/Nationalist Party) is the ruling party of the Republic of China, founded in 1912; it unified much of China in 1928. It retreated to Taiwan in 1949 after being defeated by the CCP during the Chinese Civil War in the 1940s. The KMT led by Chiang Kai-shek in the CCP's official history was condemned as a counterrevolutionary reactionary force.

11   For more discussion on Xie Jin's films in the post-Mao late 1970s and 1980s, see Ning Ma; Browne.

Works Cited   Basinger, Jeanine. *A Woman's View: How Hollywood Spoke to Women, 1930–1960*. New York: Knopf, 1993.

Braester, Yomi, and Tina Mai Chen. "Film in the People's Republic of China, 1949–1979: The Missing Years?" *Journal of Chinese Cinemas* 5.1 (2011): 5–12.

Brooks, Peter. *The Melodramatic Imagination: Balzac, Henry James, Melodrama, and the Mode of Excess*. New Haven: Yale UP, 1995.

Browne, Nick. "Society and Subjectivity: On the Political Economy of Chinese Melodrama." *Melodrama: Stage, Picture, Screen*. Ed. Jacky Bratton, Jim Cook, and Christine Gledhill. London: BFI, 1994. 167–81.

Chan, Jessica. "Translating 'Montage': The Discreet Attractions of Soviet Montage for Chinese Revolutionary Cinema." *Journal of Chinese Cinemas* 5.3 (2011): 197–218.

Chen, Tina Mai. "Socialism, Aestheticized Bodies, and International Circuits of Gender: Soviet Female Film Stars in the People's Republic of China, 1949–1969." *Journal of the Canadian Historical Association* 18.2 (2007): 53–80.

Chi, Robert. "*The Red Detachment of Women*: Resenting, Regendering, Remembering." *Chinese Films in Focus: 25 New Takes*. Ed. Chris Berry. London: BFI, 2003. 152–59.

Croll, Elisabeth. *Changing Identities of Chinese Women: Rhetoric, Experience, and Self-Perception in Twentieth-Century China*. Hong Kong: Zed, 1995.

Dai Jinhua. *Jingcheng tuwei: Nvxing, dianying, wenxue* [*Breaking Out of the City of Mirrors: Women, Film, Literature*]. Beijing: Zuojia, 1995.

Diamant, Neil. *Revolutionizing the Family: Politics, Love, and Divorce in Urban and Rural China, 1949–1968*. Berkeley: U of California P, 2000.

Donald, Stephanie. *Public Secrets, Public Spaces: Cinema and Civility in China*. Lanham: Rowman and Littlefield, 2000.

Dong Limin. "Historicizing Gender: A Study of Chinese Women's Liberation from 1949 to 1966." *differences* 24.2 (2013): 93–108.

Elsaesser, Thomas. "Tales of Sound and Fury: Observations on Family Melodrama." Landy 68–97.

Hansen, Miriam. "The Mass Production of the Senses: Classical Cinema as Vernacular Modernism." *Reinventing Film Studies*. Ed. Christine Gledhill and Linda Williams. New York: Oxford UP, 2000.

Harris, Kristine. "Re-makes/Re-models: *The Red Detachment of Women* between Stage and Screen." *Opera Quarterly* 26.2–3 (2010): 316–42.

Hershatter, Gail. *The Gender of Memory: Rural Women and China's Collective Past*. Berkeley: U of California P, 2011.

—————. *Women in China's Long Twentieth Century*. Berkeley: U of California P, 2007.

Hershatter, Gail, and Wang Zheng. "Chinese History: A Useful Category of Gender Analysis." *American Historical Review* 113.5 (2008): 1404–21.

Honig, Emily. "Iron Girls Revisited: Gender and the Politics of Work in the Cultural Revolution, 1966–76." *Re-Drawing Boundaries: Work, Households, and Gender in China.* Ed. Barbara Entwisle and Gail Henderson. Berkeley: U of California P, 2000. 97–110.

Honig, Emily, and Gail Hershatter. *Personal Voices: Chinese Women in the 1980s.* Stanford: Stanford UP, 1988.

Jones, Andrew F. *Developmental Fairy Tales: Evolutionary Thinking and Modern Chinese Culture.* Cambridge: Harvard UP, 2011.

Landy, Marcia. Introduction. Landy 13–30.

Landy, Marcia, ed. *Imitations of Life: A Reader on Film and Television Melodrama.* Detroit: Wayne State UP, 1991.

Li Xiaojiang. *Xiawa de tansuo* [*The Exploration of Eve*]. Zhengzhou: Henan renmin chubanshe, 1988.

Li Zehou and Liu Zaifu. *Gaobie geming* [*Farewell to Revolution*]. Xianggang: Tiandi tushu youxian gongsi, 1995.

Liang Xin. "Renwu, qingjie, aiqing ji qita" ["Characters, Plot, Love, and Others"]. *Hongse niangzijun: Cong juben dao yingpian* ["Red Detachment of Women": From Script to Film]. Collectively edited. Beijing: Zhongguo dianying chubanshe, 1964. 228–50.

Ma, Ning. "Spatiality and Subjectivity in Xie Jin's Film Melodrama of the New Period." *New Chinese Cinemas: Forms, Identities, Politics.* Ed. Nick Browne, Paul Pickowicz, Vivian Sochack, and Esther Yau. New York: Cambridge UP, 1994. 15–39.

Mao Jian. "Gender Politics and the Crisis of Socialist Aesthetics: The 'Room' in *Woman Basketball Player No. 5.*" *Debating the Socialist Legacy and Capitalist Globalization in China.* Ed. Xueping Zhong and Ban Wang. New York: Palgrave Macmillan, 2014. 73–84.

Marchetti, Gina. "*Two Stage Sisters*: The Blossoming of a Revolutionary Aesthetic." *Jump Cut* 34 (1989): 95–106.

McGrath, Jason. "Cultural Revolution Model Opera Films and the Realist Tradition in Chinese Cinema." *Opera Quarterly* 26.2–3 (2010): 343–76.

Pickowicz, Paul. "Melodramatic Representation and the 'May Fourth' Tradition of Chinese Cinema." *From May Fourth to June Fourth: Fiction and Film in Twentieth-Century China.* Ed. Ellen Widmer and David Der-wei Wang. Cambridge: Harvard UP, 1993. 295–326.

Red Detachment of Women. 1961. Dir. Xie Jin. Qilu yinxiang chubanshe, 2004.

Sister Flowers. 1933. Dir. Zheng Zhengqiu. Qilu yinxiang chubanshe, 2006.

Vogel, Lise. *Marxism and the Oppression of Women: Toward a Unitary Theory.* Leiden: Brill, 2013.

Wang, Ban. *The Sublime Figure of History: Aesthetics and Politics in Twentieth-Century China.* Stanford: Stanford UP, 1997.

Wang, Lingzhen. "Gender and Sexual Differences in 1980s China: Introducing Li Xiaojiang." *differences* 24.2 (2013): 9–20.

——————. "Other Genders, Other Sexualities: Chinese Differences." *differences* 24.2 (2013): 1–7.

Wang, Qi. "Those Who Lived in a Wallpapered Home: The Historical Space of the Socialist Chinese Counter-Espionage Film." *Journal of Chinese Cinemas* 5.1 (2011): 55–71.

Wang Zheng. "Call Me *Qingnian* but Not *Funv*: A Maoist Youth in Retrospect." *Feminist Studies* 27.1 (2001): 9–34.

———. "'State Feminism'? Gender and Socialist State Formation in Maoist China." *Feminist Studies* 31.3 (2005): 519–51.

Weeks, Kathi. *The Problem with Work: Feminism, Marxism, Antiwork Politics, and Postwork Imaginaries.* Durham: Duke UP, 2011.

Williams, Linda. "Film Bodies: Gender, Genre, and Excess." *Film Quarterly* 44.4 (1991): 2–13.

———. *Playing the Race Card: Melodrama of Black and White from Uncle Tom to O. J. Simpson.* Princeton: Princeton UP, 2001.

Xing Zuwen. "Woguo dianyingzhong zichanjieji sixiang biaoxian de yige genyuan" ["The Root of Bourgeoisie Consciousness in the Films of Our Country"]. 1958. *Zhongguo dianying yanjiu ziliao: 1949–1979* [*Research Materials on Chinese Film, 1949–1979*]. Ed. Wu Di. Beijing: Wenhua yishu chubanshe, 2006. 201–14.

Yeh, Emilie Yueh-Yu. "A Small History of *Wenyi*." *The Oxford Handbook of Chinese Cinemas.* Ed. Carlos Rojas and Eileen Cheng-Yin Chow. Oxford: Oxford UP, 2013. 225–39.

Yuan Wenshu. "Ping yingpian Hongse nianzijun" ["A Review of *Red Detachment of Women*"]. *Hongse niangzijun: Cong juben dao yingpian* [*"Red Detachment of Women": From Script to Film*]. Collectively edited. Beijing: Zhongguo dianying chubanshe, 1964. 414–30.

Zhang, Xudong. *Chinese Modernism in the Era of Reforms: Cultural Fever, Avant-Garde Fiction, and the New Chinese Cinema.* Durham: Duke UP, 1997.

Zhang, Zhen. *An Amorous History of the Silver Screen: Shanghai Cinema, 1896–1937.* Chicago: U of Chicago P, 2006.

———. "Urban Dreamscape, Phantom Sisters, and the Identity of an Emergent Art." *The Urban Generation: Chinese Cinema and Society at the Turn of the Twenty-First Century.* Ed. Zhen Zhang. Durham: Duke UP, 2007. 344–87.

Zhong, Xueping, and Wang Zheng et al., eds. *Some of Us: Chinese Women Growing Up in the Mao Era.* New Brunswick: Rutgers UP, 2001.

Zhu Dake. "Lun Xie Jin dianying moshi de quexian" ["On the Defect of the Mode of Xie Jin's Films"]. *Wenhui Bao* 8 July 1986. Rpt. in *Bainian zhongguo dianying lilun Wenxuan* [*Selected Essays on Chinese Film Theory in the 20th Century*]. Vol. 2. Ed. Ya Ping. Beijing: Wenhua yishu chubanshe, 2002. 235–37.

Dogville; or, On Ambiguity and Oppression: A Beauvoirian Reading

The film *Dogville*, by the polemical Danish director Lars von Trier, has a great deal to say on the subject of freedom and the role of ambiguity in understanding oppression. In order to discuss the film and its philosophical content, I will make use of some of the main ideas that shape existentialist thought, especially as they are fleshed out in the theory of Simone de Beauvoir and in her lucid and revealing treatment of the problem of oppression and its counterpart, freedom. Relying primarily but not entirely on the theory of Beauvoir, I will use "film as an example in a philosophical argument" by using "a philosophical theory as a means of interpreting films," a method described by Cynthia Freeland and Thomas Wartenberg in *Philosophy and Film* (8). First, though, it is important to clarify the value of using *Dogville* to illustrate these ideas. My claim, following Freeland and Wartenberg but also Beauvoir herself, as I will show, is that such an exemplification of a philosophical theory through film is transformational in that it leaves neither the theory nor the viewer's experience intact. The dynamics of mutual interpretation allow for a rich and complex modification of both. In his later article, "Beyond *Mere* Illustration," Wartenberg

Volume 26, Number 3   DOI 10.1215/10407391-3340408

contributes to this understanding by refining his argument, compellingly demonstrating that film not only exemplifies but can in fact *be* philosophy. In short, he argues that the use of film to "illustrate" philosophical ideas should not be dismissed by philosophers or film theorists as vacuous: sometimes, Wartenberg argues, what appears merely as an illustration of philosophy produces a real change in the philosophical theories themselves (20). In order to prove this, he reflects on different ways of illustrating texts. He shows us that some kinds of illustration are not marginal to or contingent with respect to texts but are, in fact, concretizations of abstract principles, capable of contributing significantly to the enrichment of these principles. Taking Chaplin's *Modern Times* as an example, Wartenberg shows that certain images in the movie actually embody Marx's ideas about alienation and give them a concrete sense that, it seems, could not have been arrived at through reading or thinking about Marx's theoretical reflections alone:

> *The film illustrates the mechanization of the human body by the assembly line when it shows Charlie's arms continuing to rotate in the tightening motion even when the assembly line is shut down. [. . .] Although Marx claimed that workers' bodies became machines, he did not provide a detailed account of what about factories do[es] this, nor how such mechanization is registered on and by the human body and the human mind. Part of the achievement of the film is to present a specific view of how such mechanization takes place, particularly in the new context of the assembly line. (29)*

Wartenberg concludes by emphasizing how such cinematic illustrations don't just replicate but actualize and enact the philosophical argument, enhancing its meanings and opening up more and new perspectives on abstract philosophical principles.[1]

Until very recently, film studies had not referred to Beauvoir's philosophy. That changed in 2012, however, with *Existentialism and Contemporary Cinema: A Beauvoirian Perspective*, which set out to do justice to one of the first thinkers to reflect on the "gendered 'othering' gaze" (Boulé and Tidd 1). Boulé and Tidd's introduction reflects on the possible reasons for Beauvoir's striking absence from the extensive history of feminist media studies. Among these possible reasons, the authors point out Beauvoir's reluctance to see psychoanalysis as the main resource for analyzing film as well as the fact that her contribution to structuralist anthropology was generally overlooked, so that feminist film theorists relied instead on what they found in Roland Barthes's later semiotic analyses. Even within the latest phenomenological turn in film theory, Beauvoir appears to have remained marginal. Boulé and Tidd expose the promising potential of Beauvoirian thought for film theory: aside from the clear connection between existentialism and the nature of film, best explained by its "phenomenological focus [. . .] on temporally situated 'lived experience' and its recognition of the spectacular dynamic of self and other relationships" (3), Beauvoir's idea that essence is always preceded by a temporally located and concretely situated embodied existence brought her to recognize cinema as an "authentic art form" (3), a new form of expression with a high potential to foster liberation.[2] In other words, Beauvoir, like Wartenberg, takes concretization—which is at the heart of the cinematic experience—to be in itself an irreducible part of much of philosophical thinking and potentially a powerful political tool for either reinstating oppression or delivering liberation.[3] This may, in fact, be why Beauvoir criticizes film throughout *The Second Sex*: she denounces it precisely for how it is used—in many of its Hollywood instances, for example—to reproduce systems of oppression and domination instead of opposing them.

In the following, I join these scholars in their attempt to "demonstrate the relevance of Beauvoirian existentialism (understood in its broadest sense) to film studies in the postmodern context" (Boulé and Tidd 10), showing how an analysis informed by Beauvoir might offer a new perspective on von Trier's film, one replete with philosophical and political meanings.

Dogville

Dogville tells the story of the beautiful fugitive Grace (Nicole Kidman), who arrives in the isolated township of Dogville while escaping from a team of gangsters. With some encouragement from Tom (Paul Bettany), the self-appointed town spokesman, the little community agrees to hide her; in return, Grace agrees to work for them. When the gangsters begin searching for her, however, the people of Dogville demand a better deal in exchange for the risk they run in hiding her.

Although *Dogville* originally constituted the first film in von Trier's USA: Land of Opportunities trilogy, Ilana Shiloh rightly counts the movie as an addition to the films in his Golden Heart trilogy, which includes *Breaking the Waves, The Idiots,* and *Dancer in the Dark.* Shiloh argues that *Dogville,* like *Breaking the Waves* and *Dancer in the Dark,* is a Christian movie, picking up the issue of self-sacrifice and suffering as the ultimate form of redemption. Unlike the others, though, *Dogville* ends with a sharp twist that allows it to resist becoming a film on Christian values and turns it instead into a movie that fiercely questions these values, even proposing revenge and the fight against evil as an ethical response. Carleen Mandolfo makes a similar argument, bringing these same three movies together in order to show "an appropriately complex understanding of Judeo-Christian models of salvation" (285).

The movie has evoked numerous emotional responses, mainly due to its blatant violence, that strongly involves the spectator. Caroline Bainbridge develops the argument about the complicity that von Trier's films create between film and spectator by pointing out von Trier's frequent use of filmic techniques that "confound our familiarity with fictional forms in cinema" (394). Nikolaj Lübecker also cites this complicity to justify his argument that *Dogville* is a film about the spectator rather than about the main character, Grace (159). Lübecker, like Bainbridge, believes that the film uses its cinematic strategies—in this case, a rupture between the cinematic form used throughout the movie and what is used at the very end of the movie—in order to actively manipulate the spectator. These film strategies, together with the use of "unrestricted violence" (160), pull us in as spectators and help to make us part of the violent plot. This is a "feel-bad" movie, Lübecker argues, that manipulates the spectator in order to "bring out 'the beast' in us" (159). It does this by offering us a cathartic experience to which we find ourselves strongly drawn even though it is our own suffering toward which we are being dragged. *Dogville*, in short, heavily involves the spectator by promising us a catharsis we in fact experience, but not without an accompanying punishment for wanting the catharsis to begin with. Nevertheless, Lübecker concludes, *Dogville* uses this combination of catharsis and punishment to "turn the cinematic experience into a visceral practice that pushes the spectator towards ethical reflection" (167).

Robert Sinnerbrink points out that critiques of *Dogville* have been, to a very large degree, emotionally founded, some of them even doubting whether the film can be viewed as a political film at all because it removes itself from any concrete political or historical context (turning itself instead into a conservative tale on absolute evil) and because of the extreme violence, mainly against women, that it presents and frequently seems to endorse. Von Trier's misogyny has been recognized and criticized by various authors,[4] which is one of the reasons a Beauvoirian analysis of this film is particularly challenging. I will, in fact, be using Beauvoirian concepts to view the movie as a critique of violence and women's oppression rather than as a film that merely reproduces violence and misogyny uncritically or without context. It is important to stress again here the ways in which *Dogville* is, as Shiloh and Mandolfo rightly argue, different from *Breaking the Waves* and *Dancer in the Dark*—even though its self-sacrificing female main character is made a victim of the crudest and most despicable violence throughout the film. The difference is mainly in Grace's final response to this violence, when she decides to murder the whole town before she abandons it, a reaction that clearly and emphatically uses a violent and bloody revenge to fight back against violence and oppression. On this conspicuous difference between Grace and the female protagonists of the other films in von Trier's Golden Heart trilogy, Bell argues that "Grace surpasses [von Trier's] preoccupations with madness and disabilities while remaining passionate about problems of ethical and moral agency. Where Bess, Karen and Selma were von Trier's wretched victims, Grace is his *avenging angel* who, with a casual arc of her manicured hand, threatens to sweep away a decade of obsession with naïvely feminine piety. But not, of course, until she too has been tortured" (216, my emphasis).

I approach the concept of revenge from a Beauvoirian perspective.[5] I thus agree with Sinnerbrink on the possibilities of reading *Dogville* as a political and philosophical document as opposed to a film that can only be seen as a conservative, misogynistic creation that reproduces and participates in violence. This reading also concurs with Mandolfo's in considering *Dogville* a film in search of a new female subject, one who not only is not (unlike other female characters in von Trier's filmography) a symbol of self-sacrifice, madness, or a feeble mind[6] but who challenges violence with agency and is even ready to eradicate suffering "by force—if necessary" (287).

Dogville's *Cinematic Form*

Dogville is filmed in a theatrical, quasi-Brechtian way (Sinnerbrink 3). The scene is unchanging throughout—the town with its few houses—and the minimalist production even renounces any view of the exterior façades of the houses, providing us instead with a continuous, almost pathologically voyeuristic inside view of the lives and deeds of the different characters. One reason *Dogville* is so well suited to (mainly existentialist) philosophical analysis has to do with the style in which it was filmed. Recalling some of the precepts of Dogme 95, the movie is minimalist, and the shooting is done on location and always in the present, avoiding temporal or spatial alienation. In his analysis of Dogme 95, Jean-Pierre Geuens describes the filmmaking that adheres to it as emphasizing authenticity and showing contempt for technologies that alienate the director from his or her work or the spectator from the film. By privileging the here and now, Dogme filmmaking allows spectators to be less occupied with reacting to movie techniques and more engaged in truly meeting the "world full of ambiguity and manifold diversity" (192) presented in the movie. According to Geuens, Dogme also privileges the process of filmmaking rather than the final, fixed product, making room for a welcoming of the unexpected: "In this kind of filmmaking, then, instead of putting emphasis on the constant repetition of the same (a mechanistic system sure to crush the spirit of the best individuals) Dogma [*sic*] affirms the ever-changing reality of the film work on the set" (200). Koutsourakis, in his analysis of *Dogville*, also identifies these principles in the form of the film, stressing that "the fusion of image, narrated text, and fixed narrative space" are used here in order to "negate the singularity of meaning" and produce a polyvocal space that invites ethical and political reflection and discussion.

These principles clearly reveal the existentialist character of Dogme. In "The Case for 'Thinking as a Filmmaker,'" Elyse Pepper argues that *Dogville* can be extremely useful as a model for the writing of a legal statement of facts. She bases her argument partly on the movie's formal presentation: the bare location makes the spectator feel part of the plot, a participant instead of a voyeur: "The juxtaposition of the film's inflammatory substance with its minimalist form makes the audience experience the incident—participate, rather than observe—in much the way legal writers should inspire their readers" (173). The same reasons can be used to explain the value of the film as a (mainly phenomenological and existentialist) philosophical document: the ideas it proposes reach us almost immediately, since they are presented almost "naked," with very little filmmaking paraphernalia (for instance, there are no special effects and the stage is almost completely bare). Koutsourakis agrees that this minimalism facilitates philosophical and sociological reflection on the part of the spectator. Nevertheless, he believes that the reason why such minimalist aesthetics—in the form, for instance, of *Dogville*'s bare stage or the use of a theatricalized locus—contribute to the spectator's reflection is not, as Pepper argues, that they create the experience of an absence of boundaries, of *merging* between the spectator and the film, but rather quite the opposite: it is by *estranging* the spectator from the story that this reflection is enabled. In Koutsourakis's words, "[B]y restricting the action in a bare stage, the films aim at preventing the audience from being completely absorbed by the story. Instead, the viewers are urged to focus on the examination of the portrayed relationships, and their susceptibility to change. [. . .] In these respects, the minimalist aesthetics of *Dogville* [. . .] and their impoverished conditions of production are the logical continuation of von Trier's critique of the cinematic institution through the Dogme project." Paradoxically, it is possible to describe *Dogville*'s form as based in the production of both proximity and estrangement. On the one hand, the lack of technological paraphernalia brings us extraordinarily close to the "bare facts" and allows us to concentrate on the here and now of the story. On the other hand, this proximity is always limited by the bare, stage-like location, which, in fact, prevents us from totally losing ourselves in the story and provides a certain distance, a safe perspective from which we can examine the story and the relations it presents without being totally absorbed into them.

This seems to be precisely how Beauvoir, like other phenomenological and existentialist philosophers, thinks philosophy has to be done: to think philosophically, we must ambiguously both merge with and estrange ourselves from our world and others. According to this principle, philosophy cannot be done from a position of complete absorption nor from one of complete alienation. We need to be both engaged with and at a distance from our object of research. This is one of the reasons Beauvoir has been recognized as presenting complex philosophical ideas in her plays and novels, not just in her explicitly philosophical texts. Fiction allows Beauvoir to make us *almost become* others, amply identifying with those others but also always kept at the appropriate distance for philosophical reflection to be possible.[7]

The Gift

An analysis of *Dogville*'s themes can begin with the problem of *receiving*, which Tom is trying to analyze at the town's assembly just before Grace appears.[8] Tom thinks that the people of Dogville do not know how to receive; they do not know how to accept a gift. This is why Grace's arrival makes him so happy: finally, there is a real test case for his theory.[9] Grace is the present that Dogville will have to learn to accept.[10] Here begins von Trier's critique of Western society and Western values: we (Westerners) are not capable of receiving; we are not willing to accept anything as a gift of grace (and, of course, there is nothing accidental about the fugitive's name). A present is not something we can live with, which is why we waste life (when it is given as a present), continually trying to buy and sell it. The people of Dogville do not think they lack for anything, and from the moment that they receive the present, their lives become complicated. We have learned that we must pay for things, that that is the only way they can be ours, that we can own and dominate them. A gift, then, is paradoxically not really ours. If it is given by grace, we do not have the right, so to speak, to dominate or control it. Better to pay for things so that they can really belong to us.[11]

So the people of Dogville decide to pay for Grace: they pay for her work, even though they do not necessarily need it. Von Trier shows us here a perfect example of the incongruity of consumer society. New, previously unrecognized needs are created by the people of Dogville. Suddenly, everyone needs Grace: like our smartphones, nonexistent until so recently but without which we now cannot function, Grace becomes indispensable to the people of Dogville and no one can live without her help, even though until this moment she has been entirely unknown to them.

Turning Grace from a present into property that has been paid for, then, provides the people of Dogville with a legitimate reason for domination: if they have bought Grace, Grace belongs to them, and the power they can exercise over her is limitless. The question that may be naïvely asked here is why Dogville sees itself as having the right to exploit Grace beyond the limits of the work she is supposed to do and for which Dogville is paying her. Grace is not fairly remunerated for her work to begin with, and on top of that, she is exploited in every way possible by the people of Dogville. Von Trier is reminding us here that power corrupts, that we cannot innocently believe we would be able to limit ourselves to "fair" exploitation; there is no fair use of the other. Moreover, I see von Trier as telling us something about how exploitation is always easier—practically easier and morally less bothersome—when the exploited is perfectly other, a stranger, a fugitive, with no means and no protection.

Grace is indeed the paradigm of the perfect other—of the other in general and of the feminine other in particular. This is why she is the perfect object of domination. The way in which the people of Dogville enslave Grace is clearly reminiscent of the way in which women have been exploited and dominated throughout the history of patriarchal society. She is the almost unpaid worker performing Sisyphean household labors. Nobody in Dogville really knows what her actual capacities are. Nobody asks, and nobody really cares. In Dogville, only men can be writers or doctors. It is clear from the beginning that if Grace wants to be kept on as a refugee in Dogville, the only thing she will be allowed to do will be poorly paid, almost enslaving domestic work. This, however, is only part of the domination to which Grace is subject in the town. She soon becomes the object of sexual exploitation as well, and nobody in Dogville (except for Grace's beloved, Tom) refrains from using her body. Grace is raped repeatedly and is finally put in chains when she is caught trying to escape the town. This last punishment is carried out in a clearly grotesque, exaggerated, and unrealistic way: the chains that are supposed to keep Grace from running away are totally disproportionate to her size. They are not made for humans (and certainly not for someone as poor and weak as Grace); they would be better suited to holding a wild, dangerous beast—which is exactly what the people of Dogville are trying to make the fugitive into: a beast, a dehumanized human. The bestialization of Grace makes it easier to exercise domination over her. That domination becomes a form of power that is exercised on the body of the victim, effected precisely through the negation, corruption, and humiliation of that body.

Grace becomes Dogville's scapegoat, the place where the people of Dogville can expiate their guilt and frustrations. Yet these are not especially bad people. In this respect, von Trier seems to make a point about the banality of evil.[12] Dogville is a regular town (in fact, it could be seen as the stereotype, the paradigm, of the regular town), and the people who live there are simple, well-intentioned, respectful, authority-following people. They are certainly not monsters. Nevertheless, they end up performing monstrous, unforgivable actions that (as von Trier clearly wants to show) derive not so much from their evil characters as from a typical personality constitutive of our modern capitalistic, patriarchal societies.[13]

Adorno's Authoritarian Personality

On this point, it may be useful to bring in Theodor Adorno's analysis of the authoritarian personality (see Adorno et al.). In Adorno's view, the authoritarian personality develops as a consequence of a violent and monopolized capitalism that leaves the majority of people almost powerless in the face of the administrative technologies that control their lives. This individual is highly anxious precisely because of this feeling of impotence that accompanies his or her precarious modern existence. This person is even more anxious, though, Adorno argues, when confronting the irreducible freedom that he or she still possesses, even if almost imperceptibly, despite the attempts of capitalist society to erase it completely. The authoritarian personality tries to find a way out of this anxiety by identifying with and endorsing the element that provoked the anxiety in the first place: authority. Authority, then, becomes the medium through which the impotent individual recovers strength and power; becoming an authority is what redeems the individual, so to speak, from the total loss of self brought on by anxiety.

The people of Dogville display some of the most important features of the authoritarian personality as described by Adorno:[14] a punitive attitude toward criminals, a dislike of minority groups, an instrumental attitude toward work, manipulative sexual relations, hostility to introspection, and a clear reluctance to recognize themselves as free agents responsible for their own actions and decisions (Adorno et al. 228). The authoritarian personality, Adorno remarks, eagerly defers responsibility and gives someone else the power to decide on his or her behalf. (This someone else may be a leader, but it may also be a group; in such a case, the group acts precisely to erase the individuality and free agency of the individuals taking part in it.) The people of Dogville give that authority to Tom and make decisions regarding Grace's situation only when they are gathered together at their weekly assembly. No one is really willing to dissent openly from the decisions of the majority. Decisions are, in general, made unanimously. Nobody is really an individual in Dogville; nobody really wants (or dares) to question authority. There are no free agents in the town, or rather, paradoxically, the only free agent seems to be Grace, the fugitive, the other, a free agent even while she is being enslaved, chained, and bestialized by the "humble" people of Dogville.

The people of Dogville, it seems, have never felt as powerful as when Grace comes to town. The feeling of superiority, strength, and authority they experience in dominating Grace provides them with a previously unknown sense of invulnerability. With the help of Adorno's analysis, however, we can understand this feeling as a symptom of the opposite reality: the authoritarian personality is, in fact, the projection of the weakest, most impoverished, and most obviously unfree personality. The illusory and deceptive character of the premise according to which power or freedom can be achieved through oppression can be best explained, though, through Beauvoir's philosophical ideas on the subject.

Beauvoir on Becoming Moral: The Importance of the Other's Freedom

Beauvoir's *Pyrrhus et Cinéas* and her later *Ethics of Ambiguity* and *The Second Sex* constitute central pillars in the development of her ethics. These works together elaborate a theory of ambiguity and its cardinal place in the formation of moral subjects, although it is mainly throughout *The Second Sex* that the embodied character of this subjectivity is developed and emphasized. Beauvoir agrees with Sartre that all subjects possess a kind of freedom—that is, ontological freedom[15]—that is responsible for making the world human. Thus, Beauvoir argues, similar to Sartre's argument in *Being and Nothingness*, we are condemned to be free:[16] "Every man is originally free" (Beauvoir, *Ethics* 25). Through ontological freedom, we disclose the world and give it meaning (12, 74). This ontological freedom can be denied by the subject, however, through an act of bad faith.[17] Both Sartre and Beauvoir recognize that we can be blind to our freedom, that we can attempt to escape from the responsibility implied by it. Making myself aware of my own freedom is described by Beauvoir in *The Ethics of Ambiguity* as a different kind of freedom, in this case a moral freedom that is not pure, irreducible, ontological freedom (which is, in fact, void of ethical meaning), but freedom made conscious, the freedom expressed by the desire to disclose being: "[T]o wish for the disclosure of the world and to assert oneself as free are one and the same movement" (24). This is the freedom that is created when we take full responsibility for our inescapable, ontological freedom (25, 26); this is the freedom that turns us into moral persons. At this point, Beauvoir radically separates herself from Sartrean thought. The separation becomes even sharper, though, when she argues for moral freedom as deriving precisely from the relationship with the other, from the connection with another subject. This implies not only that the other is not my enemy, as claimed in Sartrean thought, but that she or he is absolutely necessary to my moral freedom—in Beauvoir's words, "[T]he existence of others as a freedom defines my situation and is even the condition of my own freedom" (91). What Beauvoir means here is that I can only be free when another free subject recognizes my freedom. Only when the other as free subject encounters me in my own freedom and reveals it can I see myself as in possession of moral freedom. Thus, in order for me to gain my moral freedom, I need to struggle for others to achieve their freedom, since only the other as free subject can set me free.

Beauvoir argues for the recognition of the other-as-subject as nothing less than the basic condition for my becoming a free subject myself (*Pyrrhus* 299). In order for me to be free, my freedom must be recognized by another (free) subjectivity: "[W]e need the other in order for our existence to become grounded and necessary" (290, my translation). Only the other can provide meaning to my acts, to my project; we are dependent on the other's freedom: "[O]nly man can be an enemy for man; only he can rob him of the meaning of his acts and his life because it also belongs only to him alone to confirm it in its existence, to recognize it in actual fact as a freedom" (*Ethics* 82). Avoiding oppression and struggling to free the other is the only way to achieve my own free subjectivity.[18]

Oppression: Canceling Ambiguity

Confining ourselves to an illusion that we are pure subjectivities, pure freedom, with no roots in the world of materiality and objects, inevitably brings us to project our own abject immanent parts—from which we cannot escape—onto the other, making the other into a total other with no possibility of developing freedom, on the one hand, and, on the other, apparently but illusorily making ourselves into pure transcendent subjects. This, in Beauvoir's view, is the main cause of oppression and consequently the main obstacle to our development as moral subjects. "The tyrant asserts himself as a transcendence; he considers others as pure immanences: he thus arrogates to himself the right to treat them like cattle. We see the sophism on which his conduct is based: of the ambiguous condition which is that of all men, he retains for himself the only aspect of a transcendence which is capable of justifying itself; for the others, the contingent and unjustified aspect of immanence" (*Ethics* 102). The male oppression of women across history has functioned precisely in this way, in Beauvoir's view, and this is, in fact, one of her main arguments throughout *The Second Sex*: man has projected immanence onto woman, falsely believing that he is absolute transcendence while women are absolute others, pure immanence, pure flesh.

Men have projected onto women their own abjected parts, their fleshly existence, which is, in fact, their own strangeness, which is wrongly taken to threaten their absolute freedom. Men have failed to understand that by misrecognizing their own ambiguity and transferring onto the woman-other the immanence that is part of their own subjectivity, they in fact—far from becoming pure transcendence, pure freedom—lose the possibility of being truly free subjects, recognized by a free other who is not reduced to flesh.[19]

Oppression, in Beauvoir's view, is a self-defeating act that leaves me with no possibility of expressing my own moral freedom; making the other free, on the other hand, by recognizing both my own and the other's ambiguity, our complex existence as constituted both by flesh and by freedom, is the only way to become meaningfully free and to achieve morality (*Ethics* 86–87, 91, 95–96).

The struggle to free the other consists mainly in fighting oppression, given that oppression reveals itself precisely in depriving the other of her or his inherent ambiguity by objectifying the other, turning the other into pure immanence. Fighting oppression can even mean depriving the oppressor of his or her own freedom: "We have to respect freedom only when it is intended for freedom, not when it strays, flees itself, and resigns itself. A freedom which is interested only in denying freedom must be denied" (*Ethics* 90–91).

Morality, Freedom, and Authenticity

In Beauvoir's view, moral freedom is a necessary element in achieving authentic subjectivity. Authenticity is clearly linked with freedom chosen consciously and responsibly. For Beauvoir, the pursuit of moral freedom is, in fact, the only way to avoid bad faith and gain an authentic existence. In Kristana Arp's words, "In *The Ethics of Ambiguity* Beauvoir does describe an authentic mode of transcendence: it is what she calls moral freedom, which serves as an ethical ideal that all should seek" (143). Being moral, then, means recognizing ourselves and others as ambiguous and as free subjects; this is the only meaning of being authentic. Oppressing the other by thinking of myself as pure transcendence, denying my own ambiguity and the ambiguity of others, means deceiving *myself*, stripping myself of all possibility of authenticity. Ontological freedom as the theoretical possibility of gaining moral freedom always remains, but when it is not fleshed out as moral freedom, it is meaningless.

This kind of deception, through inauthentic behavior, is typical of the oppression that men exercise over women. Based on Hegel's dialectic of master and slave, Beauvoir insists that, contrary to the eventual reciprocity that Hegel's dialectic is supposed to bring about, men's positioning of women as their absolute other cancels dialectics and with it the possibility for both men and women to live an authentic existence and to develop moral freedom (*Second* 141). The firm connections between authenticity, the recognition of ambiguity, and moral freedom expressed in Beauvoir's commentaries on patriarchy and women's oppression are clearly described by Arp: "*This behavior on the part of men is wrong because it is inauthentic.* They are fleeing the challenge of establishing a free reciprocal relation with another human being by engaging in a relation with a being who is not, like them, a transcendence, but rather a being who is consigned to immanence. *The implication is that one can only achieve authenticity by struggling to maintain free reciprocal relations with others"* (144, my emphasis). Morality, freedom, and authenticity emerge in Beauvoir's philosophy as an indivisible compound of interdependent elements: moral freedom is freedom that needs to be recognized responsibly, consciously, and authentically as necessarily resulting from a moral act, a struggle to ensure that the other can also be morally free by avoiding oppression.

Thus, to deny power to the other[20]—to deny the other, through physical, economic, or political oppression, the possibility of developing moral freedom—is to fail to recognize the subject's ambiguity and to reduce her or him to pure immanence, to a condition in which the subject becomes pure flesh, a body lacking all transcendent meaning, a body with no project, no future. Fredrika Scarth emphasizes the role that turning the subject into pure, immanent body has for this cancellation of the ambiguity of the oppressed when she writes: "Tyranny is maintained not simply by committing violence against the bodies of humans, but by reducing humans to their bodies-as-immanent. [. . .] Tyranny succeeds to the extent that it can make [. . .] those it oppresses [. . .] into abject bodies" (82–83).

This immanent subject cannot recognize its own ambiguity, its freedom; it is a subject deprived of subjectivity, so to speak, who in turn cannot recognize my freedom. In confronting this being, I am turned into an object. Tyranny thus represents for Beauvoir *the cancellation of the subject's ambiguity* by turning the subject into pure immanence, pure flesh with no project and no possibility of transcendence. This is where oppression resides, and—as I have explained above—it has implications for my own condition as tyrant because, in rejecting both my own ambiguity and that of the oppressed, I, as the tyrant, become inauthentic. In Andrew's words: "Oppression is a failure, in bad faith, to recognize the other's freedom. However, *it is also a failure to recognize one's own ambiguity.* The oppressor takes her own freedom as paramount, and acting out of hubris, fails to see that she is nothing but an object without the other's recognition. [. . .] In a sense, the oppressor *uses herself as an object of force"* (36, my emphasis).[21] In other words, no matter how strong or powerful the tyrant becomes, tyranny itself, paradoxically, will rob the tyrant of his or her own subjectivity, leaving the tyrant, finally, as nothing more than a forceful object.

In *The Ethics of Ambiguity,* Beauvoir turns Sartre's concept of freedom inside out, arguing, against Sartre, that the freedom of the other does not turn me into an object, does not deprive me of my freedom. On the contrary, the other must be free, a free agent, an unalienated subject, so that I may be free as well. As long as I am faced with an unfree subject, then my freedom cannot be recognized by the other, which makes me into an object. This turns out to be a critical point for Beauvoir's theory of women's liberation. She argues that enslaving women not only deprives women of freedom but also turns their (male) oppressors into slaves. On this point (as on many others in Beauvoir's philosophical thought), she seems to be much more influenced by Hegel (especially his master-slave dialectic) and Merleau-Ponty than by Sartre.

The Ambiguity of Avenging Oppression

With the help of Beauvoir's reflections, we can better analyze the way in which Grace's oppression by the people of Dogville derives precisely from a cancellation of ambiguity: the more the people of Dogville humiliate Grace by turning her into pure immanent flesh, while themselves apparently remain pure transcendence, the more they seem to us decadent, weak, and enslaved by their new needs, their fears, and their passions.

Grace, for her part, remains stoic. Indeed, stoicism is a recurring theme in the film. Grace's goal through the entirety of her stay in Dogville is to remain untouchable, to control her feelings not by repressing them, but by not even feeling them in the first place. The stoic rationally understands the irrationality of the emotions and in this way manages to not feel them. (The only time Grace feels anything is when her kitschy clay figurines are smashed: an ironic critique of stoicism on von Trier's part?) Thus, the stoic sees him- or herself as being above others, who, unlike the stoic, surrender to the irrationality of passions and emotions and live through them. This is certainly how Grace sees herself (as we witness in the final scenes of the movie); that is, she sees herself as being above the others, who live their lives according to their particular situations and passions. She feels herself superior to all those people of Dogville, poor people who are not able to surpass their fears and frustrations. These are inferior people, according to Grace and her stoic standards, and they deserve pity and understanding, not criticism, and certainly not punishment.[22]

Up to this point, von Trier seems to have given us just another Christian movie about sacrifice, stoicism, and forgiveness in which Grace is the poor lamb (though "sainted" and thus morally superior to the others) willing to sacrifice itself so that the others can expiate their sins. But Grace is only willing to forgive because she is superior to them; she is a better person, a moral human, a free agent. Von Trier appears here once again as the sadistic filmmaker who makes us complicit in his experiment on patriarchal religious domination and in his almost pathological obsession with making women suffer and, through this self-sacrifice, "redeeming" others. Nevertheless, von Trier makes a 180-degree turn at the end of the movie, surprising us with an ambiguous reality in which it is no longer clear at all who is the victim and who is the perpetrator. Grace avenges her rape and her humiliation by absolutely demolishing the town that so violently oppressed her. This act radically changes the meanings of the film, transforming *Dogville* into a rape-revenge movie. (Alexandra Heller-Nicholas, for instance, considers *Dogville* to take part, not unambiguously, in this genre.)

According to *Dogville*, there are crimes and actions that cannot be forgiven and that must be punished, even at the price of turning ourselves into perpetrators. By punishing these kinds of crimes and actions, we are relating to their perpetrators and making them into true free agents. Not punishing them would be an act of arrogance, since it would mean that we consider ourselves owners of moral standards that others cannot be expected to live by. If we forgave them, we would be arrogantly treating these others as unfree agents who could not be expected to act morally. Beauvoir can help us make sense of this. This is the ambiguity of oppression, she argues: we will never be able to get rid of oppression by nonoppressive means, and that is all right, since the freedom of the oppressor is not a real freedom and must not be respected. It is only when we punish oppression that we restore free agency to the oppressors; it is only when we abolish oppression that we set not only the victims but also the oppressors free (*Second* 91). This may be why Beauvoir does not consider revenge to be abhorrent—in addition to the fact that, in her view, it is a powerful, visceral, and fully embodied experience that often characterizes our confrontations with violence and evil and thus deserves to be analyzed phenomenologically rather than automatically dismissed for its problematic ethical and political consequences.

Kruks makes use of Beauvoir's "eye for an eye" in order to build a "phenomenology of revenge" (151–81). Revenge has often been criticized as useless, a passion that has no place among the reasonable ways of condemning or punishing oppression. We are told that nothing is really "gained" through revenge, and yet the desire for it is often powerfully experienced. Kruks argues that although Beauvoir recognizes the self-defeating essence of revenge (it is never fully accomplished, since an equivalent or "direct reversal" of evil is never possible), she also understands that it cannot be eliminated, since it constitutes a powerful reaction by an embodied subjectivity in the face of evil. The fact that we are situated subjects, constantly bonded with others through our flesh, makes us desire revenge not only for ourselves but also on behalf of others who have suffered; the more involved we feel with the bodies of others, the more we feel in our own bodies the atrocities committed against them. For this reason, the dream of purity has to be abandoned with respect to the question of revenge and its presence in political judgments, since the other is never a neutral other, a disembodied, abstract consciousness; rather, it is always a concrete other that evokes embodied responses of hate or desire within us.

But this philosophical analysis of ambiguity and oppression is not enough, alas, to allow us definitively to settle the issue of ambiguity in *Dogville*. We still have to ask whether Grace's own terrible crime, which was clearly carried out in order to punish the cruel barbarity of the people of Dogville, should itself remain unpunished.

I am deeply indebted to the two blind reviewers of this essay, whose constructive advice and comments helped me to transform a narrow Beauvoirian reading of Dogville *into a much broader project.*

SARA COHEN SHABOT is a lecturer in women's and gender studies at the University of Haifa. She specializes in phenomenology, feminist philosophy, and philosophies of the body. Her present research and recent publications address phenomenological perspectives (mainly Beauvoirian) on the maternal embodied subject.

Notes

1 There have been many philosophical analyses of films made in this vein in recent years. Some of them have specifically dealt with the existentialist motifs that are present in those films (Dolske; Landau). These analyses usually attempt to clarify or give a more solid form to philosophical ideas that appear in "raw" form within the movie. Wartenberg's elaboration of what is valuable in these analyses helps to give this kind of philosophical move a more substantial grounding, demonstrating as it does how film does not merely reproduce but can also contribute significantly to the philosophical argument.

2 But how to attach a clear meaning to "authenticity" and the idea of cinema as an "authentic art form" within the postmodern context, where these terms—and, more broadly, the idea of "subjectivity" (i.e., of a coherent and unified subjectivity)—have lost much of their meaning? I believe Beauvoir's existentialism to be useful for dealing with this question, since, as Sonia Kruks demonstrates in her most recent work, Beauvoir is neither a "typical humanist" nor a "typical posthumanist" thinker. Kruks argues that Beauvoir sets up the basis for a new understanding of humanism, one that rejects simple definitions of human existence as intrinsically rational and offers an innovative way of comprehending humanity as inherently ambiguous, rational yet profoundly embedded in corporeality, separated from and yet constantly enmeshed with the other, free but situated, and deeply conflicted in its tendencies to embrace both violence and solidarity. This is by no means, however, an appeal

to posthumanism. Kruks rightly sees in Beauvoir a "new humanist" rather than a posthumanist. She believes that Beauvoir firmly defends core values of humanism, such as those that call for freedom and authenticity and oppose oppression; that she does not share the absolute disenchantment with these values that often characterizes posthumanist thinkers. In Kruks's view, Beauvoir does not stand with those looking for the erasure of the human, which often leads to nihilism; on the contrary, her thought has to be seen as an important contribution to the various existing attempts to widen and enrich the notion of the human, moving toward a positive reconstruction of that notion. Beauvoir's philosophy of ambiguity may be an extraordinary resource in the effort to give life to this new humanism:

> We need a humanism that acknowledges the particularities of a multiplicity of differently embodied lives; a humanism that acknowledges that we are corporeal, sentient, affective beings; that we are beings for whom freedom is not synonymous with rational will; a humanism for which flourishing is not to be confounded with the presence of the individualistic liberal order that has accompanied abstract humanism in the West. We need, in short, the kind of humanism we may draw from Beauvoir: one that affirms the ambiguity of human existence. (32)

3   Beauvoir's belief in the importance of concretizing abstract philosophical principles is crucial to an understanding of her thought. Bonnie Mann, for instance, argues that Beauvoir practices a "political phenomenology" (25), one that consists, in part, in giving a central place to imagination, to imagining the specific voices of others: "[F]or Beauvoir imaginative variation

takes on the form of a kind of relentless migration between various *points of view*, each of them bound by particular interests with ethical consequences. This results in the recently recognized, sometimes maddening polyvocality of Beauvoir's text" (25). This lends even more support to the use of Beauvoirian theory in the philosophical analysis of film.

4   See, for instance, Faber; Mandolfo; Peden. Mandolfo's analysis is especially interesting for the way it points out the direct connection between von Trier's misogyny in *Breaking the Waves* and *Dancer in the Dark* and his treatment of Christianity in those movies, a treatment in which the suffering martyr is gendered female. This move has terrible consequences for women's oppression, Mandolfo argues, since it justifies and endorses the suffering of women as a means of salvation. *Dogville* provides an alternative mainly because it uses more Jewish and apocalyptic conceptions of redemption, according to which justice is more important than suffering or self-sacrifice.

5   This is especially significant because *Dogville*, like von Trier's recent *Nymphomaniac*, has been seen as reworking the rape-and-revenge film genre. See, for instance, Heller-Nicholas. I revisit this in more detail below.

6   An interesting account of Bess in *Breaking the Waves* is Guðmundsdóttir's rendering of her as a Christ figure. Guðmundsdóttir also offers a feminist theological critique of Bess as a character who "abuses" the cross, meaning that the character is used by von Trier as a Christ figure who, instead of challenging patriarchal and religious power by way of "feminizing" Christ, is used to endorse and reproduce the domination,

suffering, and self-sacrifice of the already socially debilitated.

7 Much has been written on the important intertwining of literature and philosophy in Beauvoir. It is clear that there was no sharp difference between philosophical and literary texts for her, and she firmly believed that deep philosophical insights could be presented as successfully through fiction as through classical philosophical essays. On the tight knot connecting literature and philosophy in Beauvoir, see, for instance, Fullbrook; Moi; Mussett; Sirridge.

8 For an illuminating analysis of gift-giving in *Dogville*, see Nobus.

9 Here we can see *Dogville* practicing within itself the concretization exercise that I referred to earlier in explaining Wartenberg's and Beauvoir's approach to interpreting film through philosophy: Grace becomes Tom's "illustration," used to "prove" his argument.

10 On the idea of Grace as a gift, Nobus comments that she "personifies the gift's inexhaustible power to provoke. As a figure of the impossible and loss, the gift-object (and the process of gift-giving supporting it) is able, more than anything else, to destabilize and reorganize existing structures of power, the more so as the act of giving is spontaneous (as opposed to ritualized) and as the gift-giver is a stranger and an outsider (as opposed to a recognized member of an established social unit)" (35). We will look more closely below at Grace's power to disrupt the social order in Dogville precisely because of the strange condition she embodies as a "free gift."

11 There is an interesting connection between this idea of the impossibility of receiving a gift and some of Beauvoir's ideas on oppression, freedom, and revenge. I deal with these concepts in detail below, but I wish to state here that the idea of the gift actually clarifies Beauvoir's position regarding power relations: oppression is always an act of appropriation and exploitation, an act in which I "steal" the other's ambiguity by stealing the other's freedom and confining the other to complete immanence. Gift-giving and gift-receiving, on the other hand, transcend power relations by asking for generosity and by existing as an excess that cannot be measured in terms of price or quantitative benefit. Bergoffen thus considers the gift to be the "paradigmatic moral act" for Beauvoir (61). She believes that the only way to understand Beauvoir's alternative to violent relations is through the concept of generosity, not through that of the project: "So long as intersubjectivity is seen through the prism of the project, the other appears to me as either an obstacle, ally, or enemy. If I adopt the lens of generosity, however, these relationships disappear. [. . .] Instead of representing freedom as necessarily oriented toward something known or knowable, I see the other's freedom and represent my own as transcendence that *escapes calculation*" (62, my emphasis). Beauvoir's idea of revenge also seems to have a "gift" quality. As I explain below, although revenge is a "useless passion" in that nothing is really gained through it, Beauvoir believes that this might be precisely what makes it interesting and prone to phenomenological research. Although nothing is "gained" through revenge, this unproductive passion is strong, visceral, and undeniably human, and we cannot presume to eliminate it (Kruks 151–81).

12 Arendt develops the concept of the banality of evil in *Eichmann*

in Jerusalem to explain the evil of the Nazis not as resulting from monstrous, especially inhuman creatures who are totally different from us, but as an evil that might, under certain circumstances, develop in any one of us. The evil of the Nazi is not privileged; it does not characterize only essentially bad subjects; it is a condition that could appear time and time again, within common people, if circumstances allowed it. Arendt mainly stresses a lack of autonomous judgment and a sur-rendering to authority as the most common circumstances under which extreme evil might arise. In Arendt's words, "The trouble with Eichmann was precisely that so many were like him, and that the many were neither perverted nor sadistic, that they were, and still are, terribly and terrifyingly normal" (276).

13   Von Trier himself comments that *Dogville* was meant to show us that "evil can arise anywhere, as long as the situation is right" (Scott).

14   Using "personality" this way could be seen as a "counter-Adorno" move. If the aesthetic work (in this case the film) constitutes a her-metic monad (Hulatt), how then can the concept of "personality" (which in itself always reflects social influences rather than a particular or personal trait) be transported and concretized in such a nonrealist text? Can this mediation between theory and cultural product say something authentic regarding "personality"? On the other hand, if we see medi-ation in Adorno as "possess[ing] the revolutionary power to present new interpretations and configura-tions" (Tonon 198), and if we adopt Hulatt's argument that it is pos-sible to reconcile Adorno's view regarding "art's refusal to take an intentional stance on the external

world or to incorporate normative content from that world—with the claim that art is simultaneously critical of the heteronomous con-tent and normative structure of that world" (171), this move might be justified. My take on *Dogville* and its connection to Adorno's "authoritarian personality" is not a matter of digesting Adorno within a pseudocultural product, but of presenting a mediated analysis in which, "open and responsive to each other, [the] elements change and are changed by each other; [where] in turn, the totality or whole that emerges from them remains open and responsive to them" (Witkin 166). In this sense, it is striking how the process through which a cultural product becomes meaningful and authen-tic according to Adorno in fact recalls the way in which Warten-berg justifies philosophical analy-ses of films, a justification that also applies to my own analysis of film through Beauvoirian philosophy.

15   I follow here the concept that Arp uses (55) to more clearly explain what Beauvoir calls "natural freedom." I agree with Arp that the concept of ontological free-dom is more useful than that of natural freedom when trying to explain what existentialists mean when they refer to an inescapable freedom, a freedom on which the mere concept of subjectivity is dependent.

16   In *Being and Nothingness*, the early Sartre argues, for instance, that the slave is as free as the master (since we cannot escape freedom) (550).

17   In the second section of *The Eth-ics of Ambiguity*, Beauvoir deals with different types of individuals who deceive themselves regard-ing their ontological possession of freedom, consequently flee-ing from it and failing to achieve

moral freedom. These are the sub-man, the serious man, the nihilist, the adventurer, and the passionate man. For a discussion of these—and of a few more original examples—see Arp (55–64).

18 On this, see Arp's analysis in the section titled "Willing Others Free" (68–74).

19 See more on this in, for instance, Arp (138–40) and Scarth (99–121).

20 See Arp on the concept of power in Beauvoir as "freedom from material and social constraints" (2) and for an explanation of Beauvoir's idea of what it is that we take away when we deprive someone of the possibility of developing moral freedom (120–21, 150–51).

21 On this same issue, Arp explains: "When others are oppressed, one is cut off from free interaction with them, and thus one's own freedom is limited. [. . .] The more others are able to develop their freedom, the more I am able to develop mine, according to Beauvoir's central thesis" (114–15).

22 This might make Grace, interestingly, into an oppressor herself in Beauvoir's eyes: she is attempting to retain absolute transcendence for herself while considering the people of Dogville as embodying absolute immanence.

Works Cited

Adorno, Theodor W., Else Frenkel-Brunswik, Daniel J. Levinson, and R. Nevitt Sanford, in collaboration with Betty Aron, Maria Hertz Levinson, and William Morrow. *The Authoritarian Personality*. Ed. Max Horkheimer and Samuel H. Flowerman. New York: Harper, 1950.

Andrew, Barbara S. "Beauvoir's Place in Philosophical Thought." Card 24–44.

Arendt, Hannah. *Eichmann in Jerusalem: A Report on the Banality of Evil*. London: Faber, 1963.

Arp, Kristana. *The Bonds of Freedom: Simone de Beauvoir's Existentialist Ethics*. Chicago: Open Court, 2001.

Bainbridge, Caroline. "The Trauma Debate: Just Looking? Traumatic Affect, Film Form, and Spectatorship in the Work of Lars von Trier." *Screen* 45.4 (2004): 391–400.

Beauvoir, Simone de. *The Ethics of Ambiguity*. Trans. Bernard Frechtman. New York: Philosophical Library, 1948.

———. *Pyrrhus et Cinéas*. Paris: Gallimard, 1944.

———. *The Second Sex*. Ed. and trans. H. M. Parshley. New York: Vintage, 1989.

Bell, Emma. "The Passions of Lars von Trier." *Northern Constellations: New Readings in Nordic Cinema*. Ed. C. Claire Thomson and Scott Mackenzie. Norwich: Norvik, 2005. 205–16.

Bergoffen, Debra B. *The Philosophy of Simone de Beauvoir: Gendered Phenomenologies, Erotic Generosities*. New York: SUNY P, 1997.

Boulé, Jean Pierre, and Ursula Tidd. Introduction. *Existentialism and Contemporary Cinema: A Beauvoirian Perspective*. Ed. Jean Pierre Boulé and Ursula Tidd. New York: Berghahn, 2012.

Card, Claudia, ed. *The Cambridge Companion to Simone de Beauvoir*. Cambridge: Cambridge UP, 2003.

Dogville. Dir. Lars Von Trier. Canal+ and France 3 Cinéma, 2003.

Dolske, Gwendolyn. "More Than a Windshield Wiper: A Beauvoirian Analysis of Project and Other in *Flash of Genius*." *Film and Philosophy* 16 (2012): 1–14.

Faber, Alyda. "Redeeming Sexual Violence? A Feminist Reading of *Breaking the Waves*." *Literature and Theology* 17.1 (2003): 59–75.

Freeland, Cynthia A., and Thomas E. Wartenberg. Introduction. Freeland and Wartenberg 1–10.

Freeland, Cynthia A., and Thomas E. Wartenberg, eds. *Philosophy and Film*. New York: Routledge, 1995.

Fullbrook, Edward. "*She Came to Stay* and *Being and Nothingness*." *The Philosophy of Simone de Beauvoir: Critical Essays*. Ed. Margaret A. Simons. Bloomington: Indiana UP, 2006. 42–64.

Geuens, Jean-Pierre. "Dogma 95: A Manifesto for Our Times." *Quarterly Review of Film and Video* 18.2 (2001): 191–202.

Guðmundsdóttir, Arnfríður. "Female Christ-Figures in Films: A Feminist Critical Analysis of *Breaking the Waves* and *Dead Man Walking*." *Studia Theologica* 56.1 (2002): 27–43.

Heller-Nicholas, Alexandra. *Rape-Revenge Films: A Critical Study*. Jefferson: McFarland, 2011. Kindle file.

Hulatt, Owen. "Critique through Autonomy: On Monads and Mediation in Adorno's *Aesthetic Theory*." *Aesthetic and Artistic Autonomy*. Ed. Owen Hulatt. London: Bloomsbury Academic, 2013. 171–96.

Koutsourakis, Angelos. *Politics as Form in Lars von Trier: A Post-Brechtian Reading*. New York: Bloomsbury, 2013. Kindle file.

Kruks, Sonia. *Simone de Beauvoir and the Politics of Ambiguity*. Oxford: Oxford UP, 2012.

Landau, Iddo. "*The Nights of Cabiria* as a Camusian Existentialist Text." *Film and Philosophy* 16 (2012): 53–69.

Lübecker, Nikolaj. "Lars von Trier's *Dogville*: A Feel-Bad Film." *The New Extremism in Cinema: From France to Europe*. Ed. Tanya Horeck and Tina Kendall. Edinburgh: Edinburgh UP, 2011. 157–68.

Mandolfo, Carleen. "Women, Suffering, and Redemption in Three Films of Lars von Trier." *Literature and Theology* 24.3 (2010): 285–300.

Mann, Bonnie. *Sovereign Masculinities: Gender Lessons from the War on Terror*. Oxford: Oxford UP, 2014.

Moi, Toril. "Meaning What We Say: 'The Politics of Theory' and the Responsibility of Intellectuals." *The Legacy of Simone de Beauvoir*. Ed. Emily R. Grosholz. Oxford: Oxford UP, 2004. 139–60.

Mussett, Shannon M. "The Literary Grounding of Metaphysics: Beauvoir and Plato on Philosophical Fiction." *Beauvoir and Western Thought from Plato to Butler*. Ed. Shannon M. Mussett and William S. Wilkerson. Albany: SUNY P, 2012. 15–34.

Nobus, Dany. "The Politics of Gift-Giving and the Provocation of Lars von Trier's *Dogville*." *Film-Philosophy* 11.3 (2007): 23–37.

Peden, Knox. "'The Threepenny Shot' Review of *Dogville* (2003) and *Inside Deep Throat* (2005)." *Critical Sense* 13 (Spring 2005): 119–29.

Pepper, Elyse. "The Case for 'Thinking like a Filmmaker': Using Lars von Trier's *Dogville* as a Model for Writing a Statement of Facts." *Journal of the Legal Writing Institute* 14 (2008): 171–205.

Sartre, Jean-Paul. *Being and Nothingness.* Trans. Hazel E. Barnes. New York: Philosophical Library, 1956.

Scarth, Fredrika. *The Other Within: Ethics, Politics, and the Body in Simone de Beauvoir.* Lanham: Rowman, 2004.

Scott, A. O. "'Dogville'—It Fakes a Village." *New York Times* 21 Mar. 2004. http://www.nytimes.com/2004/03/21/movies/dogville-it-fakes-a-village.html.

Shiloh, Ilana. "*Breaking the Waves*; *Dancer in the Dark*; *Dogville*." *Modern Language Studies* 35.1 (2004): 84–88.

Sinnerbrink, Robert. "Grace and Violence: Questioning Politics and Desire in Lars von Trier's *Dogville*." *Scan* 4.2 (2007): 1–7.

Sirridge, Mary. "Philosophy in Beauvoir's Fiction." Card 129–48.

Tonon, Margherita. "Theory and the Object: Making Sense of Adorno's Concept of Mediation." *International Journal of Philosophical Studies* 21.2 (2013): 184–203.

Wartenberg, Thomas E. "Beyond *Mere* Illustration: How Films Can Be Philosophy." *Thinking through Cinema: Film as Philosophy.* Spec. issue of *Journal of Aesthetics and Art Criticism* 64.1 (2006): 19–32.

Witkin, Robert W. "Philosophy of Culture." *Theodor Adorno: Key Concepts.* Ed. Deborah Cook. Acumen: Stocksfield, 2008. 161–78.

Volume 26 Index

Volume 26, Number 3   DOI 10.1215/10407391-3340420

Wiegman, Robyn. "Eve's Triangles, or Queer Studies beside Itself." 26.1: 48–73.

—————. "Introduction: Antinormativity's Queer Conventions." 26.1: 1–25.

Wilson, Elizabeth A. "Introduction: Antinormativity's Queer Conventions." 26.1: 1–25.

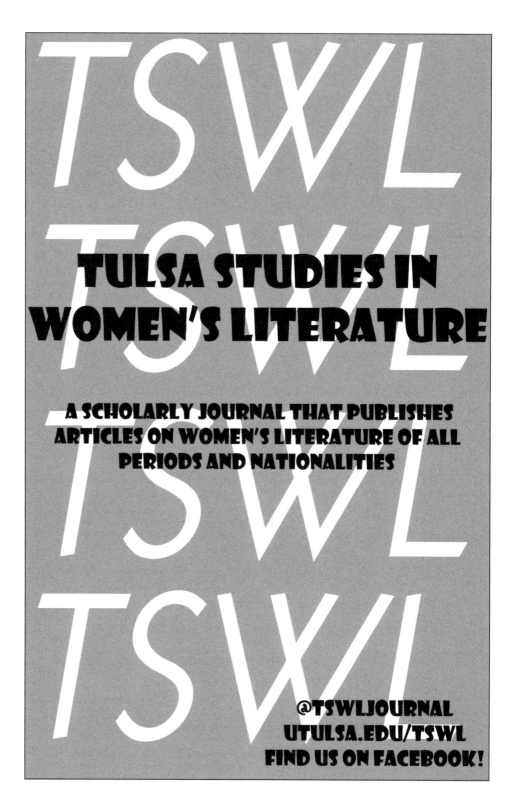

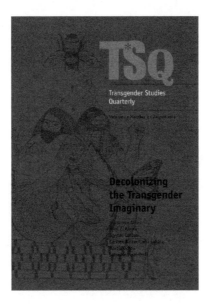

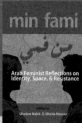